Critically Examining the Case Against the 1998 Human Rights Act

Since its inception in 1998 the Human Rights Act (HRA) has come in for a wide variety of criticism on legal, constitutional, political and cultural grounds. More recently, this criticism escalated significantly as politicians have seriously considered proposals for its repeal. This book examines the main arguments against the HRA and the issues which have led to public hostility against the protection of human rights. The first part of the book looks at the legal structures and constitutional aspects of the case against the HRA, including the criticism that the HRA is undemocratic and is used by judges to subvert the will of Parliament. The second part of the book looks at specific issues, such as immigration and terrorism, where cases involving the HRA have triggered broader public concerns about the protection of human rights. The final part of this book looks at some of the structural issues that have generated hostility to the HRA, such as media coverage and the perception of the legal profession. This book aims to unpick the complex climate of hostility that the HRA has faced and examine the social, political and legal forces that continue to inform the case against the HRA.

Frederick Cowell is a Lecturer in Law at the School of Law, Birkbeck College, University of London.

Critically Examining the Case Against the 1998 Human Rights Act

Edited by Frederick Cowell

Routledge
Taylor & Francis Group
LONDON AND NEW YORK

First published 2018 by Routledge

2 Park Square, Milton Park, Abingdon, Oxfordshire OX14 4RN
52 Vanderbilt Avenue, New York, NY 10017

Routledge is an imprint of the Taylor & Francis Group, an informa business

First issued in paperback 2019

British Library Cataloguing-in-Publication Data
A catalogue record for this book is available from the British Library

Library of Congress Cataloging-in-Publication Data
Names: Cowell, Frederick, author.
Title: Critically examining the case against the 1998 Human Rights Act / Frederick Cowell.
Description: Abingdon, Oxon [UK] ; New York : Routledge, 2017. | Includes bibliographical references and index.
Identifiers: LCCN 2017013812 (print) | LCCN 2017016552 (ebook) | ISBN 9781315310053 (ebk) | ISBN 9781138223820 (hbk : alk. paper)
Subjects: LCSH: Human rights—Great Britain. | Human rights—Europe. | Great Britain. Human Rights Act 1998. | European Court of Human Rights.
Classification: LCC KD4080 (ebook) | LCC KD4080 .C69 2017 (print) | DDC 342.4108/5—dc23
LC record available at https://lccn.loc.gov/2017013812

ISBN: 978-1-138-22382-0 (hbk)
ISBN: 978-0-367-23217-7 (pbk)

Typeset in Galliard
by Apex CoVantage, LLC

As editor I would like to dedicate this book to my mother Dr Naina Cowell, who bought 15-year-old me a poster of the Universal Declaration of Human Rights, rather than the Nirvana poster I had asked for. What was a fleeting disappointment about hanging something on my bedroom wall began a lifelong obsession resulting in many opportunities – including this book.

F. Cowell, London 2017

Contents

Notes on Contributors

Bill Bowring is a professor of law at Birkbeck College University of London and a practising barrister at Field Court Chambers. His research interests are in international law and is the author of the book *The Degradation of the International Legal Order* (2008).

Frederick Cowell is a lecturer in law at Birkbeck College, University of London.

Stephen Dimelow is a career development fellow at New College, University of Oxford. His work focuses on various aspects of constitutional law including parliamentary sovereignty.

Kanstantsin Dzehtsiarou is a lecturer in law at the University of Liverpool and the author of the book *European Consensus and the Legitimacy of the European Court of Human Rights* (2015).

Conor Gearty is a professor of law at the London School of Economics and a practicing barrister at Matrix Chambers. He is the author of *Principles of Human Rights Adjudication* (2005) and *On Fantasy Island: Britain, Europe, and Human Rights* (2016).

Nicolas Kang-Riou is a lecturer in law at the University of Salford and formerly worked for International Institute of Human Rights (Institut Cassin). He is one of the editors of *Confronting the Human Rights Act – Contemporary Themes and Perspectives* (2012).

Laura Lammasniemi is a senior lecturer in law at Anglia Ruskin University, with research interests in feminism and the law.

Siobhán Lloyd is a barrister at 1 Mitre Court Buildings specialising in immigration and housing law.

Trudy Morgan is a solicitor specialising in human rights and public law.

Colin Murray is a senior lecturer in law at Newcastle University, with research interests in security and the law.

Adam Tucker is a senior lecturer in law at the University of Liverpool.

Acknowledgements

All the contributors have made their own acknowledgements in their chapters, and many people helped get elements of the research presented in this book together in a relatively short space of time. My specific thanks go to Bill Bowring of Birkbeck College, University of London, who was very helpful with the formation of the original proposal and with advice about the project as it evolved and to the team at Routledge who very helpful and patient. Laura Lammasniemi of Anglia Ruskin University was really helpful in shaping some elements of this project and helping focus it. A huge thank-you goes to Matthew Willmore, for invaluable help with the development of the introductory chapter. Isabel Steinmetz, who assisted with the final edit of the book, has my gratitude for enabling this project to get completed.

Foreword

On Human Rights Day 2016, as this book was being completed, the leaders of more than 160 charities and civil society groups across the United Kingdom joined with the British Institute of Human Rights to ask the prime minister to drop her government's plans to 'scrap' the Human Rights Act 1998.

For these groups, the Human Rights Act is something to cherish. They see every day how it helps those delivering frontline services to make difficult ethical decisions and how it enables families to hold those in powerful positions to account. For these groups and the mostly disadvantaged people they work with the Human Rights Act makes a much-valued difference to their lives and often that difference is dramatic.[1]

We should not be surprised that those who care about those who are rendered most vulnerable by government action or inaction are amongst the most ardent supporters of the Human Rights Act. Whatever the history of human rights protection in this country, and it is a remarkable history, the Human Rights Act represented a watershed. For the first time in the UK's history, we have a charter for universal human rights that protects everyone against government action or neglect simply because they are human. The British Institute of Human Rights was formed more than 40 years ago to bring human rights to life and the Human Rights Act has been the piece of legislation which has helped the most to facilitate this mission.

How different recent history might have been if this charter, our Human Rights Act, had become popularly known as the Bill of Rights 1998, and had taken its rightful place in the UK's legal and democratic story?

Instead, the Human Rights Act has often become the story, and one within which casual mockery of human rights and human rights institutions has become normalised. The Act has been demonised by much of the press, at times abandoned by many of its progenitors, has been attacked by powerful elites, and has become surrounded by a bodyguard of lies which have at times seemed impenetrable. By the tenth anniversary of the Human Rights Act, it had become

1 This letter to the Prime Minister was published in the *Times* on 10 December 2016, the anniversary of the adoption of the Universal Declaration of Human Rights in 1948.

commonplace amongst the "commentariat" to describe the Human Rights Act as "toxic", and by the Act's 15th anniversary, a government had been elected with an overall majority on a manifesto which included a commitment to abolish the Human Rights Act. It continues to attract sustained negative media and political commentary, often in very strident terms, and in a manner which suggests that human rights themselves are some sort of oppressive alien force, rather than a mobilising spirit towards the "advent of a world in which human beings shall enjoy freedom of speech and belief and freedom from fear and want".[2]

The problem with the Human Rights Act – if there is one – was neatly summed up for me at a two-day training session for advice workers which I ran some five years ago for the British Institute of Human Rights. During the first day we had looked at how the Universal Declaration of Human Rights had been born out of the horrors of the Second World War and how Winston Churchill and the other founding fathers of the European Convention of Human Rights had sought to ensure that certain rights in the Declaration were protected across Europe as the best way of protecting the continent and its people from tyranny.[3] We had looked at how human rights are the rights that everyone has, simply because they are human, and how this universalism underpinned the very idea of human rights. We looked at how Human Rights were protected in domestic laws through various different constitutional arrangements across the nations of the world, and how here in the United Kingdom the Human Rights Act had been introduced in 1998 to give effect to the Convention. At the start of the second day I asked the delegates for feedback on the first day. One delegate immediately spoke up. She was, she said, a member of her local Conservative association and had been campaigning against the Human Rights Act. She felt embarrassed she said, because she realised that she hadn't really understood what the Human Rights Act was and what it did. She said she was going to tell all her friends that it was the bill of rights we already had.

We don't know whether she did, or whether her friends listened, but we do know that the Human Rights Act remains on the statute books and may yet survive even as the extraordinary events of the first decades of the 21st century swirl around it. Its survival is important, not only because of the role the Act plays in the UK's constitutional arrangements but also because of what it stands for: human rights protected by the rule of law – for everyone.

In this book, an attempt is made to chronicle and examine that history. In 2000, just two months before the Act came into force the Economist described it as the beginning of a "new constitutional chapter for Britain".[4] The developments across UK law since then have been enormous; rights have gone into

2 Universal Declaration of Human Rights UNGA Res 217A(III) 10 December 1948, Preamble.

3 In the words of the preamble to the Convention, "being resolved, as the governments of European countries which are likeminded and have a common heritage of political traditions, ideals, freedom and the rule of law, to take the first steps for the collective enforcement of certain of the rights stated in the Universal Declaration".

4 The Economist 'Rule of judges' (*The Economist* 24 August 2000) 3.

new spheres, judges have had to make decisions on matters that they previously had never encountered and human rights has entered into political discourse in way that would have been unknown 30 years previously. The Human Rights Act changed the UK but in so doing was subject to an unprecedented degree of hostility that has led successive governments to commit to its repeal and move towards a system of rights protection that potentially involves walking away from the European Convention on Human Rights.

It is a fascinating account of a period in which the values of decency, tolerance and respect have been sorely tested, as fears about terrorism, economic decline and dispossession have competed with more hopeful visions of our shared human future. But it is, as always, a period in which glimmers of our common humanity have continued to provide a light out of the darkness.

Stephen Bowen
Director
British Institute of Human Rights
London January 2017

Introduction

Chapter 1

Defining and understanding the case against the Human Rights Act

Frederick Cowell

The idea for this book first came about when I was looking at the comedy site *ifyoulikeitsomuchwhydontyougoandlivethere* which picked choice quotes from various discussion boards that (with some considerable hilarity) showcased a variety of ridiculous and reactionary views. I was struck by the number of comments that made increasingly furious references to human rights and reflected a world that was shaped by scare stories totally divorced from legal reality. Criticism of judges and hostility towards the legal process are nothing new, but the Human Rights Act 1998 (HRA) has served as a lightning rod for populist political anger. The HRA is the piece of legislation that brings the European Convention on Human Rights (ECHR) into British law. Prior to the HRA the ECHR was an instrument to which the UK was a state party, but the rights protected within the ECHR were not justiciable in a UK courtroom. Some of these rights were protected in other parts of UK law, and it was possible if all else failed to take a case to the European Court of Human Rights in Strasbourg. The HRA did not 'invent' or 'create' rights, but it did make their protection a lot easier.

It is fair to say that the case against the HRA is unprecedented and it is hard to find any direct parallels in British legal history of a statute exciting such high levels of opposition. The website Rights Info has identified a number of urban myths about the HRA which have included claims that prisoners have a 'right' to access to pornography and people have a 'right' to get fried chicken from the police.[1] The critics of the HRA repeat these verbatim and a never-ending list of supposed injustices originating from the Act, such as the man who claimed he had a human right to Viagra, are repeated as fact by the media. There are also a number weighty constitutional issues and concerns with the HRA, some of which have not been adequately addressed as jurisprudence on the Act has developed. Human rights and a supranational court enforcing them, are difficult concepts to square with the UK's uncodified constitution with its emphasis on civil liberties and the supremacy of Parliament. Yet, constitutional criticism of the HRA can

1 Rights Info '14 worst Human Rights myths' available at <http://rightsinfo.org/infographics/the-14-worst-human-rights-myths/> accessed 20 November 2015.

take an absolute form, describing the Act as hostile to democracy or as a mechanism for encouraging judicial law-making. Given the vocal nature of the case made against the Act, from so many different quarters, it is hardly a coincidence that 15 years after it first came into force the government considered repealing it and creating a completely different system of rights protection.

Why is there such furious criticism of the HRA? More important, does it really matter? This book sets out to assess the multitude of arguments against the HRA. It does not attempt to predict its future but rather is a history and a critical legal analysis of hostility to the HRA from its passage into law to the present day.

(1) What is the Human Right Act?

Human rights were creatures of the eighteenth century European Enlightenment and the Declaration of the Rights of Man, approved by the National Assembly of revolutionary France in 1789, was probably the world's first piece of human rights law. Eighteenth-century thinkers envisaged rights as a series of claims against the state, which had a secular foundation within the common personhood of all individuals and this, to some extent, was the model for the development of international human rights law in the twentieth century.[2] Although this conception of personhood excluded those who weren't white males, the language of rights enabled emancipation claims to be made by oppressed groups in the late nineteenth and early twentieth centuries. Some British constitutional theorists were highly sceptical of the notion of human rights; Jeremy Bentham dismissed them as 'nonsense on stilts' and A. V. Dicey viewed the concept with horror. The 1688 Bill of Rights and the 1700 Act of Settlement recognised and protected some important individual freedoms but any close analysis of either instrument invariably leads to the conclusion that they are mainly concerned with the power of Parliament and conferred limited liberties on individuals.[3] Because Britain has an uncodified constitution, constitutional traditions are an important source for understanding how the UK's constitutional framework protected rights. From the mid-eighteenth century, the doctrine of parliamentary supremacy (the concept that Parliament was the highest lawmaker) gained ascendency in UK constitutional theory. In tandem with this, as Hilaire Barnett notes, governments "encouraged the view that the liberty of the citizen [was] the fundamental hallmark of British society" and that there was no need for a written constitutional settlement which gave citizens' rights that they could assert against the state.[4] Old pieces of case law

2 See Anthony Langolis 'Human Rights: The Globalisation and Fragmentation of Moral Discourse' (2002) 28 *Review of International Studies* 479.

3 Lord Lester of Herne Hill QC and Katie Beattie 'Human Rights and the British Constitution' from Jeffery Jowell and Dawn Oliver (eds.) *The Changing Constitution* (6th ed. OUP 2007) 60.

4 Hilaire Barnett *Britain Unwrapped: Government and Constitution Explained* (Penguin 2002) 308.

such as *Entick v Carrington*, where agents of the state were forbidden from entering a private home without legal authority, illustrated how the courts were able to protect an individual's civil liberties.[5] However, as Colm O'Cinneide notes, whilst the "bedding down of a culture of individual freedom" did take place from the early eighteenth century onwards "these principles were not always respected in practice either in Britain or throughout the wider Empire."[6] The notion that the tradition of liberties within the British constitution had some form of power, somewhat collapsed in the second decade of the twentieth century as the preparation of the state for war led to the passage of legislation such as the 1911 Official Secrets Act and the 1914 Defence of the Realm Act, which radically increased the power of the state and its control over the lives of its citizens.

The first serious attempts to enshrine human rights into international law came shortly after the Second World War. The Council of Europe, a political organisation set up in 1949 with a membership of Western and non-Soviet-aligned states, was part of this process. The Council of Europe's impetus to create a binding human rights charter was driven not just by the memory of holocaust, but also by the distinctly contemporary European concern that their states were susceptible to authoritarian takeover from the left or right.[7] The Council of Europe created the 1950 European Convention on Human Rights (ECHR) which contained a series of rights protecting individuals' physical autonomy (prohibition on torture, slavery and right to life) their civil rights against the state (the right to a fair trial, liberty and privacy) and their political or participatory rights (religious freedom, freedom of speech and association). This was a relatively modest set of rights, but the onus on state parties to the new Convention was clear: they had to "secure" the rights contained within Convention for everyone living in their jurisdiction.[8] This was backed up by a notionally powerful enforcement infrastructure in the form of a European Commission and a European Court of Human Rights – contrary to the later myth which emerged in the campaign against the HRA, at the time of drafting these organs were intended to have the capacity to protect an individual's human rights within a nation state, even where the government fundamentally disagreed with the outcome.[9] The UK ratified the ECHR in 1951 and after an initial period of reluctance in 1965 took the decision to allow individuals within the UK to take cases to the ECHR. As a matter of international law the UK was obliged to protect rights under the ECHR and follow the decisions of

5 [1765] EWHC KB J98.

6 Colm O'Cinneide *Human rights and the UK constitution* (British Academy 2012) 14.

7 See the speech to the Consultative Assembly of Pierre-Henri Teitgen, August 1949 reprinted in AH Robertson and JG Merrills *Human Rights in Europe: A study of the European Convention on Human Rights* (Manchester University Press 1996) 4–5.

8 Convention for the Protection of Human Rights and Fundamental Freedoms (1950) ETS No.5, Art 1.

9 See Ed Bates *The Evolution of the European Convention on Human Rights: From Its Inception to the Creation of a Permanent Court of Human Rights* (OUP 2010) 80–100.

the Court and the Commission, but taking a case to commission was both costly and uncertain for claimants, and the ECHR could not be used to protect rights in UK courts. In the 1979 case *Malone v Metropolitan Police Commissioner*, about the tapping of telephones and the right to privacy, Sir Robert Megarry, the judge at the Court of Appeal, noted that the ECHR imposed an obligation under a treaty which meant that it was an obligation on the government in international law and not justiciable in the courts, leading him to the conclusion that "the Convention is not law here."[10]

In the 1970s a loose campaign started in favour of incorporating the ECHR into UK law. At first, these campaigners envisaged the creation of a British Bill of Rights that would allow individuals to challenge legislation, but in the 1990s the then opposition Labour Party envisaged the creation of a simple legislative mechanism to bring the ECHR directly into UK law. In October 1997, shortly after the election of a Labour government, a white paper was published titled *Rights Brought Home: The Human Rights Bill*, which envisaged a legislative framework for incorporation, not a fresh bill of rights.[11] Lord Irvine, then Lord Chancellor, in a speech in December that year argued that the bill intended to create a "shift to a rights based system" which would require administrators, legislators and judges to take rights into account when performing their respective constitutional functions.[12] In the final Act, section 1 listed the rights from the ECHR, which were now incorporated into UK law before clarifying how judges and ministers were to apply the law; section 2 required judges to take into account decisions from the European Commission and Court when deciding on human rights cases; and section 3 required them to interpret legislation in line with Convention rights. The intention behind this, Lord Irvine said, was to give courts the power to "give full effect to the substantive rights" contained in the ECHR. In 1998, during the third reading of the Human Rights Bill in the House of Lords, he was much more forceful – arguing that the proposed legislation would "enable people to enforce their human rights in the courts of the United Kingdom".[13]

The Act also placed an obligation on public-sector bodies to uphold the rights contained in the ECHR and required government ministers to ensure that any legislation proposed was compatible with the ECHR. The part of the Act that was relatively controversial, although received relatively little attention at the time, was found in section 4 – which allowed judges to declare a statute incompatible with the ECHR. This, the white paper explained, was modelled on the 1990 New Zealand Bill of Rights Act, which enabled legislation to be declared incompatible with rights rather than 'struck down' by the courts as was the case in the US Supreme Court.[14] The HRA enjoyed the support of all parties at various points in

10 [1979] Ch. 344, 378.

11 Derry Irvine 'The Development of Human Rights in Britain under an Incorporated Convention on Human Rights' (1998) *Public Law* 221.

12 Ibid. 226.

13 HL Debate 5 February 1998 vol. 585, col. 755.

14 *Rights Brought Home: The Human Rights Bill* CM 3782 (October 1997) para. 2.10–2.12.

its passage through parliament, although the Conservative Party proposed several amendments. It came into force on 15 October 2000. Given what was to come, the press barely noticed its entry into force. The *Times* printed a poem by a nine-year-old boy which said that, the human rights 'helped us stand up to bullies', but apart from that there were scant references to the HRA.

(2) What is the case against the Human Rights Act?

The term *case* seems to indicate the existence of some overarching body controlling events making a unified argument. There are in fact three broad, mutually exclusive and quite separate cases against the HRA. Little unifies them except a shared dislike of the HRA, and all three cases start from quite different intellectual premises. However, the division between all three cases is quite porous, and all three strands of argument borrow liberally from one another. First, there is the constitutional argument against the HRA, which is rooted in legal orthodoxy and is different from the other two arguments in that it is an argument about the appropriate status of the HRA as a piece of legislation. The second argument is what can be called stage one of the political case against the Act. It broadly focuses on the period between 2004 and 2010, when the HRA was perceived to limit or constrain a number of policies relating to immigration and terrorism. Whilst the concerns underpinning this argument did not dissipate, there was a distinct shift from around 2010 with the change of government after that year's general election where the wholesale abolition of the HRA was actively contemplated. This was accompanied by a focus on more general attacks on the ECHR. Both the second and third arguments are, in essence, describing the political case against the HRA; the differentiating feature is that the earlier stages were characterised by arguments that were reactive or responsive to particular issues. The latter stage of the case was characterised by hostility to supranationalism, which the European Court of Human Rights (ECtHR) became caught up in as anti–European Union (EU) sentiment increased in wider society. There was also greater agitation for outright repeal of the Act and withdrawal from the ECHR. This is not a perfect categorisation but does to some extent capture the different elements of the anti-HRA case. The constitutional argument is distinct from the political arguments although to an extent, as later chapters in this volume make clear, one has aided the other. The different political cases against the HRA have been aided by the seeming expertise of the constitutional case against the Act and the more populist elements of the political case have helped result in proposed legislative changes. The following is a brief sketch of the case against the HRA, which will be unpacked in later chapters.

(i) The constitutional case against the Human Rights Act

The UK has an uncodified constitution which is rooted in statute, institutions and institutional doctrine, such as the doctrine of parliamentary sovereignty, which maintains that Parliament is free to make and unmake any law of its choosing. This position is complicated by the existence of 'constitutional statutes' identified by Lord Justice Laws, which are subject to a greater degree of entrenchment than normal statutes.[15] The HRA is one of these statutes, with Lord Bingham describing the Act as an "important constitutional instrument".[16] When the HRA came into force in 2000 there were some who were sceptical about the relationship between the HRA and parliamentary sovereignty.[17] The vote on the 23 June 2016 to leave the EU has had and will continue to have far-reaching consequences in respect of the doctrine of parliamentary sovereignty. At the time of writing the precise legal effect of these changes is not yet clear but the constitutional case against the HRA relies on a similar orthodox defence of parliamentary sovereignty. This argument can be broken into two components: the direct impact on parliament and the increased power of the judiciary – sometimes referred to colloquially as the 'politicisation of judges'.

Section 4 of the HRA does not actually give courts the power to overrule Parliament and the consequences on Parliament for ignoring a declaration that a piece of legislation is incompatible with the ECHR are political not legal. What is meant to happen is that a 'dialogue' between Parliament and the judiciary should take place about how legislation can be reformed in order to make it ECHR compliant. Although it was far from clear what this process was meant to look like and as Alison Young noted, "the lack of clarity as to the meaning of 'democratic dialogue' led to the suspicion that it was an unstable or meaningless concept".[18] Some constitutional theorists have been concerned that the political consolidation of rights and the role of the legislature in protecting rights are undermined by the HRA, which puts the onus for rights protection on judges.[19] Some also argued that declarations of incompatibility, even though not officially striking down legislation, risked undermining the constitutional doctrine that Parliament is the supreme legal authority.[20] Whilst defenders of the Act frequently observe that the concept of parliamentary sovereignty has been changing for some time, the idea that the HRA has weakened it is appealing to constitutional conservatives and those arguing against the HRA on democratic grounds.[21] This rests,

15 *Thoburn v Sunderland City Council* [2002] 3 WLR 247.

16 *Brown v Scott* [2003] 1 AC 681 [703].

17 For an example see Jeffery Goldsworthy 'Legislative Sovereignty and the Rule of Law' from Tom Campbell, Keith Ewing and Adam Tomkins (eds.) *Sceptical Essays on Human Rights* (OUP 2001).

18 Alison Young 'Is dialogue working under the Human Rights Act 1998?' (2011) *Public Law* 773.

19 See Richard Bellamy 'Constitutive Citizenship versus Constitutional Rights: Republican Reflections on the EU Charter and the Human Rights Act' from Campbell et al. (n.17).

20 For early scepticism see Nicholas Bamforth 'Parliamentary sovereignty and the Human Rights Act 1998' (1998) 4 *Public Law* 572.

21 For an example see Mark Elliot 'United Kingdom: Parliamentary sovereignty under pressure' (2004) 4 *International Journal of Constitutional Law* 545.

however, on a very narrow definition of parliamentary sovereignty which has been increasingly questioned. In *Jackson v Attorney General* Lord Steyn described the doctrine as "a construct of the common law" created by judges and speculated that "circumstances could arise where the courts may have to qualify a principle established on a different hypothesis of constitutionalism".[22] What Lord Steyn had in mind was where Parliament proposed "to abolish judicial review or the ordinary role of the courts" in cases such as these it would be assumed that Parliament would not be able to enact such laws.[23]

The second limb of this argument is that the role of judges, whose constitutional role is to interpret legislation has been given a political dimension due to the Act's interpretative requirements in sections 2 and 3.[24] There is a divide between those who position the interpretative requirement under the HRA as simply an extension of the existing role of the judiciary and those who argue that this requires judges to essentially take a law making role.[25] There is no doubt that the interpretative requirements of the HRA have altered the power of the judiciary, but the extent to which there has been an overt or discernible politicisation of the judiciary after the HRA came into existence is somewhat more questionable. The requirement, under section 2 of the HRA, for judges to take the decisions of the ECtHR into account when deciding on cases in UK courts involving rights protection has come in for some considerable criticism for its lack of precision and for giving judges the capacity to effectively expand their role.[26] As Merris Amos notes, the creation of a privacy law through judgments in cases involving Article 8 of the ECHR, was one area where a significant new cause of action in civil cases was created effectively through litigation using the HRA.[27] The HRA has had a significant effect on judicial review by introducing proportionality (a test which examines whether the restriction of a particular right is necessary to achieve a policy aim) as a ground for review, which has made judges take a much more active role in scrutinising the substance and not just the procedure of decision-making by the executive and public bodies.[28] What section 2 of the

22 [2005] UKHL 56 [102].

23 Ibid.

24 For an example of this argument see Sir Phillip Sales and Richard Ekins 'Rights-Consistent Interpretation and the Human Rights Act 1998' (2011) 2 *Law Quarterly Review* 217.

25 For an overview of this point see Aileen Kavanagh 'The Elusive Divide between Interpretation and Legislation under the Human Rights Act 1998' (2004) 24 *Oxford Journal of Legal Studies* 259. For an argument that the HRA has empowered judges see Bellamy 'Political constitutionalism and the Human Rights Act' (2011) 9 *International Journal of Constitutional Law* 86.

26 For a concise explanation see Richard Clayton QC 'The Human Rights Act: The Good, The Bad and the Ugly' ALBA Summer Conference 2010 available at <www.adminlaw.org.uk/docs/SC%202010%20by%20Richard%20Clayton.pdf> accessed 15 November 2015, 4–5.

27 Merris Amos 'Problems with the Human Rights Act 1998 and How to Remedy Them: Is a Bill of Rights the Answer?' (2009) 72 *Modern Law Review* 883, 889.

28 For an overview of this point see Julian Rivers 'Proportionality and the variable intensity of review' (2006) 65 *Cambridge Law Journal* 174.

HRA does is make the decisions of the ECtHR have a legal status within British courts and it is certainly arguable that the way this would transform UK law was not entirely clear at the time of the HRA's creation.

Independently from this, there are a range of arguments about the type of rights protected and indeed the overall necessity of the HRA as an instrument. Keith Ewing initially expressed some scepticism about the limited range of rights protected by the ECHR and questioned whether economic and social rights ought to have been included in the HRA.[29] It has also been noted by some critics that the HRA does not contain protections or safeguards to some rights already protected in British Law, such as the right to trial by jury. Dominic Raab, MP, has taken this argument in a different direction, arguing, in the same way that constitutional theorists such as A. V. Dicey did, that it is more important to protect liberties rather than rights.[30] This broadly maintains that an individual should be free to do everything except that which is forbidden by law, although as John Wadham and others point out this bears little relationship to the way that power is distributed in modern society.[31] There is a distinct strand of constitutional conservatism in the UK that is hostile towards judicially controlled systems of rights protection leading to what Janet Hiebert describes as "court-scepticism" among critics of the HRA.[32]

(ii) The political case evolves: 2003–2010

"A strain of illiberalism had always lurked in Labour politics" the former-MP-turned-historian David Marquand observed, and "the authoritarian instinct of populist politics" came to the fore in the anti-terrorism legislation passed shortly after the terrorist attacks of 11 September 2001.[33] When the House of Lords issued a declaration of incompatibility in respect of legislation permitting the detention of foreign nationals without trial the then police minister Hazel Blears issued a statement expressing disappointment with the judgment, asserting that it was Parliament's duty to deal with these issues.[34] She went on to say that the government's "over-riding concern is the protection of this nation", linking both the constitutional issue of parliamentary supremacy with the 'headline' political concern about protection from terrorism.[35] Legislation introducing control orders – a legal tool allowing individual's suspected but not convicted of terrorism to be detained

29 Keith Ewing 'The Unbalanced Constitution' from Campbell et al. (n.17).

30 Dominic Raab *The Assault on Liberty: What Went Wrong with Rights* (Fourth Estate 2010).

31 John Wadham, Helen Mountfield QC, Elizabeth Prochaska and Raj Desai *Blackstone's Guide to The Human Rights Act 1998* (7th ed. OUP 2015) 3–4.

32 Janet Hiebert 'Parliamentary Bills of Rights: An Alternative Model?' (2006) 69 *Modern Law Review* 7, 10–11.

33 David Marquand *Britain Since 1918: The Strange Career of British Democracy* (Phoenix 2008) 392.

34 The case was *A and others v Home Secretary* [2004] UKHL 56.

35 Clare Dyer, Michael White and Alan Travis 'Judges' verdict on terror laws provokes constitutional crisis' *The Guardian* (London 17 December 2004) 6.

in their own homes – was being developed before the terrorist attacks in London on 7 July 2005. Responding to the attacks the then home secretary Charles Clarke made a speech arguing that the "right to be protected from death and destruction" at the hands of terrorists was "at least as important as the right of the terrorist to be protected from torture and ill-treatment".[36] Events over this period cemented the association between the HRA and the ability of terrorist suspects and asylum seekers to use the law to resist government policy. The home secretary from 2001 to 2004, David Blunkett was at the forefront of this, attacking judges for their supposed weakness on sentencing and for the decision in *Limbuela*, where the Court of Appeal declared that a scheme to remove support from destitute asylum seekers was unlawful and risked violating the ECHR by subjecting them to inhuman and degrading treatment.[37] Blunkett delivered a speech in June 2004 where he explicitly drew the link between individuals resisting deportation using the HRA and the threat of terrorism.[38] Between 2005 and 2006 there was a rise in human rights claims being brought in immigration appeals, which eventually permeated through into wider public perceptions about the HRA. All this was taking place in the wider context of mounting concern over immigration policy. The Labour party's pollster Phillip Gould noted that from around 1999 onwards there was a sharp rise in public concern about immigration which had the tendency to affect perceptions of other issues.[39] The HRA was affected by this general trend from around 2006 onwards.

In a speech in June 2006 the then leader of the opposition David Cameron argued that the time had come "for a new solution that protects liberties" in the UK and that there was a need for a "home-grown" human rights law that respected British legal traditions.[40] Repeal of the HRA had not featured in the Conservative Party's election manifesto at the 2005 general election and this was the first time repeal had been raised by the Conservative Party leadership. Many of the early references to the Conservatives' proposals to repeal the HRA were caught between the twin poles of being tough on crime and entrenching rights in a new constitutional settlement. The 2007 policy document setting out the plans for the repeal of the HRA and its replacement with a British Bill of Rights was titled "how a Conservative government will tackle Britain's crime crisis" and was accompanied with a press release warning of the dangers of rap music and complaints about a

36 Irene Khan 'Human rights in an age of terror' from Nicolas Kang-Rious, Jo Milner and Suryia Nayak (eds.) *Confronting the Human Rights Act: Contemporary Themes and Perspectives* (Routledge 2013) 113.

37 See John Steel 'Blunkett takes swipe at judges' *The Telegraph* (London 25 June 2003); *R (Limbuela) v Secretary of State for the Home Department* [2004] EWCA Civ 540.

38 David Blunkett 'Freedom from Terrorist Attack is also a Human Right' *The Independent* (London 12 August 2004).

39 Phillip Gould *The Unfinished Revolution: How New Labour Changed British Politics Forever* (2nd ed. Abacus 2011) 415–426.

40 David Cameron 'Balancing freedom and security – A modern British Bill of Rights', (London June 2006) available at <www.britishpoliticalspeech.org/speech-archive.htm?speech=293> accessed 15 November 2015.

lack of discipline in schools.[41] This can be contrasted with Dominic Grieve, the Conservative shadow attorney general, who in 2009 made a speech emphasising the role that a new bill of rights could play in entrenching civil liberties and protecting rights such as the right to a trial by jury, as well as extending the rights of the lesbian, gay, bisexual and transgender community.[42] Meanwhile, the capacity of convicted criminals to use the HRA was causing considerable public concern. This had been brought to the fore by the case of Learco Chindamo in 2007, a convicted murderer who successfully claimed that it would be a contravention of his Article 8 rights (the right to family life) were he to be deported.[43]

By the summer of 2007 Robert Hazel observed that the Labour and Conservative leaders were seeking "to outdo each other in attacking the Human Rights Act, echoing tabloid outrage" about immigration and crime.[44] In 2008 Jack Straw, the then Labour justice secretary, began to explore the creation of a British Bill of Rights with a section on the duties of the individual to address claims that the HRA had encouraged a culture of rights without responsibilities. A House of Commons Library research paper noted that Straw had made remarks to the *Daily Mail* that judges were too "nervous" about deporting people when they had a claim under the HRA but appeared to say the opposite when giving evidence to the Parliamentary Joint Committee of Human Rights.[45] There was a green paper on a bill of rights published in 2009, but this contained little of substance, leaving several key questions unanswered and it was widely dismissed as a legal irrelevance. In a speech shortly before the 2010 general election, Cameron contextualised the nature of his commitment to the abolition of the HRA stating that he wanted new legislation to ensure that "laws can no longer be decided by unaccountable judges" and described the abolition of the HRA as part of a

41 BBC News "Long-term' Tory pledge on crime' *BBC News* (28 August 2007) available at <http://news.bbc.co.uk/1/hi/uk_politics/6966352.stm>accessed 20 February 2016.

42 Dominic Grieve QC 'Can the Bill of Rights do better than the Human Rights Act?' *Middle Temple* (30 November 2009) available at <www.dominicgrieve.org.uk/news/can-bill-rights-do-better-human-rights-act> accessed 20 November 2016.

43 For a contemporary press report see Mark Tran 'Court rejects challenge over Chindamo deportation ruling' *The Guardian* (31 October 2007) available at <www.theguardian.com/uk/2007/oct/31/humanrights.immigrationpolicy> accessed 20 November 2016. In fact the decision did not rely solely on ECHR rights, but on the interpretation of a European Directive, it nevertheless became a totemic case for those hostile to the HRA. See Adam Wagner 'Failure to deport Philip Lawrence killer was not about human rights' *UK Human Rights Blog* (29 November 2010) available at <https://ukhumanrightsblog.com/2010/11/29/failure-to-deport-philip-lawrence-killer-was-not-about-human-rights/> accessed 20 November 2016.

44 Robert Hazell *Towards a New Constitutional Settlement: An agenda for Gordon Brown's first 100 days and beyond* The Constitution Unit, June 2007.

45 Lucina Maer and Alexander Horne 'Background to proposals for a British Bill of Rights and Duties' House of Commons Library SN/PC/04559, 3 February 2009 p. 15.

radical plan for "redistributing power in our country".[46] Alongside all of these developments were a slew of increasingly hostile articles in the press about the HRA, criticising it for providing rights to terrorists and immigrants and attacking 'rights inflation' in cases involving the HRA.

(iii) The battle for repeal: 2010–2015

The Conservative Party fought the 2010 general election with a specific commitment to replace the HRA with a British Bill of Rights but, because of the results of the election, needed to form a coalition with the Liberal Democrats in order to form a government. The Liberal Democrats had explicitly promised to protect the HRA in their election manifesto and the compromise that emerged in the Coalition Agreement of 30 May 2010 was that a "Commission to investigate the creation of a British Bill of Rights" would be created to investigate how the obligations contained in the ECHR could be entrenched in British law.[47] The Coalition Agreement was intended to supersede the manifestos of both parties and provide a framework for government.[48] The problem was that no one had voted for this document and many Conservatives did not feel that the creation of a commission on a bill of rights meant that they had to stop attacking the HRA. In her 2011 speech to the Conservative Party conference, the then home secretary Theresa May attacked the HRA, infamously (and incorrectly) claiming that having a cat could enable people to resist deportation.[49] The Commission on a Bill of Rights was formally established in March 2011 and began taking evidence shortly afterwards. In March 2012 one of the members of the Commission on a Bill of Rights, Michael Pinto-Duschinsky, resigned claiming that the commission was not focusing on the doctrine of parliamentary supremacy and following this some reports circulated that the Commission was following a pro-HRA line set by the Liberal Democrats.[50]

Overshadowing all these developments was the prisoners voting case. The ECHR gives states a five-year window to implement and enforce judgments.

46 David Cameron: Rebuilding trust in politics, Rt Hon David Cameron, Monday, 8 February 2010 available at <www.conservatives.com/news/speeches/2010/02/david_cameron_rebuilding_trust_in_politics.aspx> accessed 2 November 2016.

47 HM Gov 'The Coalition: our programme for government' HM Stationary Office, available at <www.gov.uk/government/uploads/system/uploads/attachment_data/file/78977/coalition_programme_for_government.pdf> accessed 20 November 2015 p. 11.

48 See Vernon Bogdanor *The Coalition and the Constitution* (Hart Publishing 2011) 45.

49 Total Politics 'Catgate isn't about human rights at all' *Total Politics* (4 October 2011) available at <www.totalpolitics.com/print/261092/catgate-isnand39t-about-human-rights-at-all.thtml> accessed 20 November 2015.

50 Adam Wagner 'And then there were seven: Pinto-Duschinsky quitting Bill of Rights Commission' *UK Human Rights Blog* (12 March 2012) available at <http://ukhumanrightsblog.com/2012/03/12/and-then-there-were-seven-pinto-duschinsky-quitting-bill-of-rights-commission/> accessed 20 November 2015.

In 2005 the UK had lost a case on the blanket ban on prisoners voting. The ECtHR had held that the ban was a disproportionate restriction of the right to free and fair elections and that whilst there was no obligation to grant all prisoners the vote, there was a need to review the ban to make sure any restrictions on the right to vote were only those strictly necessary for the prevention of crime and disorder.[51] Successive governments had done little to address this fearing the political consequences. In 2011 when the deadline for enforcement had been reached, the government attempted to hold a vote on a compromise solution, but this wasn't taken very seriously, and David Cameron, the then prime minister, complained that the thought of prisoners voting made him "feel physically ill".[52] In February 2011 Parliament held a backbench debate on a motion that prisoners voting should be decided by Parliament and not by the ECtHR. More than 44 MPs delivered speeches in the debate most of them attacking the ECtHR and the HRA with a significant majority of these speeches coming from Conservative MPs, who were deeply unhappy at the ECtHR and the constitutional position of the HRA.[53] Only 22 MPs voted against the motion, all of whom were 'named and shamed' in *The Sun* newspaper the following day.

The populist campaign against the HRA in the press focused increasingly on the prisoner voting row and the ongoing difficulties faced by the Home Secretary in her attempt to deport the terrorist suspect Abu-Qatada to Jordan. There was also a growing criticism of the ECtHR in the context of hostility towards the EU; a motion calling for a referendum on EU membership was narrowly defeated in Parliament in late 2011, and the rise of the UK Independence Party (UKIP) had created a political climate of increased hostility towards the EU. Much of the conflation between the EU and ECtHR was confused and legally inaccurate, but these political developments spoke to a wider political dissatisfaction with supranational government and its structures. It was around this time also that a series of preconceptions (or, less charitably, myths) began to build around the ECtHR as an institution, the most prominent ones being that the ECtHR usually ruled against the UK, the judges in the ECtHR were under-qualified and that the ECtHR was inefficient and its backlog of cases was a symptom of its inefficiency. At a 2012 conference of the Council of Europe in Brighton the UK government managed to secure agreement on institutional reforms to the ECtHR to tackle some of these issues, and within two years the backlog of cases began to decline.[54] The Commission on a Bill of Rights report in December 2012 acknowledged

51 *Hirst v UK (No.2)* [2005] ECHR 681.

52 Andrew Hough 'Prisoner vote: what MPs said in heated debate' *The Telegraph* (11 February 2011) available at <www.telegraph.co.uk/news/politics/8317485/Prisoner-vote-what-MPs-said-in-heated-debate.html> accessed 20 November 2015.

53 Danny Nicol 'Legitimacy of the Commons debate on prisoner voting' (2011) *Public Law* 682.

54 Alice Donald 'The remarkable shrinking backlog at the European Court of Human Rights' *UK Human Rights Blog* (1 October 2014) available at <http://ukhumanrightsblog.

there was a public perception that the HRA had created "expense, frivolous litigation and increased bureaucracy" and that there were those who were worried about the growth of the ECtHR's power and the lack of parliamentary control.[55] The majority of members of the commission were, in principle, in favour of the creation of a bill of rights and focused on the issue of "public ownership" of any future instrument rather than analysing why the HRA itself had come in for criticism.[56]

This was quite different from what some of the now very hostile forces in the Conservative Party and UKIP had in mind for a British Bill of Rights, which had become focused on leaving the ECHR and a much narrower conception of rights under parliamentary control. At the Conservative Party Conference in 2013 Theresa May (the then home secretary) promised to repeal the HRA and went further than before stating that "if leaving the European Convention is what it takes to fix our human rights laws, that is what we should do".[57] This was the first time that a senior government official had envisaged leaving the ECHR. As Keith Ewing noted, the increasingly strident rhetoric on repatriating rights had become synonymous with achieving the "right kind of human rights".[58] The proposals for a new British Bill of Rights published by the Conservative Party in 2014 were symptomatic of that shift. They envisaged severing the link between the Convention and the UK and replicating the rights contained within the ECHR into an instrument that would contain a list of individual duties and have greater parliamentary oversight. This was coupled with a section that stated that the new bill of rights should only apply in "serious" cases without, as Mark Elliot noted, providing "reference to what criteria seriousness and it's observe, triviality, would be determined".[59] Whilst the proposals attracted significant controversy, they nevertheless featured in the Conservative Party's manifesto at the 2015 General Election, and after unexpectedly winning a parliamentary majority the new justice secretary Michael Gove announced that a bill of rights would be drafted although proposals were put on hold in mid-summer 2015.

com/2014/10/01/the-remarkable-shrinking-backlog-at-the-european-court-of-human-rights/> accessed 20 November 2015.

55 Commission on a Bill of Rights 'A UK Bill of Rights? The Choice Before Us' Volume 1, December 2012 para. 29.

56 Ibid. para. 80–82.

57 Alan Travis 'Conservatives promise to scrap Human Rights Act after next election' *The Guardian* (London 30 September 2013) available at <www.theguardian.com/law/2013/sep/30/conservitives-scrap-human-rights-act> accessed 20 November 2015.

58 Keith Ewing 'Doughty Defenders of the Human Rights Act' from Kang-Riou et al. (n.36) 135.

59 Mark Elliot 'My analysis of the Conservative Party's proposals for a British Bill of Rights' *Public Law for Everyone* (3 October 2014) available at <http://publiclawforeveryone.com/2014/10/03/my-analysis-of-the-conservative-partys-proposals-for-a-british-bill-of-rights/> accessed 16 November 2016 as are all subsequent URLs.

(3) Assessing the causes and evidence of the case against the Human Rights Act

Since its passage, the HRA has faced a steadily escalating series of attacks, designed not just to undermine the Act but, at times, the very concept of human rights. A genuine case can be made that the HRA has faced a series of attacks without precedent for a piece of legislation in modern British history. To take just one example, Nick Herbert, MP, wrote in 2012 that under the HRA "rights are increasingly treated as a new religion" and held it responsible for creating "asymmetric – lawfare" which gave more power to criminals and terrorist suspects.[60] It is possible to view this as reactionary posturing and irrelevant to broader constitutional questions about the law and its application, but the negative campaign against the HRA has had a distinct effect on the politics of rights and the protection of human rights in the UK. The Commission on a Bill of Rights noted from its consultation process that there was a "widespread agreement that the Human Rights Act has not won the degree of public acceptance that would be desirable".[61] The campaigning group Liberty, responding to the commission's consultation, linked the lack of public ownership of the HRA with a narrative of "real and imagined litigation as reported by [a] mainly hostile media" which took root in a climate where there was a lack of education about human rights and their protection.[62] Some have argued that the creation of a bill of rights could assist in the resolution of this particular problem, but as Andrew Fordham, QC, observes, the intention of many of those advocating for a British Bill of Rights was to "water down" the UK's obligations under the ECHR.[63] A more positive gloss was put on the commission's findings by Helena Kennedy, QC, and Phillip Sands, QC, who argued that the lack of public ownership of the HRA was "neither widespread nor deep" and highlighted the very positive view of the HRA in some areas of the UK.[64]

Beyond the HRA's portrayal in the media, there are a number of different causes of hostility towards the HRA. Some of these are structural, highlighting the way the Act has been interpreted in the courts and implemented in society, and others contingent, based on historical traditions or political arguments specific to the UK. Although a variety of different explanations for the case against

60 Nick Herbert 'It would make a mockery of justice but foreign judges could rule that Britain's mass murderers have a human right to be set free' (*Mail Online* 26 November 2012) available at <www.dailymail.co.uk/news/article-2238896/It-make-mockery-justice-foreign-judges-rule-Britain-s-mass-murderers-human-right-set-free.html>.

61 Commission on a Bill of Rights (n.55) para. 7.36.

62 Ibid. p. 16, para. 32.

63 Ibid. p. 142 para. 7.32. For an articulation of this argument see Stephen Dimelow and Alison 'Young Common Sense of Confusion: The Human Rights Act and the Conservative Party' (2015) *The Constitution Society* 41–45 available at <www.consoc.org.uk/wp-content/uploads/2015/04/COSJ3217_Common_Sense_or_Confusion_WEB.pdf>

64 Phillip Sands and Helena Kennedy 'In Defence of Rights' (2013) 35 *London Review of Books* 19.

the Act will be advanced at other points in this book it is worth at this point advancing a few broad reasons why the HRA has been subject to this level of hostility and briefly reviewing some of the evidence on the hostility towards the Act.

(i) What drives criticism of the HRA? Measuring public hostility

Attempts to quantify public attitudes towards the HRA are mixed and are shaped by structural prejudices or a response to particular issues. In general, there is a distinction between England and other UK nations – which tend to be more favourable to both the HRA and the ECtHR as an institution.[65] Early polling on the HRA in 2005 found that a majority of the public thought it was doing more harm than good, but this should be treated with some caution as there had only been a handful of high-profile cases using the HRA at this point and hostility appeared to be connected to the use of the HRA by travellers to resist eviction.[66] Research undertaken the previous year by the British Institute of Human Rights identified a lack of understanding about the Act in focus groups and the tendency of many respondents to blame the HRA for "protecting the rights of terrorists or people like Myra Hindley".[67] In 2008, a poll commissioned by the Ministry of Justice found that although the overwhelming majority of the public agreed that an instrument protecting human rights was important, around 57% thought that the HRA was being abused and taken advantage of by "immigrants and asylum seekers".[68] Research undertaken by the Equality and Human Rights Commission published in 2009 showed that a large number of public bodies viewed the HRA defensively, as a regulatory framework that had to be managed. However, the report concluded that there was a clear indication from the existing data that the more people found out about the HRA the more sympathetic they became to it and that "low levels of awareness and understanding may be contributing to negative perceptions" of the Act.[69]

An additional finding of the Equality and Human Rights Commission that a majority of people favoured some form of constitutional rights protection, was supported by a 2010 ComRes poll which showed 96% support for a law that protects rights and freedoms in Britain.[70] However, the ComRes polling also showed

65 Commission on a Bill of Rights (n.55) para. 7.1–7.10.

66 Anthony King 'Human Rights Act does more harm than good, says poll' *The Telegraph* (26 March 2005) available at <www.telegraph.co.uk/news/uknews/1486471/Human-Rights-Act-does-more-harm-than-good-says-poll.html>.

67 Frances Butler 'Human rights: who needs them? Using Human Rights in the Voluntary Sector' (IPPR 2004) 24. Myra Hindley was a serial killer.

68 BBC News 'Human Rights Act 'being abused'' *BBC News* (12 January 2008) available at <http://news.bbc.co.uk/1/hi/uk/7184498.stm>.

69 Alice Donald et al. 'Human Rights in Britain since the Human Rights Act 1998: A critical review' Equality and Human Rights Commission Research Report 28 June 2009 at 183.

70 ComRes 'A public opinion poll on behalf of Liberty' (26 September 2010) available at <www.comres.co.uk/polls/liberty-human-rights-act-poll/>.

a trend picked up in YouGov polling in 2011 that whilst individual rights, such as the right to a fair trial received strong levels of support, when asked about the actual nature of the HRA, there was often high levels of ignorance and hostility.[71] Whilst support for the protection of human rights remained high 75% of the respondents to the YouGov poll agreed with the statement that the HRA "is used too widely to create rights that it was never intended to protect".[72] In 2012 in the aftermath of the political controversies over prisoners voting and the deportation of Abu-Qatada there was a strong level of support for the proposition that "human rights have become a charter for criminals and the undeserving".[73] In some ways this was just an endorsement of standard attacks on the HRA coming from the tabloid press, but this represented a hardening of attitudes towards the HRA driven by specific cases. By 2014 this had morphed into a slight majority of Britons in favour of leaving the ECtHR, a shift which pollsters from YouGov closely linked to changing views about the EU.[74] This did not automatically translate into an outright hostility for the HRA, and in spite of the Conservative government's stated aim to repeal the HRA, polling in 2015 seemed to indicate that voters did not view the Act's repeal as a priority.[75] This general trend in polling leads to two rough conclusions. First, the idea of protecting human rights and the protection of individual rights is often a lot more popular than the HRA is itself, a conclusion that can easily be used to advocate the HRA's notional replacement with a bill of rights. Second, if the HRA can be framed negatively in connection with a specific issue this is likely to result in a much more negative perception of it than an abstract question about whether a particular right is valued.

(ii) Ideological causes of hostility to the HRA

There is a question as to what sense hostility towards the HRA is in any sense ideological and here again the picture is somewhat complicated. Hostility usually falls along the authoritarian/libertarian divide, with those arguing strongly for the repeal of the HRA often following traditionally authoritarian arguments that the state needs to be able to enact greater controls on individuals. The authoritarian criticism of the HRA crosses party political boundaries often taking the form

71 Hannah Thompson 'What place for human rights?' *YouGov* (26 Aug 2011) available at <https://yougov.co.uk/news/2011/08/26/what-place-human-rights/>.

72 Ibid.

73 Jack Doyle 'Human rights laws are a charter for criminals, say 75% of Britons' *Daily Mail* (16 April 2012) available at <www.dailymail.co.uk/news/article-2130224/Human-rights-laws-charter-criminals-say-75-Britons.html>.

74 William Jordan 'Scepticism about human rights as well as the ECHR' *YouGov* (20 July 2014) available at <https://yougov.co.uk/news/2014/07/20/scepticism-about-human-rights-well-echr/>.

75 Amnesty International 'Little appetite to repeal the Human Rights Act new poll finds' *Amnesty International UK Press Release* (9 November 2015) available at <www.amnesty.org.uk/press-releases/little-appetite-repeal-human-rights-act-new-poll-finds>.

of a position divide, what some political scientists describe as tracking "the alignment of structural and attitudinal difference without an accompanying political alignment".[76] It also may be symptomatic of an emerging ideological split within Britain described by Jeremy Cliffe as a cosmopolitan divide. This envisages a political divide between conservative notions of tradition and insularity versus a cosmopolitan vision which he describes as "relatively open to the world, socially liberal and comfortable with the country's plural, multi-ethnic society" and although Cliffe does not mention the HRA explicitly, it is definitely in form closer to the cosmopolitan vision he describes.[77] The HRA is itself affected by part of a wider problem with cosmopolitanism because a cosmopolitan political order, as David Held notes, requires that allegiance is owed to the "moral realm of humanity" and not contingent on "groupings of nation, ethnicity and class".[78] Since the mid-2010s political theorists had noted that cosmopolitan politics, often associated with liberal forms of government, were in a state of crisis and increasingly losing ground to more authoritarian forms of populism, which was having a knock on effect on trust in human rights.[79]

There is, however, an additional ideological dimension to the case against the HRA that revolves around what can be described as a compound of liberal-nationalist and conservative constitutionalism that is specific to Britain and the HRA. This posits that there is a tradition of liberty that is distinctly British which is being undermined by the HRA or is an appropriate substitute for the HRA. This argument appeals both to traditionalism and traditional values whilst tapping into broad public sympathies in favour of some sort of rights protection. The important point about this sort of ideological argument is that it needs to be seen in the context of state structures and their production of ideology. Louis Althusser argued that the state superstructure, which included the "law" and "legal" ideologies of the state, formed an "ideological state apparatus", produced ideology.[80] This is important for understanding how specific institutions often produce ideological positions. In the case of the HRA, the common law legal system and uncodified constitution have produced a particular ideology underpinning hostility to the HRA. This is sometimes described as the dominant ideology thesis, which holds that within all societies there are sets of beliefs that dominate others, crowding out alternate, less dominant ideological perspectives.[81] This is

76 See Kevin Deegan-Krause 'New Dimensions of Political Cleavage' from R. Dalton and H.D. Klingemann (eds.) *The Oxford Handbook of Political Behaviour* (OUP 2009) 540.

77 Jeremy Cliffe 'Britain's cosmopolitan future: How the country is changing and why its politicians must respond' (2015) *Policy Network Paper* 1, 2.

78 David Held 'Principles of Cosmopolitan Order' from Garret Brown and Held (eds.) *The Cosmopolitanism Reader* (Polity 2010) 229.

79 See Ivan Krastev 'Liberalism's Failure to Deliver' (2016) 27 *Journal of Democracy* 35. Costas Douzinas 'The Paradoxes of Human Rights' (2013) 20 *Constellations* 51.

80 Louis Althusser *On Ideology* (3rd ed. Vesro 2008) 17.

81 See for an overview Nicholas Abercrombie and Bryan S. Turner 'The Dominant Ideology Thesis' (1978) 29 *The British Journal of Sociology* 149.

seen in the way that the constitutional case against the HRA is used by politicians to suggest that the HRA is incompatible with the dominant ideology within constitutional traditions predating the HRA. This enables the seemingly counterintuitive claim made by those attacking the HRA that the protection of rights would be better without the Act.[82] The Supreme Court has been clear that it is possible to use existing common law protections to protect human rights but was careful to acknowledge that situations exist where the Act is specifically needed as it "provides a number of additional tools enabling the courts and government to develop the law when necessary".[83] The major problem with the pre-HRA world, as one former Court of Appeal judge acknowledged, was the fact that "the rigidity of British statute-based law proved inadequate to uphold the rights of members of unpopular minorities" and therefore a more rights-based jurisprudence, which the Act facilitated, was important to deliver justice.[84] It would therefore seem that the valorisation of the pre-HRA world seems to be dependent on the dominant ideology of how the British constitution operates, one which reflects what can be described as British exceptionalism, a point that Colin Murray develops further in the second chapter of this book.

Finally, there is a broader question of ownership of rights. The HRA, as Francesca Klug notes, was simultaneously "presented as a radical departure" in UK law and as a "technical tidying up exercise", designed to rationalise the legal relationship between the ECtHR and the UK.[85] The HRA's final form was highly technocratic and was not accompanied by the kind of constitutional and social entrenchment that could enshrine rights to gain wider social acceptance. This, in part, is a problem with the concept of human rights itself, which as Benjamin Gregg notes is "grounded politically" and is "hardly the work of a cultural consensus".[86] This does not mean, Gregg argues, that there is no alternative but "moral parochialism" but that establishing a common political foundation upon which rights can then be constructed or accepted is important if they are not get caught within existing metaphysical or theological explanations for their existence.[87] In practical terms this is important because if rights are to apply to all persons equally there is a need for a social foundation to justify them applying

82 For an example see Jon Stone 'Scrapping the Human Rights Act will help protect human rights, Attorney General says' *The Independent* (25 February 2016) available at <www.independent.co.uk/news/uk/politics/scrapping-the-human-rights-act-will-help-protect-human-rights-attorney-general-says-a6894966.html>.

83 *R (Osborn) v Parole Board* [2013] UKSC 61 [57].

84 Henry Brook 'Before the Human Rights Act: The Role of the Judiciary in Protecting Human Rights in Britain' (9 November 2015) available at <https://sirhenrybrooke.me/2015/11/09/before-the-human-rights-act-the-role-of-the-judiciary-in-protecting-human-rights-in-britain/>.

85 Francesca Klug The Human Rights Act: origins and intentions' from Kang-Riouu et al. (eds.) (n.36) 35.

86 Benjamin Gregg *Human Rights as Social Construction* (CUP 2013) 35.

87 Ibid.

to everyone equally. The HRA's technocratic origins may explain why, when it is used to protect the rights of certain individuals, there is exceptionally strong opposition. In a wider context, much of the criticism of the ECtHR is itself unfounded and focused on an inaccurate presentation of what the law is, yet the court itself often lacks the political capital to defend itself.[88]

(iii) The media: Analysing the message, not the medium

The media's role in worsening perceptions of the HRA has been identified by some commentators as responsible for generating a lack of understanding about the HRA, which has fuelled subsequent hostility. Adam Wagner's 2014 paper on the 'monstering' of the HRA is an interesting overview of how the media began to create and constitute a particular version of what the Act was and, more importantly, what human rights were.[89] His argument was that the Act was being attacked by the media in a way that was completely unrelated to the issues involved in individual cases – turning the HRA itself into an object of hatred. Lieve Gies's 2014 book on the role of the media in constructing dialogue on the HRA shows how media coverage of the Act can have a direct impact on public discourse on human rights more generally.[90] Drawing on comparative examples such as the Canadian Charter of Rights and Freedoms and the 2006 Charter of Rights and Responsibilities in the Australian State of Victoria, Gies's argument is that the media does not simply play a passive role but actively creates an "accepted definition of reality" when it comes to how the law works which is sometimes actively "mischievous" or projects a particular "editorial narration" of how rights work.[91] Eleanor Drywood, Michelle Farrell and Edel Hughes's volume on human rights and the media takes this further, examining the way in which the portrayal of human rights in the media is used not only to build an understanding of what human rights are among the public but also to help entrench them within society at large.[92] The very concentrated nature of the media in the UK, which is dominated by relatively few daily newspapers that receive a disproportionate amount of political influence because of political restrictions on the editorial content of

88 For an analysis of the arguments against the ECtHR see Egbert Myjer 'Why so much criticism of the European Court of Human Rights is unfounded' from Spyridon Flogaitis, Tom Zwart and Julie Fraser (eds.) *The European Court of Human Rights and Its Discontents: Turning Criticism into Strength* (Edward Elgar Publishing 2013).

89 Adam Wagner 'The Monstering of the Human Rights Act' *Keynote Address Human Rights in the UK Media: Representation and Reality*, University of Liverpool 18–19 September 2014 available at <https://ukhumanrightsblog.com/2014/09/22/the-monstering-of-human-rights/>.

90 Lieve Gies *Mediating Human Rights: Media, Culture and the Human Rights Act* (Routledge 2014).

91 Ibid.4.

92 Eleanor Drywood, Michelle Farrell, Edel Hughes (eds.) *Human Rights in the Media: Fear and Fetish* (Routledge 2017 – Forthcoming).

broadcasters, mean that the coverage of human rights cases in a couple of papers can have a significant impact. The newspapers that are repeatedly referenced in this book – the *Daily Mail*, the *Daily Telegraph* and the *Daily Express* – have a combined circulation of only a few million but are often able to shape the political debate on particular issues. They are the newspapers that have pursued a strident anti-HRA editorial line that has in some cases led to their misreporting of human rights cases.

Criticism of the media has received some official backing; a 2006 Department for Constitutional Affairs report noted that the media blamed the HRA for a range of ills including "giving undeserving people a means of jumping the queue. . . . 'political correctness gone mad' and being a catalyst for a 'compensation culture' ".[93] Some of the coverage simply repeated common urban myths and repeated other falsehoods about the HRA, such as the notion that it protects an individual's right to fried chicken because the police once used fried chicken as a bargaining tactic to persuade someone to come off a roof.[94] A report for the Joint Committee of Human Rights in late 2006 blamed the government for not doing enough to counter negative media perceptions of the HRA and, in some cases, actively endorsing misconceptions.[95] The Human Rights Insight project noted that qualitative research showed a negative picture of human rights reflecting attitudes common in the media, such as people were "taking advantage" of the HRA and noted that where members of the public encountered the Act through interaction with public services or the law, or through a family member or friend, their perceptions were a lot more positive.[96] This would seemingly suggest that the media lens itself is the cause of many of the negative perceptions. This is, however, a somewhat narrow reading of the case being made against the HRA which often represents what the sociologist Stanley Cohen describes as a "moral panic" where the Act is "defined as a threat to societal values and interests" by forces in society, among which Cohen lists "editors . . . politicians and other right thinking people".[97] Although the concept of moral panic, as David Rowe notes, is often overused it can be a useful instrument for assessing the "complex relationship between social structure, ideology media and culture".[98] It is important in this case as the explanation that opposition to the HRA is caused by the

93 Department for Constitutional Affairs 'Review of the Implementation of the Human Rights Act' (DCA Paper 2006) 29–30.

94 Ibid.

95 Joint Committee on Human Rights 'The Human Rights Act: the DCA and Home Office Reviews' (2006) HL 278/HC 1716, 16–17.

96 Ministry of Justice 'Human Rights Insight Project' (MoJ Research Series 1/08 January 2008) p. 27.

97 Stanley Cohen *Folk Devils and Moral Panics* (3rd ed. Routledge 2002) 1.

98 David Rowes 'The Concept of Moral Panic: An Historico-Sociological Positioning' from David Lemmings and Claire Walker (eds.) *Moral Panics, the Media and the Law in Early Modern England* (Palgrave Macmillan 2009) 24.

media often takes the form of a deficit model – that the media under-informs and, where it does inform, misleads – leading to the conclusion, echoed in studies of the HRA, that greater public awareness of the law is a potential solution to the case being made against the HRA.[99]

Whilst useful in understanding how the media creates a public understanding of human rights in general, analysis such as this doesn't situate the case against the HRA in its broader socio-political context. It also doesn't investigate the way that hostility to the Act is a symptom of a broader interaction between social structures, the media and culture, which positions the HRA as the cause or a significant contributory factor to a variety of perceived social ills. Finally, legal arguments made under the HRA, and indeed the structure of the Act itself, also potentially contribute to the negative politics surrounding the HRA. This book makes extensive reference to misleading portrayals of the HRA in the media, but it is not focused on an analysis of that general issue or a detailed account of how the media might causally affect the generation of perceptions about rights in society. Rather, it is instead focused on the arguments present in these misrepresentations and what substantive point, if any, may lie behind them.

(iv) Reactionary populism

There are also broader social and cultural trends, some of them predating the HRA, which have intersected with the case against the HRA. Some of this is reactionary in nature – which, as Mark Lilla notes, is different from conservativism in that it is defined by opposition to change based on the disorder it brings rather than the preservation of the past.[100] For instance, part of the case against the HRA is a continuation of a reactionary sociocultural tradition in British politics that occasionally circles around specific statutes or pieces of law reform. In a 1955 essay titled "Crime and the Conservatives" the journalist F.W. Deeds noted the widespread public concern that "rising lawlessness has been met by feeble authority".[101] Deeds went on to note that considerable unease surrounded proposals to end capital punishment and there were calls for the return of the birch (corporal punishment used on young offenders). Some of these sentiments never really went away – in the 1980s some Conservatives were still lamenting the end of hanging. During the 1960s this synthesised with a hatred of what came to be dubbed the permissive society. This was a catch-all phrase describing the reforms introduced by Roy Jenkins when Home Secretary, which included legalising homosexuality and abortion, liberalising divorce laws and changing a variety of

99 Alice Donald, Jenny Watson and Niamh McClean 'Human Rights in Britain since the Human Rights Act 1998: a critical review' (Equality and Human Rights Commission, Research Report 28 2009).

100 Mark Lilla *The Shipwrecked Mind: On Political Reaction* (New York Review of Books, 2016) 5.

101 WF Deeds *Words and Deeds: Selected Journalism: 1931–2006* (Macmillan 2006) 122–126.

rules around criminal procedure which were criticised for creating a variety of social ills, including the rising crime rate.[102] The campaign against the permissive society started as a reactionary fringe issue in the 1970s but later informed some of the social policy of the Thatcher government in the 1980s.[103] Populist criticism of the HRA is in many ways another version of this. The parallels in popular culture are also interesting; I noted as an aside in a blog on the politics of HRA repeal in May 2015 a strange symmetry between the treatment of the 'permissive society' in a 1975 episode of the TV sitcom *Rising Damp* and 'human rights' in a 2008 episode of *Peep Show*. In both cases the terms were a cipher for reactionary views (sometimes about crime), and the laugh lines centred on the lead character lashing out at the 'permissive society'/'human rights' as a supposed symptom of the modern world. Popular television of course is not a scientific study of social attitudes, but as a cultural artefact it tells us a lot about how commonly experienced social trends can be successfully lampooned to entertain millions.

More generally, fears about crime and law and order have been a significant part of the right-wing populist case against the HRA. The populist right, John Judis notes, is different from conservatism (which is often associated with the retention of tradition – a common refrain of some opponents of the HRA). Instead, right-wing populists, Judis argues, "champion the people against an elite that they accuse of coddling a third group . . . [such as] immigrants, Islamists".[104] Criticism of judges for protecting the rights of criminals or for making it difficult for individual's to be deported is often presented as being detrimental to citizens in general.[105] This criticism is often at its most fierce when directed against ECtHR judges whose supranational and non-British status seems to add to the perception that judges are elite and out of touch.[106] Anger at ECtHR judges came to a head in 2012 in the reaction to *Othman v United Kingdom* when the European Court of Human Rights held that the UK could not deport Abu Qatada, a Jordanian terrorist suspect, because of the risk of a trial using evidence gained by torture; when prompted 60% of the public agreed with the view that the court should have been ignored and Abu Qatada deported anyway.[107] Whilst this chapter was

102 Dominic Sandbrook *White Heat: A History of Britain in the Swinging Sixties* (Abacus 2009) ch.16.

103 Brian Harrison *Seeking a Role: The United Kingdom 1951–1970* (OUP 2009) ch.9.

104 John Judis *The Populist Explosion: How the Great Recession Transformed American and European Politics* (Columbia Global Reports 2016) 4.

105 See, for example, Alasdair Palmer 'How British judges are 'overprotecting' criminals' human rights' *The Telegraph* (30 January 2011) available at <www.telegraph.co.uk/comment/columnists/alasdair-palmer/8290605/How-British-judges-are-overprotecting-criminals-human-rights.html>.

106 See, for example, Daily Express Reporter 'Judges are out of touch' *Daily Express* (20 April 2012) available at <www.express.co.uk/news/uk/315494/Judges-are-out-of-touch>.

107 *Othman v the United Kingdom* (2012) 55 EHRR 1; William Jordan 'Public: Ignore courts and deport Qatada' *YouGov* (26 April 2013) available at <https://yougov.co.uk/news/2013/04/26/brits-ignore-courts-and-deport-qatada/>.

being written, the High Court handed down its judgment in *Miller* – the so-called Brexit litigation – which held that Parliament had to be consulted prior to Britain initiating an exit from the EU.[108] The reaction from the some newspapers was to brand the three High Court judges who made the ruling "enemies of the people", demonstrating how deep populist hostility against the judiciary had become.[109] These political dynamics are shaped in part by the structures of legal arguments under the HRA and the relatively thin rights culture within British society, something that Nicolas Kang-Riou and Trudy Morgan touch on respectively in their chapters later in this book.

(v) Euroscepticism

There has been a growing scepticism of supranational institutions and their effect on existing legal institutions. As Scott Flanagan and Aie-Rie Lee noted in a 2003 study of modern Western industrial democracies, there have been subtle shifts in conventional political arguments, resulting in an increased isolation and alienation, part of which has led to widening fault lines on issues such as human rights, and has manifested itself in distrust of existing political institutions.[110] In a European context, scepticism towards European integration, often associated with a democratic deficit within the EU's institutional framework, has accompanied the growth of supranational institutionalism.[111] Mikael Madsen explicitly traces the evolution of the ECtHR in the context of its progressive institutionalisation of the organisation noting that what drove the growth of the ECtHR in the 1970s and 1980s were the "collective skills of the small legal elite" who had been charged with "institutional[ising] and juridifying human rights".[112] What Madsen captures is how the expansion of the ECtHR was not necessarily achieved through democratic consent or deliberation. As Ed Bates demonstrates in his overview of the history of the UK's relationship with the ECtHR, at several stages decisions about the jurisdiction of the commission and the court over the UK were taken without much debate or the direct consent of Parliament.[113]

108 *R (on the application of Miller and Dos Santos) v Secretary of State for Exiting the European Union* [2016] EWHC 2768.

109 Claire Phipps 'British newspapers react to judges' Brexit ruling: 'Enemies of the people'' *The Guardian* (4 November 2016) available at <www.theguardian.com/politics/2016/nov/04/enemies-of-the-people-british-newspapers-react-judges-brexit-ruling>.

110 Scott Flanagan and Aie-Rie Lee 'The New Politics, Culture Wars, and The Authoritarian-Libertarian Value Change in Advanced Industrial Democracies' (2003) 36 *Comparative Political Studies* 235.

111 This can be traced throughout the history of the EU. See Marcel Lubbers and Peer Scheepers 'Political versus Instrumental Euro-scepticism' (2005) 6 *European Union Politics* 223.

112 Mikael Madsen 'The Protracted Institutionalization of the Strasbourg Court: From Legal Diplomacy to Integrationist Jurisprudence' from Jonas Christoffersen and Madsen (eds.) *The European Court of Human Rights Between Law and Politics* (2nd ed. OUP 2013) 60.

113 See Ed Bates 'British sovereignty and The European Court of Human Rights' (2012) 128 *Law Quarterly Review* 382.

The increasing discussion of the ECtHR in terms of its status as a constitutional court across Europe has been an important factor in deciding what is *lex superior* in national law.[114] This form of constitutionalisation at the supranational level was mirrored in the growth of rights protection at the EU. In 1992 the Maastricht Treaty committed EU institutions to protecting rights contained in the ECHR, in 1998 Protocol 11 effectively increased the power of the ECtHR by giving it compulsory jurisdiction over applications from member states and the 2009 Lisbon Treaty paved the way for the EU to accede to the ECHR in 2014.[115] Whilst the EU and the ECtHR remain separate institutions, their growing relationship with one another allowed a fusing of opposition and attacks on the ECHR have correlated with the escalation of the Eurosceptic case in the UK.[116]

There are both populist and principled arguments about the relative democratic deficit of supranational organisations and the case against the HRA has married these with a much more technocratic legal case about hierarchy of legal authority. During the course of writing this book Britain voted in an advisory referendum to leave the EU. Political scientists are currently engaged in picking through the meaning of the vote and its consequences, but based on preliminary work there was a strong desire amongst those who voted to leave to regain a sense of 'control'.[117] Some of the literature on political trust in the EU had for some time been warning of the increasing disenfranchisement of voters in EU states and their scepticism of various European institutions.[118] An editorial in the *New York Times* in 2016 noted that it was not "hard to imagine" how politically motivated attacks on the ECtHR, not dissimilar to the attacks on the EU institutions, could undermine the support for the organisation a making it difficult to make a "persuasive, positive case" in its defence.[119]

114 Geir Ulfstein 'The European Court of Human Rights and national courts: A Constitutional Relationship' from Oddný Mjöll Arnardóttir and Antoine Buyse (eds.) *Shifting Centres of Gravity in Human Rights Protection: Rethinking Relations between the ECHR, EU, and National Legal Orders* (Routledge 2016).

115 Although this is in limbo after the Court of Justice of the European Union issued Opinion 2/13 in December 2014 claiming accession was incompatible with EU law. See Steve Peers 'The EU's Accession to the ECHR: The Dream Becomes a Nightmare' (2015) 16 *German Law Journal* 213.

116 See Nicholas Starin 'Have we reached a tipping point? The mainstreaming of Euroscepticism in the UK' (2015) 36 *International Political Science Review* 311.

117 Greenberg Quinlan Rosner Research 'The 21 things you need to know to understand why Britain voted Leave' available at <https://m.box.com/shared_item/https%3A%2F%2Fgqrr.app.box.com%2Fs%2F8fryc6auj1y9x3f5syp6hrwqep2xz45l> accessed 5 November 2016.

118 See, for example, Andreas Follesdal and Simon Hix 'Why there is a democratic deficit in the EU: A response to Majone and Moravcsik' (2006) 44 *Journal of Common Market Studies* 533; Hanspeter Kriesi 'The role of European integration in national election campaigns' (2007) 8 *European Union Politics* 83.

119 Thorbjorn Jagland 'Don't Caricature Europe's Court' *New York Times* (12 December 2016) available at <www.nytimes.com/2016/12/12/opinion/dont-caricature-europes-court.html?smid=tw-share&_r=0>.

This is a general phenomenon that has a specific application in the case against the HRA. Michael Arnheim outlines a series of cases where the judges in the Supreme Court described section 2 of the Act as meaning that Strasbourg has the last word on interpreting the ECHR.[120] The veracity of this interpretation aside, this has been the core element of the claim that British sovereignty is being 'undermined'.[121] Lord Sumption, in a lecture on the British Constitution, endorsed the idea that there was a conflict between democracy and the ECHR when he argued that the ECtHR had turned it from a "safeguard against despotism" into "a template for many aspects of the domestic legal order" which he concluded was giving rise to a "democratic deficit in some important areas of social policy".[122] As Richard Bellamy notes, the problem Lord Sumption seemed to have was not with the existence of rights, as he defends the existence of a core set of limited rights as the basis of democracy. Rather, Sumption's case is that the ECtHR is a supranational institution making broad-ranging interpretations of rights, which is undemocratic because it is uncoupled from any form of political accountability.[123] Whilst this argument originated in the academic sphere it is important again to observe that its themes can be transposed onto a much-wider public argument about the relative lack of control over supranational institutions.

(vi) The bill of rights cubbyhole: 'Repeal the HRA there's a better way!'

The important point to take from this brief sketch, outlined above in points (i) through (v) is that the case against the HRA is the product of deeper social and political structures rather than an objection to a specific piece of legislation or a critique of a specific juridical form. Whether it is possible that a new piece of legislation could address these issues is an open question, but to date many of the alternate proposals for a bill of rights are effectively capitulating to these deeper structural forces. As Lambrecht observes in her study of these issues in a pan-European context, there is an increasing demand for legal structures "to disrupt the trend of 'Europeanisation' of fundamental rights".[124] It is therefore appropriate, from the perspective of protecting human rights, to be cautious of alternatives to the HRA as many of them aim to weaken, not enhance, rights protection.

120 Michael Arnheim *The Problem with Human Rights Law; Is it out of control? Who is responsible? What is the solution?* (Civitas 2015) 5–7.

121 For an example of this argument see Soren Kern 'European Court Undermining British Sovereignty' *Gatestone Institute International Policy Council* (17 January 2014) available at <www.gatestoneinstitute.org/4134/echr-uk>.

122 Lord Sumption 'The Limits of Law' *27th Sultan Azlan Shah Lecture* Kuala Lumpur available at <www.supremecourt.uk/docs/speech-131120.pdf> see pages 7–9.

123 Richard Bellamy 'The Limits of Lord Sumption: Limited Legal Constitutionalism and the Political Form of the ECHR' from Nicholas Barber, Richard Ekins, Paul Yowell *Lord Sumption and the Limits of the Law* (Bloomsbury Publishing 2016).

124 Sarah Lambrecht 'Reforms to Lessen the Influence of the European Court of Human Rights: A New Strategy' (2015) 21 *European Public Law* 257.

Since at least 2007, various critics of the Act have indicated that they would replace the Act with a British Bill of Rights. The contents of a hypothetical bill of rights have alternated depending on who was advocating its creation. Some have described it as an entrenching tool designed to enhance rights protection by either further entrenching legal protections or including new rights, such as the right to a trial by jury.[125] The former attorney-general Dominic Grieve has outlined at length why a bill of rights that watered down either section 3 (the requirement of judges to read legislation in manner compatible with the ECHR) or section 4 (declarations of incompatibility) of the HRA would weaken rights protection and create more constitutional problems, leading him to the conclusion that the time had "come to consider a written constitution . . . to provide an opportunity for greater clarity, certainty and understanding as to the way power is distributed".[126] In the other direction, some have argued that a British Bill of Rights should be a more draconian instrument designed to grant rights only to people considered to be deserving of having rights.[127] Commenting on the 2014 Conservative proposals for a British Bill of Rights Stephen Greer and Rosie Slowe note that it "misrepresents the character and role of the current arrangements" under the HRA and that it is predicated on minimising "the impact of judgments of the European Court of Human Rights".[128]

Proposals for the creation of a British Bill of Rights from 2006 onwards have been a political 'cubbyhole' to park complex discussions about HRA and Britain's constitution generally. The Commission on a Bill of Rights was a classic example of exactly this; after the 2010 general election when the Conservative Party (which had a manifesto commitment to repeal the HRA) and the Liberal Democrat Party (who pledged to protect the HRA) entered into a coalition government they set up the commission to avoid having to exercise political responsibility for deciding the HRA's future. In the autumn of 2016, the Conservative government committed to delay the publication of a draft British Bill of Rights. This was the subject of some considerable speculation from legal commentators who argued that the constant delays were indicative of the difficulties that creating a replacement for the HRA poses.[129] In the Conservative Party manifesto for

125 For an example of this see JUSTICE constitution committee 'A British Bill of Rights: Informing the debate' (2007) justice available at <www.statewatch.org/news/2007/nov/uk-justice-bill-of-rights-rep.pdf>.

126 Dominic Grieve 'Can a Bill of Rights do better than the Human Rights Act?' (2016) *Public Law* 223, 233.

127 See for example Telegraph View 'A British Bill of Rights should be welcomed' *The Telegraph* (3 October 2014) available at <www.telegraph.co.uk/news/politics/conservative/11136146/A-British-Bill-of-Rights-should-be-welcomed.html>.

128 Steven Greer and Rosie Slowe 'The Conservatives' proposals for a British Bill of Rights: Mired in muddle, misconception and misrepresentation?' (2015) *European Human Rights Law Review* 372, 383.

129 David Allen Green 'The devastating Lords report on the British Bill of Rights' *Financial Times* (9 May 2016) available at <www.ft.com/content/7b0b1eea-60eb-34e8-ba86-66c681cd8c81>.

the 2017 General Election there was no mention of a British Bill of Rights and a statement clarified that Britain would remain a member of the ECHR until 2022. However, as the manifesto also contained a commitment to exempt British armed forces from the HRA, a policy which is incompatible with the ECHR, some commentators argued that this was deliberately designed to escalate conflict between the ECtHR and the UK government.[130] Whether this is correct remains to be seen as does the content of a future of a bill of rights. These however are issues slightly outside the scope of this book, which is concerned with chronicling the different aspects of the case against the HRA. The possibility of a bill of rights being able to replace the HRA is part of that story, but the precise content and nature of a future bill of rights is at the time of writing too speculative to be dwelt on at length.

(4) The structure of this book

Within 17 years of the HRA's passage into law it has become the focus of an unprecedented and multifaceted tirade of criticism and hostility. The HRA is not hated on mass, as noted above polling on the subject shows that the British public have a complex relationship with it. In fact, the desire to replace the HRA with an alternate bill of rights points towards the important role that human rights play in legitimising governmental action. However, the level and ferocity of the criticism directed against the HRA have led to the emergence of a wide variety of arguments in opposition to the HRA's continued existence. The history, origins, legality and veracity of these arguments are the subject of this book. This is primarily a retrospective account, examining how the HRA got to this position and what social and legal forces are behind it.

The first section of the book considers the deep historical factors driving the case against the HRA. The Magna Carta, as Colin Murray points out in Chapter 1, granted certain limited liberties to the subjects of the English king in the thirteenth century. It is, however, subject to a process of historic myth-making that inflates its significance paving the way for attacks on the HRA and the ECHR because of British exceptionalism. Bill Bowring examines how in the late eighteenth and early nineteenth century a particular version of the British constitution, which was focused on an unwritten constitution, parliamentary sovereignty and a mistrust of natural rights, came to be the dominant version of UK constitutionalism. This laid the foundation for later claims that the HRA was incompatible with the fundamental principles of the UK constitution, and the idea of human rights was projected as being antithetical to this process.

The second section looks at the question of sovereignty and how that relates to criticism of the HRA. Sovereignty has many different definitions, but the authors

130 See Adam Wagner 'Brexit Could Be The End Of The Phoney War Over Human Rights – The Real Fight Starts Now' *Huffpost UK* (30 May 2017) available at <http://www.huffingtonpost.co.uk/adam-wagner/brexit-human-rights_b_16872148.html> accessed 2 June 2017.

here are focused on two specific meanings of sovereignty; the constitutional doctrine of parliamentary sovereignty, outlined earlier, and what is sometimes referred to as domestic legal sovereignty, the power of states to set their own domestic laws free from external constraints.[131] Stephen Dimelow analyses the former concept in some depth, looking at the evolution of the HRA and how a particular compromise on the doctrine of parliamentary sovereignty was reached in the drafting of the Act. The problem is that the precise meaning of parliamentary sovereignty is uncertain and following Britain's vote to leave the EU has become even more contested. Kanstantsin Dzehtsiarou's chapter examines the latter conception of sovereignty and how the interface between the European Court of Human Rights and the UK courts has affected the case against the HRA. The claim commonly made by the HRA's critics is that it weakens the UK's domestic legal sovereignty – transferring powers to the ECtHR. But, as Dzehtsiarou demonstrates, the structure of the HRA facilitates a system for meaningful dialogue, with the ECtHR enabling the UK to balance its obligations under the ECHR and that it is unclear whether a better system could be put in place for facilitating this. Finally in this section, Adam Tucker analyses the veracity of the arguments made about sovereignty, arguing that they ought to be taken seriously as the HRA creates a series of trade-offs concerning parliamentary sovereignty as it is conventionally understood.

The third section looks at different categories of controversial claimants. Conor Gearty's chapter focuses on terrorism and the way that the provisions of various antiterrorism laws have been found to be incompatible with the HRA. This has created the assumption that terrorist suspects themselves are gaining rights and undermining collective security. In fact, as Siobhan Lloyd also illustrates, in relation to another set of controversial claimants – foreign nationals awaiting deportation – that the perception of what the law is, in both cases, often differs from legal reality. It also is out of kilter with attempts to reform the law which have been made to acknowledge growing public concern about the HRA and its use by particular claimants. Laura Lammasniemi observes this trend in the final chapter of this section, which looks at claims using the HRA made by benefit claimants and other individual's resisting cuts in public spending. The reaction to these cases has been highly negative and they are often portrayed as a form of rights inflation. All three chapters in this section illustrate how negative political perceptions surrounding claimants has often transcended arguments about the law and have become instead a contestation of who should and who should not possess rights. One dilemma identified by Gearty is that the protection of rights, such as the prohibition on the right to torture, is often positioned at odds to the protection of society's interests at large.

The final section tries to address some of the structural issues behind these concerns. Nicholas Kang Riou examines why discussions about rights in relation to the HRA are often structurally flawed. Discussions of cases involving the HRA

131 Stephen Krasner *Sovereignty: Organized Hypocrisy* (Princeton University Press 1999) 12.

in the media often refer to the HRA as having given rights to individuals rather than regulated the exercise of public power by state authorities. This has led to a situation where the HRA is often criticised for things that are legally untrue but nevertheless contribute to a negative public perception of the Act. In the next chapter I take up the issue of whether the question of who holds rights, which is often used to attack the HRA for protecting supposedly 'undeserving' individuals, relates to the relatively weak philosophical foundations of who is a rights holder under the HRA. The Act's technocratic origins mean that there have been weak attempts to build the political foundations for rights protection that led to the HRA, despite its relatively strong legal entrenchment, facing a variety of legitimacy challenges. In the final chapter, Trudy Morgan examines whether there is a rights culture in the UK and whether it has been embedded into the public services people use in their everyday lives. The relative failure of the HRA to accomplish this has been principally the responsibility of various governmental actors and has led it to being seen as an instrument that lawyers' use or, an instrument used to protect individuals considered socially undesirable. What this section cumulatively aims to show is how a variety of structural conditions underpin the hostility within the media discourse surrounding the HRA.

In the winter of 2016, shortly before the manuscript for this book was completed, the current attorney general seemed to indicate that although the government were still committed to repealing the Act, this would be of a lesser priority because of the constraints on legislative time involved in leaving the EU. This seemed to give the HRA a temporary reprieve but Theresa May (who became prime minister in July 2016) indicated in late December 2016 that she intended to put repeal of the HRA into a future Conservative election manifesto.[132] Towards the end of the 2017 General Election campaign the option of repealing the HRA and withdrawing from the ECHR was touted by May as a real prospect in 2023.[133] The uncertain election result means that HRA repeal was rendered impossible in the current parliament but the structural hostility towards the HRA was still present in the summer of 2017 and the Act could well be living on borrowed time. With rising nationalism and an increasingly fragmented international order, the underlying social and political forces that caused the repeal of the HRA and Britain's withdrawal from ECHR to be taken seriously seem stronger than ever.

132 Christopher Hope 'Theresa May to fight 2020 election on plans to take Britain out of European Convention on Human Rights after Brexit is completed' *The Telegraph* (28 December 2016) available at <www.telegraph.co.uk/news/2016/12/28/theresa-may-fight-2020-election-plans-take-britain-european/> accessed 15 January 2017.

133 Christopher Hope 'Britain to be bound by European Convention on Human Rights until 2022' *The Telegraph* (26 April 2017) available at <http://www.telegraph.co.uk/news/2017/04/26/britain-likely-bound-european-convention-human-rights-2022/> accessed 2 June 2017.

Part I

The historical roots of the case against the Human Rights Act

Chapter 2

The Magna Carta's tainted legacy

Historic justifications for a British Bill of Rights and the case against the Human Rights Act

*Colin Murray**

Introduction: Weaponising the Magna Carta

Events styled as celebrations often take place, as Lord Neuberger pointed out in the context of the 800th anniversary of the Magna Carta, in a "mutually self-congratulatory bubble".[1] The 2015 events proceeded on the basis of Lord Denning's oft-quoted claim that the Magna Carta is "the greatest constitutional document of all times – the foundation of the freedom of the individual against the arbitrary authority of the despot".[2] His sentiment was affirmed by Boris Johnson: "[t]he liberal spirit of Magna Carta is alive . . . in those magnificent Clauses 39 and 40 that have come to incarnate the freedoms of the individual that we uphold".[3] And who could object to a celebration on such terms? In this chapter I argue that the 2015 anniversary celebrations instrumentalised the Magna Carta for the Conservative-led government's specific political ends. Events were closely managed by ministers to emphasise the Magna Carta's place within the UK's ancient constitution as a counterpoint to the incorporation of the European Convention of Human Rights (ECHR) into UK law.[4] The celebrations therefore

* My thanks to Aoife O'Donoghue (Durham), TT Arvind (Newcastle) and Kevin Crosby (Newcastle) for their encouragement and comments on earlier drafts of this chapter. Any errors remain my own.

1 Lord Neuberger 'Speech to the Dublin University Law Society, Trinity College Dublin' (6 March 2015) para.12 available at <www.supremecourt.uk/docs/speech-150306.pdf> accessed 27 September 2016 as are all subsequent notes.

2 Magna Carta 800th Anniversary Commemoration Committee *Why Commemorate the 800th Anniversary?* (London, 2014).

3 Boris Johnson 'The Mayor of London's Keynote Speech to the Global Law Summit marking 800 years since Magna Carta' (2015) available at <www.lawgazette.co.uk/news/summit-boris-johnson-leaves-them-wanting-more/5047067.fullarticle>.

4 European Convention of Human Rights and Fundamental Freedoms 213 UNTS 222 (3 September 1953).

advanced the Conservative Party's agenda that the Human Rights Act (HRA) needs to be replaced by a "British" Bill of Rights.[5]

Having examined the significance of the 2015 celebrations I evaluate three facets of the Conservatives' efforts to employ Magna Carta as a weapon against the HRA. First, the Magna Carta's indigenous character has been used as a rallying cry against the incorporation of the ECHR's 'foreign' legal values through the HRA. Second, because the HRA has been characterised as alien to the UK's constitutional landscape, the Magna Carta supports claim that the UK has a unique history of constitutional liberty. This lays the groundwork for a bill of rights which reduces substantive rights protections and sidelines the Strasbourg court. Third, the Conservatives' claims that the UK's constitutional history makes it a particularly trustworthy country when it comes to upholding human rights challenges the underlying ethos of international human rights protections. The ultimate aim of the Magna Carta rhetoric is to persuade the UK electorate that there is little role for international human rights within the UK's governance order and, as a consequence, to ease the UK out of the ECHR.

(1) Creating the Magna Carta myth

Even if a direct line cannot be drawn between Magna Carta and the UK's current human rights protections, lawyers have historically been at the forefront of advancing this national foundation myth. Whereas the 'historian's view' of 1215 "has tended to emphasise the self-interested motives of the barons and has generally been sceptical about the charter's constitutional significance", according to Lord Sumption the 'lawyer's view' treats the charter as "a major constitutional document, the foundation of the rule of law and the liberty of the subject in England".[6] The divergence between the popularised Magna Carta myth and the historical reality owes much to the efforts of lawyers, from Lord Coke in the seventeenth century onwards, to instrumentalise the charter in the service of contemporary political causes.[7] The Magna Carta's usefulness lies the generality of its supposed challenge to unaccountable authority, making the detail of its terms and context of its drafting irrelevant. The pope's swift annulment, rendering the 1215 settlement ineffective, matters little to the celebrations of its significance for the rule of law. That the security clause, a mechanism for constraining absolute monarchical authority, was stricken from the subsequent 1216 version need not hamper claims that the Magna Carta founded the separation of powers.[8] Trial

5 This chapter uses the term *British Bill of Rights* in line with the rest of the book, even though UK Bill of Rights better reflects the geographical scope and cultural sensitivities involved in a measure which would likely extend to cover Northern Ireland.

6 Lord Sumption 'Magna Carta Then and Now' (9 Mar 2015) p. 1 available at <www.supremecourt.uk/docs/speech-150309.pdf>.

7 See Max Radin 'The Myth of Magna Carta' (1947) 60 *Harvard Law Review* 1060, 1088.

8 Magna Carta 1215, Cl.61.

by jury came to be read into the text retrospectively.[9] In the 2015 celebrations Conservative ministers regurgitated this Whiggish narrative, casting the Magna Carta as the start of the "bending of the arc in favour of individual rights and freedoms" in the history of England and ultimately the UK.[10]

The Global Law Summit of 2015 was not intended to reflect on the Magna Carta's place in history but to refresh its "iconic, even mythical value".[11] Cass Sunstein has described this process as the creation of a "usable past" which underpins national political self-consciousness.[12] As the following extract from a *Guardian* editorial indicates, the resulting constitutional foundational myth has been generally accepted:

> David Cameron has called it the 'foundation of all our laws and liberties'. Historically speaking, this is bunk. But in so far as it supports the idea that individual freedom is precious and must be defended and passed on, it is genuinely ennobling. Myth it may be, but a virtuous national myth that speaks to the belief that the timeless and magisterial law stands above the flawed ruler, whether medieval or modern.[13]

Nevertheless, because the principles said to be at work in the Magna Carta are so underdeveloped they can easily be overlooked or even entirely hollowed out. In 1878, in opposition to the deployment of Indian troops in Malta, Gladstone directly invoked clause 51 of the original 1215 charter (calling for foreign knights and mercenaries to leave the kingdom), even though the provision had not been included in the later statutory versions of the charter. By grounding his opposition in the 'ancient constitution' Gladstone evidently "still thought of Magna Carta as something modern".[14] As little as 50 years later, however, such claims would have marked him out as a crank. As a sovereign Parliament overlaid the

9 On the range of rights read into Magna Carta by later writers, see Claire Breay *Magna Carta: Manuscripts and Myths* (British Library, 2002) 7 and Lord Neuberger 'Magna Carta: The Bible of the English Constitution or a disgrace to the English nation?' para. 23 available at <www.supremecourt.uk/docs/speech-150618.pdf>.

10 Justine Greening 'How DFID is promoting the rule of law, property rights, access to justice and good governance in the countries we work in' (2015) available at <www.gov.uk/government/speeches/justine-greening-global-law-summit >.

11 Jeremy Wright 'The Attorney General's Keynote Speech to the Global Law Summit marking 800 years since Magna Carta' (2015) available at <www.gov.uk/government/speeches/global-law-summit-keynote-address>.

12 Cass Sunstein 'The Idea of a Usable Past' (1995) 95 *Columbia Law Review* 601, 603.

13 Editorial 'The Guardian View on Magna Carta: The Magic of Myth' *The Guardian* (12 June 2015) available at <www.theguardian.com/commentisfree/2015/jun/12/guardian-view-on-magna-carta-magic-of-myth>.

14 P. Blass *Continuity and Anachronism: Parliamentary and Constitutional Development in Whig Historiography and in the Anti-Whig Reaction Between 1890 and 1930* (Martinus Nijhoff, 1978) 194.

ancient constitution with modern statute, the legal force of the Magna Carta was lost. In Peter Linebaugh's scathing assessment, "[the Magna Carta] ceased to be an active constitutional force and became a symbol characterized by ambiguity, mystery, and nonsense . . . it became an idol of the ruling class".[15] Today the charter has become more useful as a means to legitimatise UK human-rights exceptionalism than as a rallying cry for individual liberties.[16]

(2) Human rights as an invasive species

The supposedly exceptional nature of the UK's constitutional order was, in the decades before the HRA's eventual enactment, employed by the opponents of the ECHR to limit its role within the UK's constitutional order.[17] Although he was a leading human rights advocate Lord Scarman had to acknowledge that "the legislative sovereignty of Parliament . . . makes it difficult for the legal system to accommodate the concept of fundamental and inviolable human rights".[18] In drafting the HRA the New Labour government focused on overcoming the narrative that domestic human rights legislation could not be compatible with the notion of parliamentary sovereignty as the keystone principle of the UK's constitution.[19] For Jack Straw, this difficulty in mapping the HRA to the requirements of parliamentary sovereignty was, above all others, the "elephant in the room" during the drafting process.[20] The drafters tackled this conundrum by favouring a reinterpretation clause and declarations of incompatibility over any judicial strike-down power.[21] As a result, most constitutional commentators have joined Lord Steyn in accepting that "[i]t is crystal clear that the carefully and subtly drafted Human Rights Act 1998 preserves the principle of parliamentary sovereignty".[22] The HRA's requirement that domestic courts "take into account" Strasbourg jurisprudence was also intended to walk a fine line.[23] On one hand, it restricted the UK courts from developing novel and activist approaches to human rights and, on the other, it did not impose an obligation upon domestic judges to slavishly adhere to Strasbourg's position.[24]

15 Peter Linebaugh *The Magna Carta Manifesto: Liberties and Commons for All* (University of California Press, 2008) 192.
16 See Natalie Riendeau 'Michael Oakeshott, the Legendary Past and Magna Carta' from Robert Hazell and James Melton (eds.), *Magna Carta and its Modern Legacy* (CUP, 2015) 212, 230–231.
17 See John Griffith 'The Political Constitution' (1979) 42 *Modern Law Review* 1, 16.
18 Lord Scarman *English Law – The New Dimension* (Steven & Sons, 1974) 15.
19 HM Government *Rights Brought Home: The Human Rights Bill* (HMSO, 1997) para. 2.13.
20 Jack Straw *Aspects of Law Reform: An Insider's Perspective* (CUP, 2012) 28.
21 HRA 1998, s.3(1) and s.4(2).
22 *R v Director of Public Prosecutions, ex parte Kebilene* [2000] 2 AC 326, 367.
23 HRA 1998, s.2(1).
24 Lord Irvine, 'The Development of Human Rights in Britain under an incorporated Convention on Human Rights' (1998) *Public Law* 221, 232.

That the HRA simply incorporated some of the UK's commitments under the ECHR into domestic law was not a mainstay of the Conservative Party's criticism at the time of the HRA's enactment. Their 1997 manifesto described the introduction of any enumerated list of human rights in domestic law as a "radical" change which "could unravel what generations of our predecessors have created".[25] The legacy of successive high-profile defeats for the UK before Strasbourg's institutions, however, blunted claims that fundamental rights were already adequately protected in UK law.[26] The incorporation approach was, nonetheless, a visible effort by Tony Blair's government to emphasise the limited ambitions of this legislation in an effort to smooth its integration into the UK's Constitution. Some human rights advocates, such as Sydney Kentridge, QC, complained that the HRA was too timid and that "a new, home-grown, British Bill of Rights would have looked rather different".[27] To justify incorporation, the government's refrain was that the HRA was 'bringing home' "rights, originally developed with major help from the United Kingdom Government, [which] are no longer actually seen as British rights".[28] In an unfortunate turn of phrase, given the nature of the criticisms which would follow, Lord Irvine went so far as to describe the HRA as the "domestication of freedom".[29] Crucially he appreciated that the HRA would need to be accepted as compatible with the UK's constitutional traditions.[30] The Conservatives, for their part, were not concerned that the HRA would leave the UK courts constrained to follow Strasbourg but that the new law would give too much freedom of action to UK judges.[31]

David Cameron played a personal role in shifting the critique of the HRA onto its 'foreign' character. From his earliest contributions in Parliament, he sought to advance an indigenous account of rights and liberties stretching back to the Magna Carta. In 2001 he challenged New Labour's legislative response to the 9/11 attacks as an attempt to conform to the ECHR but neglecting ancient protections of liberties in domestic law: "In many ways the Government had a choice between this country's ancient rights of habeas corpus and the right not be detained without trial; between Magna Carta and the ECHR."[32] In the summer of 2006 the idea of replacing the HRA with a "British Bill of Rights" became

25 Conservative Party, *The Conservative Manifesto* (1997) Pt 10 available at <www.politics resources.net/area/uk/man/con97.htm>.
26 See, for example, Lord Donaldson HL Deb, vol.560, col.1154 (25 January 1995).
27 Sydney Kentridge QC 'The Incorporation of the European Convention on Human Rights' from University of Cambridge Centre for Public Law (ed.), *Constitutional Reform in the United Kingdom: Practice and Principles* (Hart, 1998) 69, p. 69.
28 HM Government *Rights Brought Home: The Human Rights Bill* (HMSO, 1997) para. 1.14.
29 Irvine 'The Development of Human Rights in Britain' (above n.24) 225.
30 Ibid. 235.
31 See Francesca Klug 'A Bill of Rights: Do we need one or do we already have one?' (2007) *Public Law* (hereafter *PL*) 701, 706–707.
32 David Cameron HC Deb, vol.375, col.145 (19 November 2001).

one of David Cameron's first major policy initiatives as leader of the Conservative Party. In a speech to the Centre for Policy Studies he cast this proposal as responding to the HRA being both too foreign, arguing for a bill of rights which was "home-grown and sensitive to Britain's legal inheritance", and too restrictive upon government policy, criticising the HRA for failing to "strike a common-sense balance between civil liberties and the protection of public security".[33]

This critique of the HRA's restrictiveness should have gained little traction. A 2006 review noted that the HRA had "not seriously impeded the achievement of the Government's objectives on crime, terrorism or immigration and has not led to the public being exposed to additional or unnecessary risks".[34] Because the HRA remained, according to the Joint Committee on Human Rights (JCHR), "a convenient scapegoat for unrelated administrative failings within Government", the legislation nonetheless continued to take 'friendly fire' from the very administration which had enacted it.[35] As a result Cameron's assault on the European basis of the HRA's rights protections met with little resistance. The Conservatives offered a bill of rights "designed and drafted with reference exclusively to British values and priorities".[36] Lord Falconer, Labour's then Lord Chancellor, responded with technocratic concerns as to the potential for confusion between the terms of such legislation and the scope of the UK's international human rights commitments.[37] Although Labour insisted that the ECHR was a UK inspired treaty this defence focused too heavily on Strasbourg institutions and did little to deflect Cameron's claims that the HRA "obliges British courts to base their judgments (sic) on the ECHR and the case law . . . that goes with it".[38] When the UK's most senior judges accepted in *Ullah* that "[t]he duty of national courts is to keep pace with the Strasbourg jurisprudence as it evolves over time: no more, but certainly no less",[39] the intention seems to have been to emphasise that the HRA would not lead to judicial activism. The effect, however, was to promote an image of the UK courts as subservient to Strasbourg.[40] Even as the UK Supreme Court moved away from any notion of strict adherence to the interpretation of the ECHR rights adopted by Strasbourg,[41] Conservative politicians did not allow the judges to shed the perception of subservience generated by *Ullah*.

33 Cameron 'Balancing Freedom and Security – A modern British Bill of Rights' (26 June 2006) available at <www.theguardian.com/politics/2006/jun/26/conservatives.constitution>.

34 Department of Constitutional Affairs *Review of the Implementation of the Human Rights Act* (HMSO, 2006) p. 4.

35 Joint Committee on Human Rights *The Human Rights Act: The DCA and Home Office Reviews* (2006) HL 278/HC 1716, para.40.

36 DCA *Review of the Implementation of the Human Rights Act* (above n.34) 5.

37 Ibid. 6.

38 *R (Ullah) v Special Adjudicator* [2004] UKHL 26; [2004] 2 AC 323.

39 Ibid. 20 (Lord Bingham).

40 See Lord Irvine 'A British Interpretation of Convention Rights' (2012) *PL* 237, 252.

41 *R v Horncastle* [2009] UKSC 14; [2010] 2 AC 373.

"[W]hat ebbs may flow" the then Lord Chancellor Michael Gove tartly remarked in late 2016, maintaining that "[w]e cannot necessarily rely on a future court or future judges to take this approach".[42] The Conservative mantra remained that a British Bill of Rights would restore the supremacy of the UK Supreme Court, whether the Court wanted it or not.[43]

For David Cameron, the Magna Carta was the standard under which this indigenous approach to human rights marched: "Human rights is a cause that runs deep in the British heart . . . Magna Carta set down specific rights for citizens, including the right to freedom from unlawful detention."[44] The alignment of the anniversary of the Magna Carta with his 2015 election victory, which freed him from the constraints of a governing coalition with the pro-HRA Liberal Democrats, therefore became an opportunity to advance this view:

> For centuries, Magna Carta has been quoted to help promote human rights and alleviate suffering all around the world. But here in Britain ironically, the place where those ideas were first set out, the good name of human rights has sometimes been distorted and devalued. It falls to us in this generation to restore the reputation of those rights – and their critical underpinning of our legal system.[45]

For the Conservative leadership, a British Bill of Rights would realise this aim by limiting the direct influence of the ECHR rights. As the 2015 Conservative manifesto made clear, the HRA's repeal was primarily intended to "break the formal link between British courts and the European Court of Human Rights, and make our own Supreme Court the ultimate arbiter of human rights matters in the UK".[46]

Claims that the HRA is somehow alien to the UK's legal traditions have spearheaded efforts to undermine this legislation. In this cause, the Magna Carta has been invoked as a particularly potent weapon. The charter remains a point of pride which judges, even without the impetus of the anniversary, repeatedly

42 European Union Committee *The UK, the EU and a British Bill of Rights* (2016) HL 139, Q79.

43 See, for example, James Forsyth 'Chris Grayling: I want to see our Supreme Court supreme again' *The Spectator* (28 September 2013) available at <www.spectator.co.uk/2013/09/the-echr-is-unacceptable/ >.

44 Cameron 'Speech on the European Court of Human Rights' (25 January 2012) available at: <www.gov.uk/government/speeches/speech-on-the-european-court-of-human-rights.>

45 Cameron 'Magna Carta 800th Anniversary' (15 June 2015) available at: <www.gov.uk/government/speeches/magna-carta-800th-anniversary-pms-speech>.

46 Conservative Party *The Conservative Party Manifesto* (2015) p. 60. available at: <https://s3-eu-west-1.amazonaws.com/manifesto2015/ConservativeManifesto2015.pdf>.

reference.[47] Perhaps the clearest sign of the effectiveness of this approach was Lord Neuberger's acceptance that

> it is important that any change in the way in which we are governed, whether in the legislature, the executive or the judiciary, is conceived and developed in a way which harmonises with our present established arrangements. For instance, one can't simply graft on an aspect of a foreign system which seems to work abroad: like a perfectly sound stranger's organ transplanted into another's body, the foreign aspect may simply be rejected by our home grown system.[48]

Although the reference was in the abstract, he followed it up by declaring that "[w]ith the bringing into UK law of the Human Rights Convention in 1998, we have gone some way down the road towards having a sort of crypto-constitution".[49] It is small wonder, therefore, that the majority of the Coalition government's Commission on a UK Bill of Rights accepted that "many people feel alienated from a system that they regard as 'European' rather than British" and that "this lack of 'ownership' by the public . . . [provides] the most powerful argument for a new constitutional instrument".[50] Persistent complaints over the HRA's foreignness, emphasised by the Conservative Party under David Cameron's leadership, have therefore created a pretext for its repeal with far more traction within public opinion, in England at least, than any substantive critique of the HRA's operation.

(3) Hollowing out human rights protections

Although David Cameron resigned in the late summer of 2016, there is every sign that rhetorical allusions to the Magna Carta will continue to play a role in the bill-of-rights debate. Theresa May's animus towards the HRA, on grounds of its inhibiting effective government action against terrorism, has been long standing.[51] In the course of the Brexit campaign, however, she adapted her critique to incorporate Cameron's Magna Carta narrative:

> [H]uman rights were not invented in 1950 when the Convention was drafted, or in 1998 when the Convention was incorporated into our law

47 See, for example, Lord Irvine of Lairg 'The Spirit of Magna Carta continues to resonate in Modern Law' (2003) 119 LQR 227; Tom Bingham *Lives of the Law: Selected Essays and Speeches: 2000–2010* (OUP, 2011) pp. 3–12; and Lady Justice Arden, 'Magna Carta and the Judges – Realising the Vision' (2011) available at <www.royalholloway.ac.uk/aboutus/documents/pdf/magnacarta/magnacarta8711.pdf>.

48 Neuberger 'Speech to the Dublin University Law Society' (above n.1) para. 5.

49 Ibid. para. 16. See also Merris Amos 'Transplanting Human Rights Norms: The Case of the United Kingdom's Human Rights Act' (2013) 35 *Human Rights Quarterly* 386.

50 Commission on a UK Bill of Rights *A UK Bill of Rights: The Choice Before Us* (December 2012) vol.1, para. 80.

51 See Patrick Hennessy 'Home Secretary: Scrap the Human Rights Act' *The Telegraph* (1 October 2011).

> through the Human Rights Act. This is Great Britain, the country of Magna Carta, parliamentary democracy and the fairest courts in the world. And we can protect human rights ourselves in a way that doesn't jeopardise national security or bind the hands of parliament.[52]

The myth of the UK's "liberty-drenched ancient past" is sufficiently obscure to enable May to invoke it in the cause of rebalancing rights protections in favour of Parliament's supremacy.[53] Invocations of the Magna Carta often serve as a crypto-heritage by which to justify weakening domestic human rights arrangements and minimising the role of pan-European protections.

When David Cameron first mooted the idea of a British Bill of Rights the Labour government scoffed that human rights could not be better reconciled with the UK's principle of parliamentary sovereignty than under the HRA's mechanisms.[54] What Labour ministers did not appreciate is that the Conservative leadership would quietly abandon Cameron's early suggestions of an "entrenching" bill, in favour of legislation which would sustain the doctrine of parliamentary sovereignty.[55] By the time the Conservative Party came to develop its ideas for a bill of rights ahead of the 2015 General Election, it was adamant that "[i]n all matters related to our international commitments, Parliament is sovereign".[56] As Lord Chancellor Michael Gove was even magnanimous enough to recognise that in legislating "[w]e need to ensure that we uphold parliamentary sovereignty, which, to be fair, the Human Rights Act affirms, and make Parliament's view clear on these issues".[57] Far from enhancing the limited powers the HRA gave the courts with regard to primary legislation, the Conservatives' British Bill of Rights would "[p]revent our laws from being effectively re-written through 'interpretation' ".[58] The Magna Carta is therefore the ideal avatar for the Conservatives' proposals as it is the nearest thing to an "irrepealable 'fundamental statute' that England has ever had".[59] Nonetheless, as the courts have consistently affirmed, this reverence has not made it immune "from development or improvement", to the extent that very little of the charter remains on the statute

52 Theresa May 'The United Kingdom, the European Union, and Our Place in the World' (25 April 2016) available at <www.gov.uk/government/speeches/home-secretarys-speech-on-the-uk-eu-and-our-place-in-the-world>.

53 Linda Colley *acts of Union and Disunion* (Profile, 2014) 35.

54 Department of Constitutional Affairs *Review of the Implementation of the Human Rights Act* (HMSO, 2006) 5.

55 Cameron 'Balancing Freedom and Security' (n.33).

56 Conservative Party *Protecting Human Rights in the UK: The Conservatives' Proposals for Changing Britain's Human Rights Laws* (2014) p. 5 available at <www.conservatives.com/~/media/Files/Downloadable%20Files/HUMAN_RIGHTS.pdf>.

57 EU Committee *The UK, the EU and a British Bill of Rights* (n.42) Q82.

58 Conservative Party *Protecting Human Rights in the UK* (n.56) 6.

59 Frederick Pollock and Frederic Maitland, *The History of English Law before the Time of Edward I* vol. 1 (2nd ed. CUP: 1923) 173.

book.[60] The Conservatives' proposals envisage removing the teeth from existing HRA protections, all the while wrapping their reforms under a title of Bill of Rights, with its implication of strike-down powers.[61]

So seductive was the pull of the Conservatives' Magna Carta rhetoric that Gordon Brown's administration even tried to steal its clothes by mooting the possibility that, although the HRA incorporated "rights which build on British values as old as Magna Carta", it could be built on by a new bill of rights and duties.[62] However, the Conservative Party's 2014 Policy Paper on Human Rights seeks to hollow out rights protections, claiming that "over the centuries through our Common Law tradition, the UK's protection of human rights has always been grounded in real circumstance".[63] This claim reheats Dicey's Victorian hyperbole that the Habeas Corpus acts have "done for the liberty of Englishmen more than could have been achieved by any declaration of rights".[64] David Cameron, moreover, has maintained that fair hearing rights, habeas corpus and protections against torture are "sewn into the fabric of our nation, so deep we barely even question it", suggesting that adherence to the ECHR is distorting this understanding of rights.[65] In claiming that "this country has always been a beacon for liberty and democracy", government ministers have reached back centuries to the "tradition embodied in Magna Carta, the Petition of Right, the Bill of Rights, the Claim of Right and other statutes".[66] Such statements, in sum, amount to an 'Enlightenment' approach to human rights, which treats the protection of a limited range of negative liberties as the only "legitimate purpose of a Bill of Rights".[67]

The Conservatives' reliance on the Magna Carta is to some extent mirrored in judicial pronouncements. Some senior judges have responded to the threat to the HRA by reasserting the common law's utility as a tool for dealing with human rights abuses. In Osborn, the Supreme Court maintained that the HRA did not necessarily "supersede the protection of human rights under the common law or statute, or create a discrete body of law based upon judgments of the European court".[68] In *HS2*, Lord Neuberger and Lord Mance insisted that fundamental constitutional principles, such as those contained in the Magna Carta, were protected

60 *Chester v Bateson* [1920] 1 KB 829, 834 (Darling J).

61 Baroness Hale, for one, regards strike-down powers as inherent in a "proper" Bill of Rights; Baroness Hale 'Magna Carta: Our Shared Heritage' (2015) p. 11 available at: <www.supremecourt.uk/docs/speech-150601.pdf.>.

62 HM Government *The Governance of Britain* (2007) Cm 7170, para. 207 and para. 209–210.

63 Conservative Party *Protecting Human Rights in the UK* (n.56) p. 2.

64 AV Dicey *An Introduction to the Study of the Constitution* (Liberty Classics, 8th ed., 1915) p. 134.

65 Cameron 'Magna Carta 800th Anniversary' (n.45).

66 Lord Faulks HL Deb 24 May 2016 vol.773, col.281.

67 Joint Committee on Human Rights *A Bill of Rights for the UK?* (2008) HL 165-I/HC 150-I, para. 15.

68 *R (Osborn) v Parole Board* [2013] UKSC 61; [2014] AC 1115, [57] (Lord Reed).

against implied repeal.[69] Baroness Hale has also recounted how the principles underpinning the Magna Carta could continue to be relied upon even if the HRA had never entered force.[70] The judges' message seems to be that many UK judges perceive conflicts between public policy concerns and individual interests through a human rights lens and that repealing the HRA will not change their underlying frame of reference.[71] But these statements, in their attempt "to undercut perceptions that the Convention is a dominant 'alien' appendage which will necessarily override pre-existing domestic norms", nonetheless create the impression that the HRA's repeal would not jeopardise rights protections.[72] Reliance on the ancient constitution will all-too-often promise more than it delivers in terms of rights protection. This tradition, to take one prominent example, did little to curtail the flow of successful human rights claims against abuses perpetrated by the police, military and security agencies in Northern Ireland in the 1970s and 1980s.[73]

The ECHR's text is, however, not the Conservatives' main target. In light of a decade of lambasting the ECHR for not being "home-grown and sensitive to Britain's legal inheritance",[74] it might appear ironic that the Conservatives' 2014 policy paper did not propose introducing any new rights reflecting this inheritance but, rather, building "the text of the original Human Rights Convention into primary legislation".[75] This approach is, however, in keeping with the notion that most of the rights "originally protected under the Convention were and are . . . a classic exposition of the 'liberties' which successive generations of British politicians and the British public have claimed as our shared inheritance".[76] This view of the ECHR has deep roots within Conservative thinking. In 1987 one senior Conservative MP, proposing the ECHR's incorporation into UK law, insisted that the ECHR's language "echoes right down the corridors of history . . . as far back as [the] Magna Carta".[77] Although enumerated rights might have marked something of a departure from common law traditions, it was the ECHR's protection mechanisms and particularly the Strasbourg court,

69 *R (Buckinghamshire County Council) v Secretary of State for Transport* [2014] UKSC 3, [2014] 1 WLR 324, [207].

70 Hale 'Magna Carta' (n.61) 16–18.

71 See Kate Malleson, 'The Evolving Role of the Supreme Court' (2011) *PL* 754, 763.

72 See Roger Masterman and Se-shauna Wheatle, 'A Common Law Resurgence in Rights Protection?' (2015) *European Human Rights Law Review* 57, 61.

73 For examples, see *Ireland v United Kingdom* [1978] 2 EHRR 25 (inhuman and degrading treatment of internees suspected of involvement in IRA activity); *Brogan v United Kingdom* (1989) 11 EHRR 117 (in which police pre-charge detention powers in Northern Ireland were found to breach the right to liberty); *McCann v United Kingdom* (1996) 21 EHRR 97 (breach of the right to life as a result of inadequate planning in an SAS operation in which three IRA members were shot dead).

74 Cameron 'Balancing Freedom and Security' (n.33).

75 Conservative Party *Protecting Human Rights in the UK* (n.56) p. 5.

76 Dominic Grieve 'Can a Bill of Rights do better than the Human Rights Act?' (2016) *PL* 223, 223.

77 Edward Gardner HC Deb 6 Feb 1987 vol.109, col.1224

which made the Convention a novel development.[78] It is Strasbourg's role which the Conservatives are so eager to challenge; as David Cameron argued, "when controversial rulings overshadow the good and patient long-term work that has been done . . . it has a corrosive effect on people's support for human rights".[79] The 2014 policy paper was particularly scathing about the manner in which the Strasbourg court has interpreted rights in light of contemporary values through its "living-instrument" doctrine.[80] For the Conservatives this doctrine has generated the very human rights 'mission creep' which is responsible for a swathe of adverse judgments against the UK.[81] Similar sentiments were expressed by Jack Straw, who as home secretary had piloted the HRA through the House of Commons but who came to insist that the ECHR provided Strasbourg with the role of protecting "basic rights" but not with developing them.[82] Some of this opposition has been influenced by the ECtHR's prisoner voting jurisprudence, described by David Davis as something "we emphatically did not sign up for".[83]

The Conservatives' central message is that they remain committed to truly fundamental rights, embodied in the Magna Carta, but aim to closely circumscribe protections in light of what they regard as unacceptable extensions to the ambit of human rights. During her campaign for the leadership of the Conservative Party after David Cameron's resignation, Theresa May put on hold her intention to withdraw the UK from the ECHR, on the basis that "this is an issue that divides people, and the reality is there will be no parliamentary majority for pulling out".[84] Nonetheless, the idea behind a British Bill of Rights remains to redefine or, euphemistically, to "clarify" the UK's relationship with Strasbourg.[85] In one of his earliest speeches on HRA reform David Cameron insisted that a British Bill of Rights, by establishing "a clearly set out domestic constitutional doctrine", will oblige Strasbourg to grant the UK a more extensive margin of appreciation on controversial human rights questions.[86] The 2012 Brighton Declaration, however, calls into question the need for domestic legislation in this regard.[87]

78 See Klug 'A Magna Carta for All Humanity: Homing in on Human Rights' (2015) *European Human Rights Law Review* 266, 267–268.
79 Cameron 'Speech on the European Court of Human Rights' (n.44).
80 *Tyrer v United Kingdom* [1978] 2 EHRR 1, [31]. See George Letsas 'Two concepts of the margin of appreciation' (2006) 26 *Oxford Journal of Legal Studies* 705.
81 Conservative Party *Protecting Human Rights in the UK* (n.56) 3.
82 Straw *Aspects of Law Reform* (n.20) 46.
83 David Davis HC Deb 10 Feb 2011 vol.523, col.496–497.
84 See Jason Parkinson 'The Human Rights Act helps us hold power to account. We must defend it' *The Guardian* (26 Jul 2016) available at <www.theguardian.com/commentisfree/2016/jul/26/theresa-may-repeal-human-rights-act-defend-it>.
85 Grieve 'Can a Bill of Rights do better?' (n.76) 224.
86 Cameron 'Balancing Freedom and Security' (n.33).
87 Committee of Ministers of the Council of Europe 'High Level Conference on the Future of the European Court of Human Rights' (2012) available at <www.echr.coe.int/Documents/2012_Brighton_FinalDeclaration_ENG.pdf>.

The declaration, pushed for by the Coalition government during the UK's period chairing the Council of Europe, has arguably already expanded public authorities' room for manoeuvre by encouraging the court "to give great prominence to" the doctrines of subsidiarity and margin of appreciation.[88] It has also been embodied in Protocol 15 ECHR, which builds margin of appreciation doctrine into the preamble of the Convention.[89] The Coalition government experimented with accessing a wider margin of appreciation for the UK through the Immigration Act 2014, which redefines the relationship between the public interest and individual and family rights in deportation cases.[90] Proposals for a British Bill of Rights seek to extend this approach across a wider range of rights and also attempt to ring-fence certain activities, such as combat deployments of the UK Armed Forces, from human rights scrutiny.[91]

(4) Justifying UK human rights exceptionalism

National foundation myths supposedly provide a unique source of authority for a political order.[92] If this is the case then the process by which individual liberties 'came to be attributed, in origin, to the victory of the barons over King John' has generated a particularly potent myth.[93] In the foundation story of the US, the War of Independence is often recast as a struggle to recapture the Magna Carta's inheritance.[94] In former US Attorney General Eric Holder's telling of this story these liberties, lost because of the oppressive power wielded by George III's governments, were ultimately reaffirmed and 'broadened' by the US Bill of Rights.[95] These US foundation myths have been used as part of US Government efforts to promote international human rights law abroad, despite the resistance of successive governments to "complying with human rights standards at home".[96] The Magna Carta's 800th anniversary therefore gave the HRA's detractors the opportunity to take advantage of what John Alder has described as the charter's

88 Ibid. para. 12(a). See Grieve, 'Can a Bill of Rights do better?' (n.76) 228.
89 Protocol 15 ECHR (2013) CETS No.213, Article 1.
90 See chapter eight of this volume.
91 Ibid. Q79.
92 See Michael Oakeshott *The Vocabulary of a Modern European State: Essays and Reviews 1952–88* (Imprint Academic, 2008) 194.
93 Brian Simpson *Human Rights and the End of Empire: Britain and the Genesis of the European Convention* (OUP, 2001) 24.
94 See Claire Palley *The United Kingdom and Human Rights* (Sweet & Maxwell, 1991) 71–73.
95 Eric Holder 'Remarks at the Global Law Summit to Commemorate the 800-Year Anniversary of Magna Carta' (2015) available at: <www.justice.gov/opa/speech/attorney-general-holder-delivers-remarks-global-law-summit-commemorate-800-year>.
96 Michael Ignatieff, 'Introduction: American Exceptionalism and Human Rights' from Ignatieff (ed.), *American Exceptionalism and Human Rights* (Princeton University Press, 2009) 1, 1.

"iconic significance" to invigorate reactionary opposition within the UK, not only to the legislative arrangements contained within HRA but also to the international human rights project as a whole.[97] By promoting the UK's constitutional history as uniquely imbued with a spirit of liberty, Conservative ministers are in essence claiming that international human rights have little role to play in UK governance and apply instead to "less happier lands".[98]

Chris Grayling, when Lord Chancellor/Justice Secretary, took the opportunity of the Global Law Summit staged to mark the 800th anniversary to enthuse that the "Magna Carta has been one of the UK's greatest exports: it has inspired and formed the basis of so many legal systems".[99] Less was made in his speech about how often this export of constitutional liberties was intertwined with the UK's imperial project.[100] Such contributions nonetheless establish a theme of fundamental rights protections being transmitted from the UK to the rest of the world. As David Cameron declared on the Magna Carta's anniversary the concept of government under the law, "taken for granted here in Britain . . . is what others are crying out for, hoping for, praying for".[101] Embarrassing Strasbourg judgments may have threatened this complaisant superiority and energised the Conservative backlash against the ECHR, but the friction between the UK's governance arrangements and post-war international constitutionalism, which Cameron sought to tap into, is deep rooted.[102] Successive UK governments have struggled to define the UK's place in a post-war order in which it is a declining world power.

The senior Conservative MP Peter Lilley, long a vocal detractor of the HRA, has characterised the UK's post-war contribution to drafting the ECHR as an effort to "bring the advantage of British liberties to 'lesser breeds without the law', as Kipling had it".[103] His quotation from Kipling in part emphasises the condescending attitude of some of the UK politicians and officials involved in drafting the ECHR towards the legal systems of continental Europe and their confidence that the UK conformed in all important respects to the ECHR's requirements.[104] But this should not disguise Lilley's belief that international

97 John Alder 'The Sublime and the Beautiful: Incommensurability and Human Rights' (2006) *PL* 697, 699.

98 Richard II, Act II, Scene 1.

99 Chris Grayling 'Lord Chancellor speaks at the Global Law Summit, marking 800 years of the Magna Carta' available at <www.gov.uk/government/speeches/lord-chancellor-speech-at-the-global-law-summit-23-february-2015>.

100 See, for example, Edmund Burke *The Works of the Right Honorable Edmund Burke Vol.2*, (Little, Brown & Company, 1865–67) 441.

101 Cameron 'Magna Carta 800th Anniversary' (n.45).

102 G. de Freitas HC Deb 22 August 1945 vol. 413, col. 692–693.

103 Peter Lilley HC Deb 10 February 2011 vol.523, col.551 quoting R. Kipling, *Recessional* (1897).

104 See Geffory Marston 'The United Kingdom's Part in the Preparation of the European Convention on Human Rights, 1950' (1993) *42 International and Comparative Law Quarterly* 796, 811.

human rights mechanisms were far removed from the UK's historic protections for civil liberties: "[o]ur liberties did not result from giving courts the right to explicate an abstract list of rights".[105]

Even if the ECHR drew on civil liberties which were part of the UK's constitutional history, the ancient constitution's proponents maintain that the human rights project diverged unacceptably from the UK's constitution in allowing an international tribunal to Act as the ultimate interpretative authority on the scope of these rights. The UK is above such scrutiny; "[i]t is only because this country was prepared to take on the might of Nazi Germany that there is a European Court".[106] This is not a novel argument but, rather, a reprise of A.V. Dicey's nineteenth-century claims that parliamentary sovereignty should prevail over particular civil liberties and that liberty would be secured by "the manners of the nation".[107] In other words, Dicey was confident that the UK electorate would not support despotic governments and juries would not convict suspects tried under oppressive criminal offences, but this provides little meaningful constraint on UK government action.[108] Nonetheless, such concerns are irrelevant to an account which treats "real" human rights abuses as impossible in the UK because, as Giovanni Sartori satirised, "the British people are clever and fine people who know how to go about in politics".[109] In light of the underlying premise of the UK being exceptional as a font of liberty, a British Bill of Rights becomes a means by which to decouple the UK from international human rights projects.

Magna Carta exceptionalism, by confirming the UK as a uniquely long-standing 'rights-respecting' democracy, transforms human rights into values which are not directly relevant to government policy making, except in relation to foreign policy. Even as he issued veiled threats against the UK's ongoing commitment to the ECHR system, David Cameron continued to invoke human rights abuses as a basis for justifying military interventions, declaring that "[w]e are not and never will be a country that walks on by while human rights are trampled into the dust".[110] He was, however, employing the term to cover the use of massive force by Colonel Gaddafi's military against a near-defenceless civilian population in Benghazi. In explaining the UK's intervention in Libya in these terms, David Cameron was treating 'real' human rights abuses as being synonymous with crimes against humanity. As one former minister reiterated when military action was proposed against President Assad's regime in Syria in 2013, "failure by the international community to Act would be far more dangerous than taking evidence-based, proportionate and legal military action as a clear lesson to

105 Lilley HC Deb 10 February 2011 vol.523, col.552.
106 Philip Hollobone HC Deb 10 February 2011 vol.523, col.538.
107 Dicey *Law of the Constitution* (n.64) 120.
108 Simpson *Human Rights and the End of Empire* (n.93) 37.
109 Giovanni Sartori 'Constitutionalism: A Preliminary Discussion' (1962) 56 *American Political Science Review* 853, 854.
110 Cameron 'Speech on the European Court of Human Rights' (n.44).

human rights abusers and dictators who murder and terrorise innocent civilian populations".[111] The implication is that the ambit of human rights should extend to only to cover rights abuses which cause "extreme humanitarian distress on a large scale".[112] The UK government maintains that such circumstances are capable of justifying humanitarian intervention but is implying that domestic legal systems should be left to tackle lesser infringements.

Conclusion: The Magna Carta as a Trojan horse

In 1915, at the height of the First World War, the pressure to trumpet the heritage of the Magna Carta was acute, with commemorative events intended to provide a not-too-subtle affirmation of the ongoing 'democratic' struggle against the 'authoritarian' central powers.[113] One hundred years later it should perhaps be more surprising to find that the Magna Carta is still being co-opted into struggles over how to define the UK polity, with Elizabeth Truss claiming, soon after her appointment as Lord Chancellor in Theresa May's Government in July 2016, that "[w]e have a strong record, as a country, of human rights, dating back to Magna Carta, and the British Bill of Rights is going to be the next step in enshrining those rights in our laws".[114] This contribution has sought to expose the connection between the Conservatives' oft-avowed commitment to the spirit of Magna Carta and their efforts to undermine the HRA. Magna Carta rhetoric has proved useful to these ends because it camouflages the government's ultimate aim of weakening rights protections.

Magna Carta rhetoric is a device used by the Conservatives to critique the HRA as being too foreign to the UK's legal traditions and too threatening to parliamentary sovereignty to warrant its place within the UK Constitution. In asserting an indigenous rights tradition stretching back to 1215, the Conservative government is, in the first instance, justifying at least the rebranding of the HRA, to prevent human rights from being "seen as something that are done to British courts and the British people as a result of foreign intervention".[115] Having unleashed such powerful nationalistic arguments against the ECHR system the government might well, in the political climate prevailing in the wake of the EU referendum result, see little additional cost in hollowing out the HRA's protections. This does not necessarily mean returning to a diaphanous web of civil liberties in place of a

111 Andrew Mitchell HC Deb 29 August 2013 vol.566, col.1474.

112 Dominic Grieve 'Guidance: Chemical Weapon Use by Syrian Regime: UK Government Legal Position' (29 August 2013) para. 4 available at <www.gov.uk/government/publications/chemical-weapon-use-by-syrian-regime-uk-government-legal-position/chemical-weapon-use-by-syrian-regime-uk-government-legal-position-html-version>.

113 See H. Malden (ed.) *Magna Carta Commemoration Essays* (Royal Historical Society, 1917).

114 Elizabeth Truss HC Deb 6 September 2016 vol.614, col.186.

115 See EU Committee *The UK, the EU and a British Bill of Rights* (n.42) para. 36.

system of enumerated rights, but proposals for a bill of rights are moving towards limiting the scope of some existing rights, carving out exceptions to others, and restricting the remedies available to the courts. Magna Carta rhetoric is even being advanced as a basis for abandoning the UK's international human rights commitments as an unnecessary encumbrance on the UK's unique constitution. Too often the Magna Carta has been invoked in the bill of rights debate as a Trojan horse, burnishing the Conservative Party's supposed commitment to fundamental freedoms even as it tries to unpick the ECHR from the UK Constitution.

Chapter 3

England's terror of the French Revolution

The historical roots of resistance to the Rights of Man and the case against the Human Rights Act

Bill Bowring

Introduction

In this chapter I argue that the roots of English (nowadays British) unease and in some cases downright hostility towards the Human Rights Act (HRA), and the European Convention on Human Rights (ECHR) which it partially incorporates into UK legislation, is to be found in the sharp, even intemperate, responses to the *Déclaration des Droits de l'Homme et du Citoyen* of 1789 by the fathers, respectively, of English conservatism and English liberalism: Edmund Burke and Jeremy Bentham. I also seek to show that their tone and their arguments found their way into the influential writing of Albert Venn Dicey in the late nineteenth century, into the mindset of the proponents of 'political constitutionalism' in contemporary Britain and underlie contemporary opposition to the HRA.

I start in the recent past with some remarks on the drafting process for the ECHR in 1949–50, and the reasons why the ECHR is, as the UK desired, a much more limited document than the Universal Declaration of Human Rights adopted by the United Nations in 1948. The ECHR contains 'first generation', 'justiceable', human rights, in a concise form which is remarkably similar to that of the *Déclaration*, even if this is not expressly noted by contemporary scholars.

Second, I turn to A.V. Dicey's remarks on the *Déclaration* and indeed all written constitutions especially those containing declarations or definitions of rights: his targets were the French and Belgian Constitutions of his time. I note that he commences with a quotation from Edmund Burke, from 1791, and that in passing he praises Bentham for having refuted the supremacy of natural rights. Third, I examine Burke both in his writings of 1790 and in the posthumous construction of his thought into a foundation of English conservatism. Fourth, I explore Jeremy Bentham's posthumously published frontal attack on the *Déclaration* and the reasons why he may have reacted in this way. Fifth, I trace the echoes of Burke, Bentham and Dicey in the work of Richard Bellamy, a leading contemporary exponent of 'political constitutionalism'.

It is my case that this colourful history is at the root of the opposition to or at least unease with the HRA which is the subject matter of this book. In conclusion,

I find support for my argument in the cover of a collection, focusing on one of the most outspoken opponents of the ECHR and HRA, Lord Sumption, published in 2016. The cover shows a print from 1794; and the note on the print brings my argument full circle.

(1) The drafting of the ECHR

The Universal Declaration of Human Rights (UDHR)[1] was adopted by the United Nations General Assembly on 10 December 1948 at the Palais de Chaillot in Paris.[2] Even a cursory glance at this document reveals that its 30 articles, with 26 substantive rights, contain many more rights than those listed in the ECHR. These include the right to social security (Article 22); the right to work, to equal pay for equal work and just and favourable remuneration and the right to form and join trade unions (Article 23); the right to rest and leisure including paid holidays (Article 24); the right to an adequate standard of living including food, clothing, housing, medical care, social services and social protection (Article 25); the right to education (Article 26); and the right to participation in the cultural life of the community (Article 27). That is, the social, economic and cultural rights which are noticeably absent from the ECHR. I have argued elsewhere that the UK and the other common-law countries share a profound scepticism concerning or even an allergy towards social and economic rights, not least because they are thought not to be susceptible to adjudication.[3]

Morsink not only highlights the "question of whether or not there are two kinds of rights in the Declaration, "real" civil and political rights and "utopian" social, economic and cultural ones", and observes that "[s]ome delegations thought that no cuts should be made in the area of social and economic rights, for they were the new and recently accepted rights".[4] These newer rights, it was thought, should be spelled out in greater detail than the older eighteenth-century civil and political ones.[5] He also notes that ". . . a cursory reading of the Declaration might suggest that the drafters did not think of these 'new', nineteenth-century rights as having the same status as the older and more established civil and political rights that hail from the eighteenth century."[6]

Brian Simpson relates that during the 1949–1950 negotiations in the Council of Europe which produced the ECHR, the UK's Foreign Office position was to

1 Universal Declaration of Human Rights UNGA Res 217A(III) 10 December 1948.
2 Johannes Morsink *The Universal Declaration of Human Rights: Origins, Drafting and Intent* (University of Pennsylvania Press 1990).
3 Bill Bowring 'Forbidden Relations? The UK's Discourse of Human Rights and the Struggle for Social Justice' (2002) 1 *Law, Social Justice, and Global Development* available at <http://elj.warwick.ac.uk/global/issue/2002-1/bowring.htm> accessed 14 October 2016.
4 Morsink (n.2) 84.
5 Ibid. 164. The delegations in favour of cutting were those from the USA, UK and India.
6 Ibid. 222

emphasise that the approach of the Council of Europe "should be on the right lines".[7] The initial plan was for "a statement in concise form" of fundamental personal rights based mainly on the UDHR.[8] The issue was which rights were capable of legal enforcement,[9] and the proposal was for a "minimum list of rights susceptible of legal enforcement".[10] That is, the cutting of the "utopian" and non-justiciable social and economic rights in the UDHR. Simpson does not note the rather striking fact that that the final text of the ECHR, with its twelve substantive rights, was remarkably similar to the eighteenth-century civil and political rights to which Morsink referred. That is, the rights set out in the *Déclaration des Droits de l'Homme et du Citoyen* adopted by the National Assembly of France on 26 August 1789.[11] Furthermore, these are precisely the substantive rights to be found in the HRA, and although the authors of much contemporary criticism of the HRA may not be in any way conscious of it, their hostility echoes the outspoken condemnation of the English critics of the eighteenth and nineteenth centuries. I do note, with approbation of their historical sense, if not approval for their arguments, commentators such as Professor Guglielmo Verdirame, who recalls Edmund Burke as follows:[12]

> The British genius, as Burke understood, was to entrench liberty in the beliefs, traditions and habits of the British people, realising that this matters even more than abstract pronouncements. The association of liberty with tradition instils a sense of individual and collective ownership of those rights. It connects the individual with past and future generations. It minimises the atomising effect of purely individualistic entitlements.

Furthermore, Conservative politicians have also cited Burke with approval when calling for repeal of the HRA. In a Westminster Hall Debate, concerning a "British Bill of Rights", Bill Cash MP described Burke as having identified "a proper kind of freedom" which he contrasted unfavourably with the "entirely abstract and in the event utterly destructive approach" represented by natural rights.[13] I show in this chapter that opposition to the Rights of Man,

7 Brian Simpson *Human Rights and End of Empire: Britain and the Genesis of the European Convention* (OUP 2001) 649.
8 Ibid. 650.
9 Ibid. 658.
10 Ibid. 661.
11 Jeremy Waldron *Nonsense upon Stilts: Bentham, Burke and Marx on the Rights of Man* (Methuen 1987) 24.
12 Guglielmo Verdirame "Why Britain should scrap the Human Rights Act" *The Spectator* (3 October 2014) available at <http://blogs.spectator.co.uk/2014/10/why-britain-should-scrap-the-human-rights-act/ accessed 24 November 2016>.
13 WH Deb 17 March 2011 vol. 525, col. 116.

to the French *Déclaration* of 1789, and latterly to the HRA, has a long and distinguished pedigree in English conservatism.

(2) Dicey and the 1789 *Déclaration*

In the appendix to his 1885 *Introduction to the Study of the Law of the Constitution* (*The Law of the Constitution*), Albert Venn Dicey (4 February 1835–7 April 1922) commented on the "rigidity" of the French Constitutions, starting with the constitution of 1791 which contained the *Déclaration*, and the 12 French constitutions up to the 1875.[14] He commented that "[a]n English critic smiles at the labour wasted in France on the attempt to make immutable Constitutions which, on an average, have lasted about the years apiece."[15] Each one contained the *Déclaration*. The very first line of the preamble to the 1958 French constitution (of the Fifth Republic) is as follows:

> The French people solemnly proclaim their attachment to the Rights of Man and the principles of national sovereignty as defined by the Declaration of 1789, confirmed and complemented by the Preamble to the Constitution of 1946.[16]

Dicey is frequently referred to today by English constitutional lawyers, an example being Alison Young in her 2008 *Parliamentary Sovereignty and the Human Rights Act*, who discusses Dicey at length.[17] The issue in her text is the compatibility of the HRA with Dicey's doctrines of parliamentary sovereignty and the rule of law. But it is symptomatic of such contemporary engagements with Dicey, and hers in particular, that there is no reference to the eighteenth-century antecedents to Dicey's nineteenth-century theorisation of the English Constitution, no mention of Burke or Bentham, and no mention of his constant engagement with the 1789 *Déclaration* in its contemporary (to him) manifestations on the continent. In fact, throughout *the Law of the Constitution*, Dicey referred, adversely, to both the French and Belgian Constitutions. The whole book should, in my view, be read as a polemical refutation of the call for protection of rights

14 A. V. Dicey *Introduction to the Study of the Law of the Constitution* (first ed. 1885; 8th ed. Macmillan 1931) 469.

15 Ibid. 474.

16 English translation approved by the French authorities, available at <www.thisnation.com/library/france.html> accessed on 14 October 2016.

17 Alison Young *Parliamentary Sovereignty and the Human Rights Act* (Hart 2009). In her Conclusion, Young (p. 161) makes it clear that her book argues for possible ways in which rights can be entrenched while preserving parliamentary sovereignty. She contends (p. 162) that Dicey's theory has been regarded as the "prevailing conception of sovereignty".

by way of written declarations or lists of rights. I do not apologise, therefore, for quoting Dicey at some length.

Belgium adopted its first constitution in 1831, drawing on French, Dutch and English models.[18] As Lefebvre pointed out, the Belgian Constitution differed from the French and American Constitutions in that it did not have a separate *Droits de l'homme et du citoyen* or Bill of Rights but incorporated most of them into the main body of the Constitution so as to make them legally binding.[19] Dicey commented that

> . . . it is a mistake to think that the whole law of the English constitution might not be reduced to writing and be enacted in the form of a constitutional code. The Belgian constitution indeed comes very near to a written reproduction of the English constitution, and the constitution of England might easily be turned into an Act of Parliament without suffering any material transformation of character, provided only that the English parliament retained – what the Belgian Parliament, by the way, does not possess – the unrestricted power of repealing or amending the constitutional code.[20]

That is, parliamentary sovereignty or supremacy. This passage immediately preceded the statement by Dicey of the

> . . . three traits of Parliamentary sovereignty as it exists in England: first, the power of the legislature to alter any law, fundamental or otherwise, as freely and in the same manner as other laws; secondly, the absence of any legal distinction between constitutional and other laws; thirdly, the non-existence of any judicial or other authority having the right to nullify an Act of Parliament, or to treat it as void or unconstitutional.[21]

This formulation brought Dicey straight to his point of comparison. In chapter IV, "The Rule of Law: its Nature and General Applications", Dicey commented,

> . . . the English constitution . . . was not created at one stroke, and far from being the result of legislation, in the ordinary sense of that term . . . [is] the fruit of contests carried on in the Courts on behalf of the rights of individuals. Our constitution, in short, is a judge-made constitution, and it bears on its face all the features, good and bad, of judge-made law . . . Hence

18 Edwige Lefebvre "The Belgian Constitution of 1831: The Citizen Burgher" (ZERP Diskussionspapier, Bremen 4/97) available at <www.jura.uni-bremen.de/lib/download.php?file=13752639d7.pdf> accessed 14 October 2016.

19 Lefebvre (n.18) p. 27

20 A. V. Dicey *Introduction to the Study of the Law of the Constitution* (first ed. 1885; 8th ed. Macmillan 1931)() 86.

21 Ibid. 87.

> flow noteworthy distinctions between the constitution of England and the constitutions of most foreign countries. There is in the English constitution an absence of those declarations or definitions of rights so dear to foreign constitutionalists.[22]

Later in the book, Dicey was even more explicit as to what he was opposing. In chapter VI "The Right to Freedom of Discussion", Dicey wrote,

> The Declaration of the Rights of Man and the French Constitution of 1791 proclaim freedom of discussion and the liberty of the press in terms which are still cited in text-books as embodying maxims of French jurisprudence . . .[23]

And later in the same chapter,

> [t]he Revolution (it may be fancied) put an end to restraints upon the press. The Declaration of the Rights of Man proclaimed the right of every citizen to publish and print his opinions . . . the Constitution of 1791 guaranteed to every man the natural right of speaking, printing and publishing his thoughts without having his writing submitted to any censorship or inspection prior to publication. But the Declaration of Rights and this guarantee were practically worthless.[24]

Even more significant for the purposes of this chapter is the quotation with which Dicey started his book, on page 1, under the heading "The True Nature of Constitutional Law". Dicey's quotation was as follows:

> "Great critics," writes Burke in 1791, "have taught us one essential rule . . . It is this, that if ever we should find ourselves disposed not to admire those writers or artists, Livy or Virgil for instance, Raphael or Michael Angelo, whom all the learned had admired, not to follow our own fancies, but to study them until we know how and what we ought to admire; and if we cannot arrive at this combination of admiration with knowledge, rather to believe that we are dull, than that the rest of the world has been imposed on. It is as good a rule, at least, with regard to this admired constitution (of England). We ought to understand it according to our measure; and to venerate where we are not able presently to comprehend.[25]

The reference given by Dicey in his footnote is simply "Burke, *Works*, iii (1872 ed.), p. 114". This was in fact a quotation from Burke's *From an Appeal from*

22 Ibid. 192.
23 Ibid. 234.
24 Ibid. 252.
25 Ibid. 1.

the New to the Old Whigs, in Consequence of some late Discussions in Parliament, Relative to the Reflections on the French Revolution, of 1791.[26] Dicey did not refer to Burke much in his text but added in the same chapter:

> The present generation must of necessity look on the constitution in a spirit different from the sentiment either of 1791 or of 1818.[27] We cannot share the religious enthusiasm of Burke, raised, as it was, to the temper of fanatical adoration by just hatred of those "doctors of the modern school", who, when he wrote, were renewing the rule of barbarism in the form of the reign of terror . . .[28]

What I have shown is that throughout the *Law of the Constitution* Dicey was arguing with the continental tradition of constitutionalism with its roots in the French Revolution and the *Déclaration* of 1789. And Dicey was most certainly following in Burke's footsteps, as I show, and as the quotation at the start of his book made absolutely clear.

(3) Edmund Burke on the French Revolution

Edmund Burke (1729–1797) is often referred to as the 'founder of modern conservatism'. The work which Dicey cited was written towards the end of his life, when he was 63 years old, and one year after his *Reflections on the Revolution in France*, which Burke wrote from February to the summer of 1790.[29] It was, as Jeremy Waldron points out, an immediate success, selling more than 17,000 copies by the end of the year.[30] Burke was publicly congratulated by the king and other political leaders. But in 1794 his case for the impeachment of Warren Hastings (the then governor of Bengal) for maladministration in India failed, his

26 Edmund Burke *From An Appeal from the New to the Old Whigs, in Consequence of some late Discussions in Parliament, Relative to the Reflections on the French Revolution* (London 1791) facsimile available at https://archive.org/details/appealfromnewtoo00burkiala accessed 14 October 2010, 140–141.

27 This is a reference to the work of the historian Henry Hallam (1777 to 1859) *View of the State of Europe during the Middle Ages* (12th ed.), Volume 2, p267: "No unbiased observer who derives pleasure from the welfare of his species, can fail to consider the long and uninterruptedly increasing prosperity of England as the most beautiful phaenomenon in the history of mankind . . .".

28 Dicey (n.20) 3.

29 Its full title was *Reflections on the Revolution in France and on the proceedings in certain societies in London relative to that event. In a letter intended to have been sent to a gentleman in Paris by the right honourable Edmund Burke* facsimile of the 2nd edition available at <https://archive.org/details/reflectionsonre04burkgoog> accessed 17 October 2016.

30 Jeremy Waldron (ed.) 'Nonsense upon Stilts. Bentham, Burke and Marx on the Rights of Man' (London, Methuen 1987) ch. 4 "*Edmund Burke's Reflections on the Revolution in France*" (1790) 82.

son died that year, and the French revolution had apparently achieved victory, and he died a bitter and troubled man in 1797. Burke's starting point in his *Reflections* was to characterise English constitutionalism in terms of property and inheritance, terms which would be at once recognisable to his aristocratic and landed readers:

> You will observe, that from Magna Carta to the Declaration of Right, it has been the uniform policy of our constitution to claim and assert our liberties, as an *entailed inheritance* derived to us from our forefathers, and to be transmitted to our posterity . . .[31]

This was to be contrasted to the "rights of man" philosophy of the French revolutionaries:

> I shall only say here, in justice to that old-fashioned constitution, under which we have long prospered, that our representation has been found perfectly adequate to all purposes for which a representation of the people can be desired or derived . . . To detail the particulars in which it is found so well to promote its ends, would demand a treatise on our practical constitution, I state here the doctrine of the Revolutionists, only that you and others may see, what an opinion these gentlemen entertain of the constitution of their country . . .[32]

In passing, he noted that the revolutionaries considered the English House of Commons as only a "semblance", "a form", "a theory", "a shadow", "a mockery", perhaps "a nuisance" – though he did not disclose the source of these epithets. Like Jeremy Bentham, to whom I turn next, he regarded the ideas of the French revolutionaries as intellectual terrorism, or more precisely an underground mine to blow up everything of value in a grand explosion:

> It is no wonder therefore, that with these ideas of everything in their constitution and government at home, either in church or state, as illegitimate and usurped, or, at best as a vain mockery, they look abroad with an eager and passionate enthusiasm. Whilst they are possessed by these notions, it is vain to talk to them of the practice of their ancestors, the fundamental laws of their country, the fixed form of a constitution, whose merits are confirmed by the solid test of long experience . . . They despise wisdom as the wisdom of unlettered men; and as for the rest, they have wrought under-ground a mine that will blow up at one grand explosion all examples of antiquity, all precedents, charters and acts of parliament. They have 'the rights of men'.

31 Ibid. 100.
32 Ibid. 102.

> Against these there can be no prescription; against these no agreement is binding; these admit no temperament, and no compromise: anything withheld from their full demand is so much fraud and injustice. Against these their rights of men let no government look for security in the length of its continuance, or in the justice and lenity of its administration.[33]

Thomas Schofield, professor of the History of Legal and Political Thought and director of the Bentham Project at University College London, where Bentham's 'auto-icon' is preserved, analysed the effect of Burke's polemic on contemporary English conservative thought.[34] He pointed out that the rights-of-man doctrine of the French revolutionaries posed as much of a danger to social order as the more tangible military threat posed by revolutionary France.[35] Indeed in his *Letter to a Member of the National Assembly* and *Thoughts on French Affairs*, Burke argued that the Britain and other European powers "should aid counter-revolution and expurgate rights-of-man philosophy".[36] After the events of 1792 Burke's polemic convinced conservatives that the proponents of rights-of-man philosophy, with its central principle of the sovereignty of the people, believed it should be universally applied, to every European state:

> There was now widespread agreement with Burke's view that these doctrines tended 'to the utter subversion, not only of all government, in all modes, and to all stable securities to rational freedom, but to all the rules and principles of morality.'[37]

Democratic principles and the threat of sedition were now inseparable. In 1792 William Pitt the Younger (1759–1806),[38] the British prime minister who was a ferocious opponent of the French Revolution and led Britain in the wars against France (which declared war against Britain in 1793) and Napoleon, explained to the House of Commons,

> This whole system of insurrection . . . would appear . . . to be laid in the Rights of Man, that monstrous doctrine, under colour of which the weak and ignorant, who are most susceptible of impression from such barren abstract

33 Ibid. 103–4.
34 Thomas Philip Schofield 'Conservative Political Thought in Britain in Response to the French Revolution' (1986) 29 *The Historical Journal* 601.
35 Ibid. 601
36 Ibid. 603
37 Ibid. 603, and Edmund Burke *The works of the Right Honourable Edmund Burke: A new Edition* (12 vols., London 1808–13), VI, 148.
38 He became the youngest prime minister in 1783 at the age of 24. He left office in 1801 but was prime minister again from 1804 until his death in 1806. He was also the chancellor of the exchequer throughout his premiership. See <www.bbc.co.uk/history/historic_figures/pitt_the_younger.shtml> accessed on 22 November 2016.

> speculations, were expected and attempted to be seduced to overturn Government, law, property, security, religion, order, and everything valuable in this country, as they had already overturned and destroyed everything in France, and endangered every nation in Europe.[39]

In my view Pitt's denunciation of the rights of man as a "monstrous doctrine" continues to resonate in the debates concerning the HRA. Benedict Douglas has noted that the intellectual legacy of both Bentham and Burke and their scepticism towards rights has contributed to the perception that there is a lack of popular 'ownership' over the contents of the HRA.[40] It is noteworthy, however, that the antagonists in the debate over the future of the HRA rarely refer to this history and speak as if they are ignorant of it. Schofield sums up the convictions of conservatives as follows:[41]

> Conservatives proceeded to argue that the inequalities of property and rank, as they existed in Britain, were perfectly just, in conformity with nature, and promoted both the individual and general welfare. This form of government, founded on property, guaranteed stability, equal civil rights and proper reward to industry and skill. The revolutionary government of France however had an unnatural basis, the sovereignty of the people. The revolution had destroyed security of property and instituted tyranny. By attacking property, it had assaulted the true principles of government, and because it was universal in its doctrines, it was universal in its application. The revolution was more than the destruction of the ancient monarchy of France; it constituted a world-wide onslaught upon civilization.[42]

The historian Emily Jones has recently shown that by 1914 Burke had been firmly established as a 'conservative' political thinker whose work was directly associated with British conservatism.[43] She observes that 'Burkean conservatism' centres on key concepts, drawn primarily from his *Reflections on the Revolution in France* (1790), such as 'the authority of tradition'; the organic, historic conception of society; and the necessity of order, religion, and property. Thus, she observes, Burke, who never produced a theory of government, is now generally referred to as the "founder of modern conservatism."[44]

39 Schofield (n34) 604; and *The Parliamentary Register* (2nd series, 45 vols., London, 1781–96)XXXVIII, 247.

40 Benedict Douglas 'Why Human Rights Have Not Been Accepted in the UK' *U.K. Constitutional Law Blog* (4th May 2015) available at <http://ukconstitutionallaw.org> accessed 20 November 2016.

41 Schofield (n.34) 621.

42 Ibid. 621.

43 Emily Jones 'Conservatism, Edmund Burke, and the Invention of a Political Tradition, c. 1885–1914' (2015) 58 *The Historical Journal* 1115.

44 Ibid. 1116.

Indeed, Burke never set out to be a political theorist, let alone a theorist of conservatism. As the title of his 1791 text shows, he saw himself as a Whig. He was an example of a polemicist and politician whose status as a "political philosopher of conservatism" was constructed by a "burgeoning literature in higher education", systematising his letters and speeches, at the same time as a substantial number of political Conservatives appropriated his "conservatism". Thus, Burke's thought was moulded into "a much baggier but more polemically useful 'theory' of conservatism which eventually became seen as the basis of political Conservatism."[45] Jones points out that Dicey defended the existing constitution against revolutionary 'Jacobins' in a series of books and articles. In these texts, Burke's "Reflections", a defence of the liberty of aristocrats and clergymen against atheists and the multitude, as well as a eulogy of the British constitution, became a key source. The *Fortnightly Review* claimed that '[i]t is the fashion in these days to quote Burke.' In this perspective, says Jones, Home Rulers became "French Jacobins, intent on destruction and not reform."[46]

I agree with Jones's estimation that 'Burkean conservatism' came to symbolise relatively vague concepts, such as hostility to constitutional change (including the critique of abstract ahistorical thought in politics, and the need for balance in the constitution), and support for private property, religion, historicism and the organic nature of society.[47] Jones, however, does not focus on Burke's specific attack on the "rights of man", nor does she refer to Schofield's publication in the same journal. However, the influence of Edmund Burke on Dicey and on the British attitude – and hostility towards – the Rights of Man cannot be denied, in the context of his role as the "father of English conservatism".

(4) Jeremy Bentham and 'anarchical fallacies'

Dicey did not refer in his *Law of the Constitution* to Edmund Burke's younger contemporary Jeremy Bentham (1748–1832), except in the introduction, where he stated that the "dogma of natural rights" was in England condemned and confuted (refuted) by Bentham and his disciples. In Dicey's view the declining influence of utilitarianism appeared to have given new strength to this doctrine.[48] Dicey did not tell his readers how Bentham had performed this service. Bentham's attack on 'rights-of-man philosophy' was written in much stronger terms even than Burke's. Bentham began working on his response to the 1789 *Déclaration* in 1795 and finished them in 1796. The document was originally titled *Pestulance Unmasked*, but remained unpublished, though offered to an

45 Ibid. 1118.
46 Ibid. 1121.
47 Jones (n.43) 1123.
48 Dicey (n.20) lxii.

anti-Jacobin magazine under the splendid title *No French Nonsense: or a Cross Buttock for the first Declaration of Rights: together with a kick of the A – for the Second . . . by a practitioner of the Old English Art of Self Defence.*[49]

But it was not published under this title or any other until after Bentham's death in 1832, and although there was a publication in French, it did not appear in English until my ancestor John Bowring edited *The Works of Jeremy Bentham* in 11 volumes in 1843.[50] There it appeared under the title *Anarchical Fallacies; being an examination of the Declaration of Rights issued during the French Revolution.*[51] Jeremy Waldron sets it out in full in his collection already mentioned.[52] Bentham's vigorous condemnation of the *Déclaration* is well known:

> *Natural rights* is simple nonsense: natural and imprescriptible rights, rhetorical nonsense, – nonsense upon stilts . . . But this rhetorical nonsense ends in the old strain of mischievous nonsense; for immediately a list of these pretended natural rights is given, and those are so expressed as to present to view legal rights. And of these rights, whatever they are, there is not, it seems, any one of which any government *can*, upon any occasion whatever, abrogate the smallest particle.

So much for terrorist language.[53] In another text which Waldron includes in his collection, Bentham's *Supply without Burden*,[54] first published in 1795, Bentham wrote,

> When I hear of natural rights . . . I always see in the background a cluster of daggers or of pikes introduced in the National Assembly with the applause of the President Condorcet for the avowed purpose of exterminating the King's friends.[55]

49 Waldron (n.30) 32.

50 Hugo Bedau mistakenly gives the date of publication in English as 1834 – see Hugo Adam Bedau 'Anarchical Fallacies": Bentham's Attack on Human Rights' (2000) 22 *Human Rights Quarterly* 261.

51 Jeremy Bentham 'Anarchical Fallacies' from John Bowring (ed.) *The Works of Jeremy Bentham* (Edinburgh, William Tait, 1843) vol II, p. 489–535, facsimile edition available at <http://oll.libertyfund.org/sources/2124-facsimile-pdf-bentham-the-works-of-jeremy-bentham-vol-2/download> (accessed on 17 October 2016)

52 Waldron (n.30) 46–76.

53 Ibid. 55.

54 Jeremy Bentham 'Supply without Burden' from John Bowring (ed.) *The Works of Jeremy Bentham* (Edinburgh, William Tait 1843) vol. II, p. 585–598, facsimile edition available at <http://oll.libertyfund.org/sources/2124-facsimile-pdf-bentham-the-works-of-jeremy-bentham-vol-2/download> accessed on 17 October 2016.

55 Waldron (n.30) 74.

Hugo Bedau also refers to Bentham's opinion, citing his colourful phrases, that the *Déclaration:*

> . . . consists of "execrable trash," that its purpose is "resistance to all laws" and "insurrection," that its advocates "sow the seeds of anarchy broad-cast," and, most memorably, that any doctrine of natural rights is "simple nonsense: natural and imprescriptible rights, rhetorical nonsense,-nonsense upon stilts.[56]

In his later essay Philip Schofield noted that while Bentham was, until 1789, actively engaged in putting forward proposals for the reform of the French electoral and constitutional systems, Bentham was increasingly shocked by the violence of the Terror in France, and became ever more convinced of the superiority of the British preference for slow evolution, representative democracy through a sovereign parliament and rights defined and determined by the courts.[57]

These events were the insurrection of 10 August 1792 when the Tuileries was attacked and the royal family forced to flee, the September Massacres, the success of the French armies in Europe following the Battle of Valmy on 20 September 1792 and the abolition of the monarchy two days later. Bentham noted that the 'characteristic properties' of democratic government were ignorance, violence, extravagance, discontent, frequent wars and danger of violent revolution.[58] Indeed, the feature which Bentham criticised most severely was the lack of intelligence in the people to conduct the business of government.

Schofield concludes that Bentham was edging towards the development of a radical utilitarian politics until the excesses of the French Revolution persuaded him to abandon this course and, instead, to defend the existing institutions of the British polity. The historian J. H. Burns also noted[59] the divergence between the hopes of reformers and the reality of revolution in France. Even at his most sympathetic to the cause of radical reform Bentham was, according to Burns, already aware of the ideological gulf between his doctrines and those of the National Assembly. "The phrase natural right", he remarked in one of the unfinished letters to Mirabeau, "when opposed to utility is altogether an unmeaning one." At that time Bentham had not yet turned his attention to the *Déclaration*, but his opinion of it was not in doubt.[60]

The American philosopher Hugo Adam Bedau asked why Bentham described the *Déclaration* as containing "anarchical fallacies".[61] He turned directly to why

56 Bedau (n.50) 263.

57 Philip Schofield 'Jeremy Bentham, the French Revolution and political Radicalism' (2004) 30 *History of European Ideas* 381, 396.

58 See University College London Library, Bentham Papers, xliv. 5.

59 J. H. Burns 'Bentham and the French Revolution' (1966) 16 *Transactions of the Royal Historical Society* 95.

60 Ibid. 103.

61 Hugo Adam Bedau '"Anarchical Fallacies": Bentham's Attack on Human Rights' (2000) 22 *Human Rights Quarterly* 26.

Bentham thought that the French "Declaration sow[s] the seeds of anarchy broad-cast," and that it is a doctrine of "the rights of anarchy – the order of chaos." According to Bentham, the French *Déclaration* did this because of its tacit message: "People, behold your rights! If a single article of them be violated, insurrection is not your right only, but the most sacred of your duties."[62] As Bedau pointed out that this was a startling remark, since no such radically anarchic language actually appeared in the preamble or in any of the seventeen articles of the French *Déclaration*. The only language coming at all close to this was to be found in the second article, where all persons are told they have ". . . natural and imprescriptible rights . . . [including the right of] resistance to oppression" (*la résistance à l'oppression*).[63] Bedau pointed out that this was not to be found either in the American "Bill of Rights" of 1791 or in the 1948 UDHR. However, this assertion led Bentham to heap scorn on the very idea of an "imprescriptible" right – a right that no political or legal authority may or can suspend, modify, or nullify.64 Furthermore, Bedau pointed out that Bentham never explained why an insistence on "natural rights" as they were affirmed in the French *Déclaration*, were the sole or the dominant cause of political unrest in France.[65]

(5) The footprints of Burke, Bentham and Dicey in contemporary "political constitutionalism"

In this section I trace some of the lasting effects, the continuing resonance, of English and British hostility to the rights of man, in present-day scholarship. Richard Bellamy is a leading contemporary exponent of "political constitutionalism" – as opposed to the "legal constitutionalism" of those who believe that it is high time that the UK followed the example of the rest of the world and adopted a written constitution.[66] He points out that the UK presents a rather intractable puzzle to scholars of constitutionalism. Despite the absence to this date of a written constitution or even entrenched constitutional provisions – or even the equivalent

62 Ibid. 266.

63 Article 2: "Le but de toute association politique est la conservation des droits naturels et imprescriptibles de l'Homme. Ces droits sont la liberté, la propriété, la sûreté, et la résistance à l'oppression."

In French on the web-site of the French Conseil Constitutionnel, available at <www.conseil-constitutionnel.fr/conseil-constitutionnel/francais/la-constitution/la-constitution-du-4-octobre-1958/declaration-des-droits-de-l-homme-et-du-citoyen-de-1789.5076.html> accessed 18 October 2016. In English, "The goal of any political association is the conservation of the natural and imprescriptible rights of man. These rights are liberty, property, safety and resistance against oppression."

64 Bedau (n.61) 267.

65 Ibid. 268.

66 See Richard Bellamy 'Political constitutionalism and the Human Rights Act' (2011) 9 *International Journal of Constitutional Law* 86.

of Israel's Basic Laws[67] – the UK (or, more accurately, England) can claim to be the inspirer and originator of two key elements of modern "legal constitutionalism": the separation of powers (the inspiration for Montesquieu's 1748 *De l'esprit des lois*) and a bill of rights (as found in the 1689 *Act Declaring the Rights and Liberties of the Subject and Settling the Succession of the Crown*). Bellamy notes that "from more or less the same period" Parliamentary sovereignty emerged as the distinctive constitutional feature of the UK.[68]

I would say (which Bellamy does not) that this was fixed in constitutional practice in England in the seventeenth rather than the eighteenth century, and I would contend that parliamentary sovereignty is the direct consequence of Parliament's victory in the English Revolution (or Civil War). This was noted in 1993 by Lord Templeman in the House of Lords in *M v Home Office*,[69] when he characterised the submissions of the Home Office as "a proposition which would reverse the result of the Civil War". This war culminated in the execution of King Charles I in 1649 and led to the first and last attempt at a written constitution for England, the Instrument of Government, drafted by Major-General John Lambert in 1653.[70] Bellamy goes on to argue that parliamentary sovereignty has been a characteristic of the English constitutional order that "commentators from the late eighteenth century onward have believed negated, or at least trumped, both of these attributes of a legal constitution" – the separation of powers and a bill of rights. At this point Bellamy turns to Dicey:

> As Dicey, who became this doctrine's chief ideologist, famously and approvingly noted, there is 'in the English constitution an absence of those declarations or definitions of rights so dear to foreign constitutionalists.'[71]

And he mentions in passing Burke:

> However, from Edmund Burke onward, a host of defenders of the Westminster system have regarded it as offering a distinct and superior model of political constitutionalism, which protects British liberties far more effectively than could the paper parchment of a "legal" Constitution.[72]

Bellamy is clear that his aim is "less to assess if current judicial practice suggests the HRA is compatible with a distinctly political conception of the constitution

67 See *Basic Laws* available at <www.knesset.gov.il/description/eng/eng_mimshal_yesod.htm> accessed 18 October 2016.
68 Bellamy (n.66) 87.
69 *M v Home Office* [1993] UKHL 5.
70 See Peter Gaunt 'Drafting the Instrument of Government, 1653–54: a reappraisal' (1989) 8 *Parliamentary History* 28.
71 Bellamy (n.66) 86–7.
72 Ibid. 87.

and more to explore if it could be so".[73] At this point he returns to his opening paradox:

> In this way, skepticism about the possibility of a political constitution turns into skepticism about constitutionalism itself. And so we come back to the opening apparent paradox, the resolution of which arises by virtue of the British constitution's remaining true to its history in successfully combining both the separation of powers and a bill of rights not in despite of but because of Parliamentary sovereignty.[74]

Bellamy has returned to this theme in his contribution to a collection devoted to Lord Sumption's 2013 lecture "The Limits of Law".[75] In expressing his trenchant views concerning the Human Rights Act 1998 and the dangers of "judicial lawmaking", Lord Sumption did not mention Burke, Bentham or Dicey, though their ghosts, I suggest, are always present at his shoulder. Bellamy's contribution is titled *The Limits of Lord Sumption: Limited Legal Constitutionalism and the Political Form of the ECHR*.[76] According to the book's index, Burke, Bentham or Dicey are nowhere referred to in the collection. Bellamy is highly critical of Lord Sumption's "conservative" approach:

> However, whereas his arguments are institutionally and to some degree politically conservative, this is less so with regard to political constitutionalism. By and large, political constitutionalism has been proposed by those on the left of the political spectrum as much concerned by the judiciary's failure to uphold rights as by their propensity to discover new rights. From the political constitutionalist perspective, Lord Sumption's limited legal constitutionalism is as contentious and as open to abuse as the more extensive versions he criticises, such as those he associates with Ronald Dworkin, John Rawls and the 'living instrument' doctrine of the ECtHR.[77]

Conclusion

However, even if the index is notable for the absences I refer to in the preceding discussion, the cover illustration and the anonymous "A Note on the Cover" of *The Limits of Lord Sumption*, serve to help me to make my point. The illustration

73 Ibid. 88.
74 Ibid.111.
75 Lord Sumption *the 27th Sultan Azlan Shah Lecture* (Kuala Lumpur 20 November 2013) available at <www.supremecourt.uk/docs/speech-131120.pdf> accessed 18 October 2016.
76 Richard Bellamy "The Limits of Lord Sumption: Limited Legal Constitutionalism and the Political Form of the ECHR" from Nicholas Barber, Richard Ekins and Paul Yowell (eds.) *Lord Sumption and the Limits of the Law* (Hart Publishing 2016).
77 Ibid. 195.

is the 1793 print by James Gillray, "Fashion before ease; or, a good constitution sacrificed for a fantastic form". The note reads,

> The print shows an unhappy Britannia being laced into a corset by Thomas Paine. Paine was the author of, amongst other books, *The Rights of Man* – and the title of this volume can be seen on the measuring tape, which dangles from his pocket next to his tailor's shears. *The Rights of Man*, published a couple of years before Gillray's print, called for the introduction of a written constitution for the United Kingdom (sic), the recognition that natural rights constrain the state . . . Paine's intellectual rival, Edmund Burke, would have sympathised with the manner in which Gillray has chosen to depict the scene. For Burke, the British state was an organic entity, one that had developed over time, intertwined with the community of which it was a part. The rationalist attempt to draw up a set of rights that limited the states was bound to create discomfort: the protection of liberties is a function of a well-formed state, and not something that can be imposed on it from outside.[78]

Gillray's print and the note support, I think, my argument that the case against the HRA has a great deal to do with the historical development of English constitutionalism. The intellectual origins of both conservatism and liberalism in their English manifestations, and with the horror felt by Burke and Bentham not only towards the French Revolution itself, were characterised against the idea of natural rights, in particular the intellectual 'terrorism' of the *Déclaration*. This led to a cultural scepticism of the concept of natural rights which were often cast as the direct antithesis of British constitutional traditions. In a similar way the contemporary debate about HRA repeal frames supposedly British traditions, such as parliamentary sovereignty, against European notions, such as the protection of rights by the ECHR.

78 Ibid.

Part II

Sovereignty

Chapter 4

An ingenious failure? The Human Rights Act 1998 and parliamentary sovereignty

*Stephen J. Dimelow**

Introduction

In his introduction to the Human Rights Bill's second reading in the House of Commons, the then Home Secretary Jack Straw was unequivocal about the Government's continued commitment to parliamentary sovereignty. According to Straw, having decided that the European Convention on Human Rights (ECHR) should be incorporated into UK law, "how to do that in a manner that strengthened, and did not undermine, the sovereignty of parliament" was "the most fundamental question" the government faced.[1] While "[s]ome . . . argued that the courts should have the power to set aside primary legislation . . . on the grounds of incompatibility with the convention",[2] Straw was clear; the bill he was championing would not "call into question" the "constitutional arrangements that . . . make us one of the world's most stable democracies".[3] Notwithstanding the government's desire to give further effect to the ECHR, the sovereignty of parliament was to remain "paramount".[4]

Following the bill's enactment as the Human Rights Act 1998 (HRA), the government's efforts were frequently praised for their ingenuity, particularly in the way they balanced the so-called "key-stone of the constitution"[5] with the

* Career Development Fellow, New College, University of Oxford.

1 HC Deb 16 February 1998, vol. 306, col. 769.

2 HC Deb (n.1). For subsequently expressed unhappiness of this sort, see eg Mark Evans, *Constitution-Making and the Labour Party* (Palgrave Macmillan 2003) 186; Robert Wintemute 'The Human Rights Act's First Five Years: Too Strong, Too Weak or Just Right?' (2006) 17 *King's College Law Journal* 209; Rodney Brazier *Constitutional Reform* (3rd ed. OUP 2008) 129.

3 HC Deb (n.1) col 770.

4 HC Deb (n.1) col 770. This point was reiterated in Paul Boateng and Jack Straw 'Bringing Rights Home: Labour's plans to Incorporate the European Convention on Human Rights into UK Law' (1997) *EHRLR* (*European Human Rights Law Review*) 71, 77. For similar, see also Lord Irvine HL Deb 3 November 1997, vol. 582, col. 1228; Home Office *Rights Brought Home: The Human Rights Bill* (Cmd 3782, 1997) para. 2.13.

5 AV Dicey *An Introduction to the Study of the Law of the Constitution* (10th ed. Macmillan 1959) 70.

protection of fundamental rights.[6] While some continued to view the Act as either unnecessary or imprudent,[7] few raised doubts about the continued supremacy of Parliament in the new legal landscape.[8] Lord Steyn went so far as to say that he believed it "crystal clear" that the HRA preserved the principle of parliamentary sovereignty before the Act had even come into force,[9] so convinced was he that the government had achieved its aim.

As time has gone on, and the full breadth of the Act's consequences have gradually become clear, the HRA's s relationship with parliamentary sovereignty has become one of a number of increasingly divisive topics among constitutional and political commentators.[10] While many continue to think that the effort which went into the Act's drafting has not been wasted, and Parliament's powers remain undiminished,[11] a number of academic and political figures have expressed doubts about the extent to which Parliament can really be described as sovereign while the HRA remains in force. When one looks closely, they suggest, it is clear that the balance of power in the legal system is very different from that which some would have us believe. It is the judiciary, not Parliament, who really hold the trump card.[12]

6 KD Ewing, 'The Human Rights Act and Parliamentary Democracy' (1999) 62 *Modern Law Review* (*MLR*) 79, 79. For use of the term 'ingenious' see Ian Leigh and Laurence Lustgarten 'Making Rights Real: The Courts, Remedies and the Human Rights Act' (1999) 58 *Cambridge Law Journal* 509, 536; Stephen Sedley 'Foreword' from Stephen Grosz, Jack Beatson and Peter Duffy (eds.) *Human Rights: The 1998 Act and the European Convention* (Sweet & Maxwell 2000) vii; Louis Blom-Cooper 'Government and the Judiciary' from Anthony Seldon and Dennis Kavanagh (eds.) *The Blair Effect 2001–5* (CUP 2005) 238. For early, detailed analysis of the relationship between parliamentary sovereignty and the HRA see Nicholas Bamforth 'Parliamentary Sovereignty and the Human Rights Act 1998' [(998) *Public Law* (*PL*) 572; Ewing 'The Human Rights Act'; David Feldman 'The Human Rights Act 1998 and Constitutional Principles' (1999) 19 *Legal Studies* (*LS*) 165.

7 Tom Campbell, KD Ewing and Adam Tomkins (eds.) *Sceptical Essays on Human Rights* (OUP 2001).

8 Aileen Kavanagh *Constitutional Review under the UK Human Rights Act* (CUP 2009) 313. For some exceptions, see eg Tom Campbell 'Incorporation through Interpretation' from Tom Campbell, KD Ewing and Adam Tomkins (eds.) *Sceptical Essays on Human Rights* (OUP 2001); Jonathan Morgan 'Law's British Empire' (2002) 22 *Oxford Journal of Legal Studies (OJLS)* 734, 737–38; Mark Elliott 'Parliamentary Sovereignty and the New Constitutional Hypothesis: Legislative Freedom, Political Reality and Convention' (2002) 22 *LS* 340, esp 346–52; Mark Elliott 'United Kingdom: Parliamentary Sovereignty under Pressure' (2004) 2 *International Journal of Constitutional Law* (*ICON*) 545, 552–54.

9 *R v DPP, ex parte Kebilene* [2000] 2 AC 326, 327. Except with respect to the devolved administrations, the implementation of the Act was delayed until 1 October 2000 to allow for necessary preparations to be made.

10 For discussion, see generally Tom Hickman *Public Law after the Human Rights Act* (Hart Publishing 2010).

11 Hickman (n.10) 63; Colm O'Cinneide *Human Rights and the UK Constitution* (British Academy 2012) 48; O'Cinneide 'Human Rights and the UK Constitution' from Jeffrey Jowell, Dawn Oliver, and O'Cinneide (eds.) *The Changing Constitution* (8th ed. OUP 2015) 99.

12 Morgan 'Law's British' (n.8); Nick Herbert 'Rights without Responsibilities – A Decade of the Human Rights Act' British Institution of Human Rights Lecture (London 24

In this chapter I explore the debate that has developed around the HRA's relationship with the principle of parliamentary sovereignty. After outlining the principal grounds of disagreement, I suggest that these competing claims are much less concerned with the HRA's relationship to parliamentary sovereignty than it might first appear. While arguments are often framed as if parliamentary sovereignty is their central focus, in reality there is far less disagreement about the Act's drafting, how it has been applied, and how it interacts with this constitutional principle than might be thought. Instead, the primary source of disagreement might be better characterised as the nature and requirements of the principle itself, and what exactly should be considered an intrusion on it. How this insight, if correct, could be used to inform the debate that surrounds the future of the HRA, and the idea that the best way to reinvigorate Parliament is to adopt a British Bill of Rights of some sort, is briefly explored in the chapter's penultimate section.

(1) Conflicting claims

Much has been written about the HRA's relationship to UK constitutional principles, particularly that of parliamentary sovereignty. In this section I offer a little context for the debate that surrounds the Act's relationship to the principle of parliamentary sovereignty, before going on to outline and evaluate the current shape of the disagreement as I see it.

(i) Parliamentary sovereignty: An overview

The first problem that confronts anyone attempting to write about the compatibility of any aspect of the UK legal system with parliamentary sovereignty nowadays is determining which understanding of parliamentary sovereignty to employ. As much as it might be possible to summarise the essence of the principle in eight words – whatever the Queen in Parliament enacts is law[13] – lurking behind these eight words is a great deal of disagreement.[14] For my purposes, it is best I rely

November 2008) available at <www.nickherbert.com/media_centre.php/76/rights-without-responsibilities-a-decade-of-the-human-rights-act> accessed 6 July 2016; Kavanagh *Constitutional Review* (n.8) ch. 11; Michael Pinto-Duschinsky *Bringing Rights Back Home: Making Human Rights Compatible with Parliamentary Democracy in the UK* (Policy Exchange 2011); Michael Pinto-Duschinsky 'Commission Must Not Compromise by Recommending Bill Identical to HRA' *The Guardian* (London 13 March 2012) available at <www.theguardian.com/law/2012/mar/13/bill-of-rights-commission-compromise-hra> accessed 6 July 2016; Vernon Bogdanor 'Magna Carta, the Rule of Law and the Reform of the Constitution' from Robert Hazell and James Melton (eds.) *Magna Carta and Its Modern Legacy* (CUP 2015) 32–33; Graham Gee 'Reforming the Human Rights Act' (2015) 3 *Quaderni Costituzionali* 808.

13 NW Barber 'The Afterlife of Parliamentary Sovereignty' (2011) 9 *ICON* 144, 145.

14 For a concise overview of some of the areas of disagreement, see, for example, Barber (n.13) 145–49. For recent writings defending slightly different accounts of parliamentary

chiefly on Albert Venn Dicey's account from *An Introduction to the Study of the Law of the Constitution*, though, for reasons I briefly touch on later, the fact that this is the most suitable option is itself perhaps illustrative of some of the problems which have come to afflict the literature in this area. In Dicey's oft-quoted account, parliamentary sovereignty means

> . . . neither more nor less than this, namely, that Parliament . . . has, under the English constitution, the right to make or unmake any law whatever; and, further, that no person or body is recognised by the law of England has having a right to override or set aside the legislation of Parliament.[15]

This definition is commonly said to contain both a positive and a negative dimension.[16] The positive element can be found in the claim that, from a legal perspective, Parliament has the power to enact primary legislation on any subject matter it desires through the ordinary legislative process,[17] whereas the negative element can be found in the claim that, once an Act of Parliament has been enacted, and for as long as it remains on the statute book, neither the courts nor any other institution can question that Act's legal authority.[18] So because an earlier Parliament cannot limit the legislative authority of a future Parliament, Dicey also endorsed the idea that one Parliament cannot bind its successors.[19] In Dicey's words, "one law, whatever its importance can be passed and changed by exactly the same method as every other law".[20]

This account of parliamentary sovereignty influenced the debates on UK human rights reform in two important ways. First, it created a legal and political culture which was often sceptical of, and sometimes outrightly hostile towards, the idea of a statutory protection of human rights.[21] Second, it was widely thought to create a significant limit on the potential authority of any rights

---

sovereignty, see eg Jeffrey Goldsworthy *The Sovereignty of Parliament: History and Philosophy* (Clarendon Press 1999); Jeffrey Goldsworthy *Parliamentary Sovereignty: Contemporary Debates* (CUP 2009); Alison Young *Parliamentary Sovereignty and the Human Rights Act* (Hart Publishing 2009); Alison Young, 'Parliamentary Sovereignty Re-Defined' from Richard Rawlings, Peter Leyland and Alison Young (eds.) *Sovereignty and the Law: Domestic, European, and International Perspectives* (OUP 2013); Michael Gordon *Parliamentary Sovereignty in the UK Constitution: Process, Politics and Democracy* (Hart Publishing 2015); Han-Ru Zhou 'Revisiting the "Manner and Form" Theory of Parliamentary Sovereignty' (2013) 129 *Law Quarterly Review* (*LQR*) 610.

15 Dicey (n.5) 39–40.

16 Ibid. 39–40; Young (n.14) 2; cf Goldsworthy *The Sovereignty of Parliament* (n.14) 10.

17 Dicey (n.5) 40.

18 Dicey (n.5) 40.

19 Dicey (n.5) 64ff.

20 Dicey (n.5) 90.

21 See Hickman (n.10) 12–20; Janet L Hiebert and James B Kelly *Parliamentary Bills of Rights: The Experiences of New Zealand and the United Kingdom* (CUP 2015) 238ff.

protecting enactment through entirely prohibiting entrenchment.[22] Thus, even if strong enough reasons could be found to justify the enactment of a rights protecting instrument, and a move away from the approach to rights protection that had developed under the UK's traditional constitutional framework, it was not entirely clear that this could be achieved in any meaningful way without the full-scale abandonment of parliamentary sovereignty.[23]

Placed in this broader context, it is of little surprise that some commentators have been so effusive in their praise of the HRA's drafting.[24] For those who view the Act as having successfully balanced the protection of human rights and parliamentary sovereignty, the HRA's draftsmen and women appear to have achieved something remarkable. A belief that just such a feat has been achieved tends to be justified as follows.[25] Beginning with the positive dimension of Dicey's definition, it is clear that Parliament still remains free 'to make or unmake any law'. Although there is now a requirement that the minister in charge of a bill must make a statement before its second reading which either confirms that the bill is, in the minister's view, compatible with ECHR rights,[26] or that it might not be ECHR compliant but the government wishes to proceed anyway,[27] Parliament

22 See O Hood Phillips *Reform of the Constitution* (Chatto & Windus 1970) 151ff; Lord Hailsham *The Dilemma of Democracy: Diagnosis and Prescription* (Collins 1978) ch. 26. For a fuller account of the lead up and reform process, see Francesca Klug 'The Human Rights Act: Origins and Intentions' from Nicolas Kang-Riou et al. (eds.) *Confronting the Human Rights Act: Contemporary Themes and Perspectives* (Routledge 2012).

23 Stephen Gardbaum *The New Commonwealth Model of Constitutionalism: Theory and Practice* (CUP 2013) 156. This is why writers often portray the relationship between the HRA and parliamentary sovereignty as the key question that faced proponents of a bill of rights–type enactment. See, for example, Bamforth 'Parliamentary Sovereignty' (n.6) 572; Brazier (n.2) 129–30; Mike Finn and Anthony Seldon 'Constitutional Reform Since 1997' from Matt Qvortrup (ed.) *The British Constitution: Continuity and Change* (Hart Publishing 2013) 30; Aileen Kavanagh 'What's So Weak About "Weak-Form Review"? The Case of the UK Human Rights Act 1998' (2015) 13 *ICON* 1008, 1014.

24 For instance, on top of people referring to it as 'ingenious' or similar, during its parliamentary debates Lord Lester described the bill as 'brilliantly conceived and exquisitely well executed' (HL Deb 5 February 1998, vol. 585, cols. 834–35). For similar from Earl Russell see HL Deb 3 November 1997, vol. 582, col. 1286; HL Deb 5 February 1998, vol. 585, col. 838. In extra-judicial writings, Lord Bingham described it as 'one of the outstanding achievements, if not *the* outstanding achievement, of the first Blair government.' See Lord Bingham 'The Human Rights Act' (2010) *EHRLR* 568, 574.

25 See, for example, Stephanie Palmer 'The Human Rights Act 1998: Bringing Rights Home' (1998) 1 *Cambridge Yearbook of European Legal Studies* 125, 136–39; Bamforth 'Parliamentary Sovereignty' (n.6); Ewing 'The Human Rights Act' (n.6); Adam Tomkins *Public Law* (Clarendon Press 2003) 120–21; Bingham (n.24) 570–71; Richard Bellamy 'Political Constitutionalism and the Human Rights Act' (2011) 9 *ICON* 86, 98; Gardbaum *The New* (n.23) 157–61; Hiebert and Kelly (n.21); Gordon *Parliamentary Sovereignty* (n.14) 120–121.

26 Human Rights Act 1998 (HRA 1998) s 19(a).

27 Ibid. s 19(b).

remains free to enact legislation that is incompatible with the ECHR whenever it wishes to. So far as the negative dimension of the definition goes, the HRA does not give the judiciary a right to 'override' or 'set aside' legislation so it remains the case that neither the courts nor any other institution can question the legal authority of a validly enacted Act of Parliament. The Act, it is true, instructs the judiciary to "take into account" the relevant jurisprudence of the European Court of Human Rights and other related bodies,[28] and it does allow the judiciary to either reinterpret a piece of legislation which is deemed incompatible with the ECHR[29] or declare that piece of legislation incompatible with the ECHR,[30] but importantly, the Act stops short of allowing the judiciary to ignore or strike down that legislation and declare it invalid in the way that many constitutional courts can, and many believe is undemocratic.[31] Rather, section 4(6)(a) of the HRA makes clear that a declaration of incompatibility "does not affect the validity, continuing operation or enforcement of the provision in respect of which it is given" and section 4(6)(b) makes it clear that the declaration "is not binding on the parties to the proceedings in which it is made". Whether or not any action is taken will depend on how the government decides to respond. Under section 10(2) the relevant minister is given the power to respond to a declaration of incompatibility, should there be compelling reasons to, by way of a fast-track remedial order, but there is no legal requirement that action must be taken. Finally, so far as the idea that one Parliament cannot bind its successors goes, unlike most rights-protecting enactments, the HRA is an ordinary Act of Parliament which can be amended or repealed through the normal legislative process. As a result, should political decision makers decide to alter the HRA in some way, they are neither prevented from nor do they face additional restrictions beyond the normal legislative process.

Doubts have been expressed about almost all aspects of the above account, albeit not always at the same time, and there is not always a straightforward link between a particular line of criticism and a single element of Dicey's definition. The wide-ranging and multifaceted debate that has come to surround the UK Constitution means that competing claims or evidence about the HRA's relationship to parliamentary sovereignty can be found in a wide range of different places, and drawn from commentators who have very different views about the merits and demerits of any supposed intrusion on constitutional principle,[32] as well as very different views about the merits and demerits of legally protected human

28 Ibid. s 2(1).

29 Ibid. s 3(1).

30 Ibid. s 4(2).

31 See for example Jeremy Waldron 'The Core of the Case Against Judicial Review' (2006) 115 *Yale Law Journal* 1346. For an argument against this, see Kavanagh *Constitutional Review* (n.8) ch 13.

32 For an exploration of the complicated relationship between the HRA and UK constitutional principles, see Gavin Phillipson 'The Human Rights Act, Dialogue and

rights at all.[33] For present purposes, it suffices to briefly highlight three aspects of the above account of the relationship between parliamentary sovereignty and the HRA which have attracted a good degree of criticism.[34] The first concerns the issue of whether or not the HRA is entrenched. The second concerns the power of the courts under section 3(1) of the HRA. The third concerns the presentation of section 4 as a weak form of constitutional review.

So far as the issue of entrenchment goes, it has been claimed that the enactment of the HRA has limited Parliament in a way that most, if not all, other acts of Parliament do not and in a way that simply cannot be reconciled with parliamentary sovereignty. This is because, although the Act has not been formally ascribed a different authority, or formally entrenched, it has developed a special legal and political status which makes it harder to change than most, if not all, other acts of Parliament.[35]

The argument that the HRA has a special legal and political status has been justified on two grounds. The first justification builds on the idea that the common law now views some statutes differently because they have a "constitutional" nature.[36] This idea finds support in cases such as *Thoburn v Sunderland City Council*,[37] *H v Lord Advocate*,[38] and *R (on the application of HS2 action Alliance Ltd) v Secretary of State for Transport*,[39] and is of particular importance in the present context because not only is it clear that the HRA would qualify as such an enactment,[40] it is widely thought that constitutional statutes are immune from implied repeal.[41] If this is the case, and Parliament must express any intention to

Constitutional Principles' from Roger Masterman and Ian Leigh (eds.) *The United Kingdom's Statutory Bill of Rights: Constitutional and Comparative Perspectives* (OUP 2013).

33 A number of scholars argue that the values and interests that are normally protected through a bill of rights–type enactment are best left to the political process. This thinking is normally traced back to JAG Griffith 'The Political Constitution' (1979) 42 *MLR* 1.

34 My argument applies to any claim that the domestic court's duty to take into account the ECHR under section 2 of the HRA is a challenge to parliamentary sovereignty, albeit this is claim that is much less frequently made.

35 For an extended argument of this sort, see Kavanagh *Constitutional Review* (n.8) ch 10, esp 293ff. For discussion of this sort of thinking, see Gardbaum *The New* (n.23) 160–61; Hickman (n.10) 24–25. Some have suggested its status is not superior but actually inferior. See Douglas W Vick 'The Human Rights Act and the British Constitution' (2002) 37 *Texas International Law Journal* 329, 330–31.

36 Kavanagh *Constitutional Review* (n.8) ch. 10, esp 293ff.

37 [2002] EWHC 195; [2003] QB 151.

38 [2012] UKSC 24; [2013] 1 AC 413.

39 [2014] UKSC 3 [2014] 1 WLR 324.

40 *Thoburn* (n.37) 186–87 (Laws LJ); *HS2* (n.39) [207]-[208] (Lord Neuberger and Lord Mance).

41 *Thoburn* (n.37) 186–87 (Laws LJ); Andrew Blick *Beyond New Magna Carta: A Constitution for the United Kingdom* (Hart Publishing 2015) 189. For critical evaluation, see eg Tomkins *Public Law* (n.25) 123–25; Young *Parliamentary Sovereignty* (n.14) ch. 2; Gordon *Parliamentary Sovereignty* (n.14) 169ff.

change such a statute clearly, doubts arise about whether the HRA and parliamentary sovereignty can truly be reconciled in the way described earlier. If it is no longer true that "one law, whatever its importance can be passed and changed by exactly the same method as every other law",[42] and any Parliament seeking to alter the HRA would have to navigate a more arduous legislative process, then surely any attempt to reconcile the Act and constitutional principle predicated on the HRA having an ordinary status must be fundamentally flawed?

The second justification is premised on an assessment of the political and constitutional landscape that surrounds the Act, the suggestion being that when one looks at this it quickly becomes apparent that any change to the HRA is so hard to achieve in practice that it is better or more accurate to view the Act as having a separate legal and political status.[43] Considerations like the political cost of repealing the Act, and it being unlikely that a government would be willing to appear hostile towards human rights; the implausibility of a UK government withdrawing from the ECHR system, and the harmful impact that remaining a party to the ECHR system would have on any attempt to alter human rights protection; and the difficulties that the devolved administrations would cause any UK government that attempted to change the HRA without its support – support which at present looks unlikely to be forthcoming – are all said to radically increase the degree to which the HRA is embedded into the UK legal system. For some, the HRA's position in the modern constitutional settlement is such that it is the Act, rather than parliamentary sovereignty, that is now the cornerstone of the constitution, and thus, the idea that the two sit side by side in the way described earlier is clearly wrong.[44]

In the case of section 3(1) of the HRA, and the court's duty to interpret legislation 'so far as it is possible to do so' in accordance with the ECHR, a number of commentators have raised doubts about the way in which the courts power under this provision is represented in the above account. Of particular importance is the way in which it has been used to ignore Parliament's clearly expressed intention.[45] Rather than understand the word possible in section 3(1) narrowly, and thereby limit the scope of their power to something more constitutionally justifiable, the

42 Dicey (n.5) 90.

43 Kavanagh *Constitutional Review* (n.8) ch. 10, esp 303ff.

44 See Vernon Bogdanor *The New British Constitution* (Hart Publishing 2009) ch. 3 cf Aileen McHarg 'Rights and Democracy in UK Public Law' from Mark Elliott and David Feldman (eds.) *The Cambridge Companion to Public Law* (CUP 2015) 123.

45 See Kavanagh *Constitutional Review* (n.8) 318–19; James Allan 'Statutory Bills of Rights: You Read Words In, You Read Words Out, You Take Parliament's Clear Intention and You Shake it All About – Doin' the Sankey Hanky Panky' from Tom Campbell, KD Ewing and Adam Tomkins (eds.) *The Legal Protection of Human Rights: Sceptical Essays* (OUP 2011); Jonathan Morgan 'Amateur Operatics: The Realisation of Parliamentary Protection of Civil Liberties' from Tom Campbell, KD Ewing and Adam Tomkins (eds.) *The Legal Protection of Human Rights: Sceptical Essays* (OUP 2011) 430–33; Gee (n.12); Kavanagh "What's so Weak' (n.23) 1015–23.

courts have instead interpreted it as allowing them to depart from the clear intention of Parliament in pursuance of ECHR compatibility and thereby 'override or set aside' its legislation. Thus, in the leading case in this area, the House of Lords held that it was within their power to depart "from the unambiguous meaning the legislation would otherwise bear"[46] by, for instance, reading "in words which change the meaning of the enacted legislation".[47] In one particularly controversial case, the provision was held to allow the court to read an entire subsection into the Youth Justice and Criminal Evidence Act 1999 in an attempt to protect their understanding of the right to a fair trial, despite the fact that the provision in question was extremely detailed and clearly showed Parliament's intention to be otherwise.[48] Surely Parliament cannot truly be said to remain sovereign if the courts now have a power to rewrite legislation in circumstances where Parliament's intention has been clearly expressed as different?[49]

So far as section 4 of the HRA goes, and the presentation of the declaration of incompatibility as a weak form of constitutional review, a number of commentators have suggested that the difference between a declaration of incompatibility and the power to strike down legislation that legislators were so keen to avoid is overplayed in the preceding account.[50] As a result, it is commonly said that, in reality, a declaration that a piece of legislation is incompatible leaves politicians with such little scope to disagree with the judiciary's view on the meaning and application of the ECHR that Parliament cannot be fairly described as able to Act as it wishes free from question.[51] It is only in exceptional circumstances that politicians would refuse to implement such a ruling,[52] and even then it is not clear that they can do much more than delay the inevitable. Take the blanket ban on prisoner voting. It presently feels like it is a matter of time before the Representation of the People Act 1983 will be amended to implement the Grand Chamber

46 *Ghaidan v Godin Mendoza* [2004] UKHL 30, [2004] 2 AC 557 [30] (Lord Nicholls). For more detailed overviews of the case law in this area, see Brice Dickson *Human Rights and the United Kingdom Supreme Court* (OUP 2013) 63–72; Christopher Crawford 'Dialogue and Rights-Compatible Interpretations under Section 3 of the Human Rights Act 1998' (2014) 25 *King's Law Journal* (*KLJ*) 59.

47 *Ghaidan* (n.46) [32] (Lord Nicholls).

48 *R v A* [2001] UKHL 25, [2002] 1 AC 45.

49 Allan (n.45); Conservative Party *Protecting Human Rights in the UK: The Conservatives' Proposals for Changing Britain's Human Rights Laws* (2014) 4.

50 See Christopher Crawford 'Dialogue and Declarations of Incompatibility under Section 4 of the Human Rights Act 1998' (2013) 25 *The Denning Law Journal* 43; Chintan Chandrachud 'Reconfiguring the Discourse on Political Responses to Declarations of Incompatibility' (2014) *PL* 624; Gee (n.12).

51 See Nevil Johnson *Reshaping the British Constitution* (Palgrave Macmillan 2004); Kavanagh *Constitutional Review* (n.8) 320–22; Morgan 'Amateur Operatics' (n.45).435–38; Crawford 'Dialogue' (n.50) 88.

52 Philip Sales and Richard Ekins 'Rights-Consistent Interpretation and the Human Rights Act 1998' (2011) 127 *LQR* 217, 230; Gee (n.12).

decision in *Hirst v United Kingdom (no 2)*,[53] even if at present it might look like a useful illustration of Parliament's continued freedom to Act in contravention of the ECHR.[54]

(ii) Evaluation

At times, those on both sides of this debate can appear to have little sympathy for those who have expressed a different view to their own. Take, for instance, Jeffrey Goldsworthy's view that "[l]ike most commentators, I fail to see the difficulty" with reconciling the HRA and the new judicial role under it with parliamentary sovereignty,[55] or Adam Tomkins view that the challenge posed by the HRA to parliamentary sovereignty is "nothing like as big or as complex a challenge" as that posed by UK membership of the European Union, and can therefore be dealt with "relatively swiftly",[56] and compare them with James Allan's view that it is "[o]nly in an incredibly formalistic and legalistic sense" that "a jurisdiction with judges openly and explicitly engaged in . . . [section 3 reinterpretation] . . . [can] . . . be said to retain parliamentary sovereignty".[57] In one view, it is easy to reconcile parliamentary sovereignty and the HRA, and relatively little time or effort need be spent establishing how this is achieved, whilst in the other view it is a far more complicated issue which we would do well not to approach narrow-mindedly. Disagreements within academic literature and political discourse are, of course, not unusual, even if such a pronounced disagreement over such a fundamental aspect of an important legislative scheme might strike some as a little surprising. What marks this disagreement out as being perhaps a little more unusual is that the key issue of concern for those who dispute the HRA's congruence with parliamentary sovereignty often appears to differ from the key issue of concern for those who do not. As a result, there is a problem when we try

53 [2005] ECHR 681.

54 See Stephen Gardbaum 'What's so Weak about "Weak-Form Review"? A Reply to Aileen Kavanagh' (2015) 13 *ICON* 1040, 1042–44; Gordon *Parliamentary Sovereignty* (n.14) 124–25.

55 Goldsworthy *Contemporary Debates* (n.14) 299. For similar sentiments, see Jeffrey Goldsworthy 'Is Parliament Sovereign? Recent Challenges to the Doctrine of Parliamentary Sovereignty' (2005) 3 *New Zealand Journal of Public and International Law* 7, 30–31; Gordon *Parliamentary Sovereignty* (n.14) 121.

56 Tomkins *Public Law* (n.25) 121. Tomkins appears slightly more sympathetic in Adam Tomkins 'The Rule of Law in Blair's Britain' (2007) 26 *University Queensland Law Journal* 255, 266–69. For similar, see Nicholas Bamforth 'Courts in a Multi-Layered Constitution' from Nicholas Bamforth and Peter Leyland (eds.) *Public Law in a Multi-Layered Constitution* (Hart Publishing 2003) 290–91.

57 Allan (n.45) 115–16. This division between the possibility of the formal doctrine and the reality of the legal system is also the broad idea I take from Vernon Bogdanor's claim that Jeffrey Goldsworthy has become imprisoned by the doctrine of parliamentary sovereignty. See, generally, Vernon Bogdanor 'Imprisoned by a Doctrine: The Modern Defence of Parliamentary Sovereignty' (2012) 32 *OJLS* 179.

to play one view off against the other because it appears that any debate largely takes place at cross-purposes.[58]

The best way to illustrate this is through a comparison of the material that each approach takes into consideration. One of the things that binds together the three grounds of challenge outlined earlier and can also be said to distinguish all three from the conventional explanation of how the HRA can be reconciled with parliamentary sovereignty, is how tightly the boundary between what is relevant or irrelevant to the argument is drawn. In essence, the three challenges all employ a much broader view of what should be taken into account when we assess the HRA – parliamentary sovereignty relationship than the more sympathetic account. Thus, in the case of the claim that the HRA limits parliamentary sovereignty by virtue of its special status, factors such as the implausibility of the government running the political gauntlet of repealing or significantly restricting the Act, the unlikelihood that the government would divorce itself entirely from the ECHR, and the political makeup and perspectives of the devolution settlement are brought into play. In the case of the claim that the judiciary's power under section 3 of the HRA poses a challenge to parliamentary sovereignty, the broader political reality that surrounds the court's application of the provision is said to provide an important addendum to the more conventional picture. Similarly, in the case of the judiciary's power to issue a declaration of incompatibility, the consequences which follow such a declaration, and the attenuated freedom that Parliament enjoys to disagree with the courts verdict, are highlighted as of especial importance to a proper understanding of the Act's operation. When we shift attention shift to those accounts which accept the HRA's adherence to the constitutional principle, there is no need to mention this array of factors at all; the relationship is determined by looking at the structure and background of the Act, and the various elements which go together to make up the principle. Beyond that, little else is especially important.

The importance of this reliance on a broader range of materials for present purposes is that it indicates a different intellectual pursuit underlies the three challenges to that which underlies the move favourable explanation. This is because the broader material outlined above is largely irrelevant when parliamentary sovereignty is the yardstick against which the HRA is being assessed. It has long been accepted that Parliament is subject to a range of powerful extra-legal or external constraints that serve to limit its theoretically unlimited power to legislate[59] – Dicey recognised such limitations himself[60] – so at least for the purposes of rec-

58 This in itself is, of course, not unique. Within UK public law, the debate that surrounds the constitutional foundations of judicial review is another area in which some argue that a far less pronounced disagreement may exist in reality than aspects of the literature might suggest.

59 See Colin Munro *Studies in Constitutional Law* (2nd ed. OUP 1999) 133–37; Gordon *Parliamentary Sovereignty* (n.14) 14–15.

60 Dicey (n.5) 72ff.

onciling the HRA with parliamentary sovereignty it does not matter a great deal that such factors exist, even if they have increased in number or complexity.[61] They fall outside the legitimate scope of analysis because it shifts our attention from 'Can the HRA be reconciled with the principle of parliamentary sovereignty and its requirements?' towards the principle itself, what should be considered an intrusion on it and even whether it should be the yardstick at all.

This is not to say that the material employed in the three challenges, but not in the more favourable account, is entirely irrelevant to a proper understanding of the HRA 's relationship to the rest of the UK legal system. It certainly helps to illustrate how the HRA might arguably have had an impact on the balance of power between the elected and unelected institutions of government, and, if correct, it might raise a range of interesting questions about the principle and its role in the future. The HRA is not the only development that might be argued to have had an impact on the role or the position of the courts in recent years – the UK's membership of (and now exit from) the European Union, devolution and an apparent change in attitude amongst some senior judiciary, for instance, all raise questions of their own[62] – and it is possible that the impact of these developments, particularly when viewed cumulatively, may lead some to question the continued utility of a principle which places Parliament at the heart of the legal and political landscape when that landscape has changed so dramatically.[63] However, this is to highlight a more complicated and multifaceted issue in legal and political culture and one which is significantly different to suggesting that there is a problem reconciling the HRA with constitutional principle.

It might seem like this is splitting hairs, or perhaps labouring over a relatively trivial matter. However, once we accept that the three challenges are largely targeted at a different issue to the more favourable account, it becomes easier to see a couple of important, interrelated, points. First, there is a greater degree of mutual ground here than might sometimes be thought. On one hand, too much

61 Albeit a very significant increase of such factors might diminish the practical relevance of the doctrine. See Goldsworthy *Contemporary Debates* (n.14) 303.

62 For an overview, see, for example, Nicholas Bamforth and Peter Leyland 'Public Law in a Multi-Layered Constitution' from Nicholas Bamforth and Peter Leyland (eds.) *Public Law in a Multi-Layered Constitution* (Hart Publishing 2003) 4–10; Dawn Oliver 'The United Kingdom Constitution in Transition: From Where to Where?' from Mads Andenas and Duncan Fairgrieve (eds.) *Tom Bingham and the Transformation of the Law: A Liber Amicorum* (OUP 2009); Stephen Sedley 'The Long Sleep' from Mads Andeans and Duncan Fairgrieve (eds.) *Tom Bingham and the Transformation of the Law: A Liber Amicorum* (OUP 2009).

63 See Jeffrey Jowell 'Beyond the Rule of Law: Towards Constitutional Judicial Review' (2000) *PL* 671, 671–72; Lord Hope 'Is the Rule of Law Now the Sovereign Principle? from Richard Rawlings, Peter Leyland and Alison Young (eds.) *Sovereignty and the Law: Domestic, European and International Perspectives* (OUP 2013); Roger Masterman and Jo Eric Khushal Murkens 'Skirting Supremacy and Subordination: The Constitutional Authority of the United Kingdom Supreme Court' [2013] *PL* 800.

emphasis on the broader material can lead us to overlook the fact that when only the narrower material is taken into account, most writers agree that the HRA and parliamentary sovereignty can be reconciled. This can be seen particularly clearly in accounts which employ a division between the formalities of the HRA and the substance of its operation and, in the process, admit that it can be formally reconciled with parliamentary sovereignty but go on to suggest that a range of problems develop when one looks a little deeper into the substance of the Act's operation.[64] On the other hand, too much emphasis on the importance of a narrow approach can distract from the fact that even those who believe that the HRA can be reconciled with parliamentary sovereignty accept that outside the narrow confines of this particular question there is an important debate to be had about both the best way to explain this reconciliation and the best way to understand parliamentary sovereignty's parameters.[65] Dicey's account may have played a prominent role in both the discussions which led to the HRA, and the debates which have taken place since the Act's enactment, but it is not the only or last word on the subject.[66] As long ago as 1980, Dicey's account of parliamentary sovereignty was described as having been subjected to "a veritable onslaught of criticism", with the result that "revision and qualification has proceeded in many directions".[67] This body of literature has only continued to grow in the years since.

Second, the principal difference between the three challenges and the more conventional account is that there is a more comprehensive, and ultimately misplaced, understanding of what it means to be sovereign. Rather than parliamentary sovereignty being understood as just a legal rule which conveys a very particular point about the legal relationship between the legislature and the courts, it is taken to be a more comprehensive account of the balance of power in the UK or an explanation of the UK's position within supranational and international legal and political organisations, as a shorthand for saying that Parliament, or even the government, can Act as it pleases free from any influence or shackles of one sort or another. It is true that both the divide between political and legal sovereignty, and the idea of sovereignty itself, has been subjected to a barrage of criticism over the years,[68] and this is not the only debate in which confusion has

64 Elliott 'Parliamentary sovereignty' (n.8); Elliott 'United Kingdom' (n.8); Kavanagh *Constitutional Review* (n.8) ch 11.

65 See Goldsworthy *The Sovereignty of Parliament* (n.14); Goldsworthy *Contemporary Debates* (n.14); Young *Parliamentary Sovereignty* (n.14); Gordon *Parliamentary Sovereignty* (n.14).

66 For evidence of the continuing influence of Dicey's account, see Blick (n.41) 106–7.

67 Richard Cosgrove *The Rule of Law: Albert Venn Dicey, Victorian Jurist* (University of North Carolina Press 1980) 75. cf John McEldowney 'Dicey in Historical Perspective – A Review Essay' from Patrick McAuslan and John McEldowney (eds.) *Law, Legitimacy and the Constitution: Essays Marking the Centenary of Dicey's Law of the Constitution* (Sweet & Maxwell 1985) 42.

68 For discussion, see Martin Loughlin *Foundations of Public Law* (OUP 2010) ch. 7.

developed over how we should understand the principle – the use of the term in the recent referendum on UK membership of the European Union is a striking example of this, as, in the words of Michael Gordon, a number of "very different" understandings of sovereignty collapsed "into a single murky soup"[69] – but, whatever the superficial attractiveness of the more comprehensive approach, it is important that we do not conflate two very different things.

(2) Future directions: Parliamentary sovereignty and HRA reform

For over a decade there have been calls for reform of the HRA, including a number of calls for the Act's total repeal and replacement by some form of British Bill of Rights. Not everyone who doubts the HRA's compatibility with parliamentary sovereignty considers this to be a drawback, and amongst those who do consider it a drawback it is rarely the only reason used to justify reform. However, a belief that the HRA has undermined parliamentary sovereignty has unquestionably played a prominent role within the UK Bill of Rights debate thus far. In the run up to the last 2015 General Election, for instance, the Conservative Party published a policy document which suggested the HRA should be replaced with a British Bill of Rights and Responsibilities,[70] in part because the HRA "undermines the sovereignty of Parliament, and democratic accountability to the public".[71] If I am right in my analysis, and at the heart of what might appear to be conflicting perspectives over the relationship between the HRA and parliamentary sovereignty is, in fact, a very different disagreement about parliamentary sovereignty's requirements and what can be rightfully termed an intrusion on the constitutional principle, then an important question arises as to how my argument might inform the active debate on the HRA's future.

It follows from the preceding that there is a relatively straightforward answer to the question at the heart of this chapter: the HRA does not cause a significant problem for parliamentary sovereignty when that principle is properly understood. There may be scope to debate whether refinements should be made to our understanding of the principle, and its requirements, in light of both the HRA and other legal and political developments that have occurred in recent years. There may also be scope to debate whether a more fundamental change of some sort is necessary. However, these are distinct issues from the idea that the Act itself and the principle are in conflict, and so any suggestion that the HRA conflicts with parliamentary sovereignty as conventionally understood is simply

69 Michael Gordon 'The UK's Sovereignty Situation: Brexit, Bewilderment and Beyond . . .' (2016) 27 *KLJ* 333, 335. See also Graham Gee and Alison Young 'Regaining Sovereignty? Brexit, the UK Parliament and the Common Law' (2016) 22 *European Public Law* 131.

70 Conservative Party (n.49).

71 Conservative Party (n.49) 4. See also Pinto-Duschinsky 'Commission' (n.12).

mistaken, whether or not it is made in the context of an attempt to justify reform of some kind.

Rather than summarily dismiss all arguments to the contrary, though, a more constructive approach might be to recognise that there are better ways to understand the threat posed by the three challenges outlined earlier. After all, if it is true that these challenges are premised on a very different understanding of what it means to be sovereign, then while they might not pose much of a challenge to parliamentary sovereignty itself, this is not to see them in their best light. Instead, we must take as our starting point the idea that the HRA has created a political and legal culture which limits Parliament's ability to Act.

If we repackage the three challenges in this way, is there a dramatic increase in their merits? As much as the overall balance of power in the legal system may now differ from the balance which existed before the HRA, I do not believe this offers grounds for change. Regardless whether the HRA managed to leave parliamentary sovereignty intact, it was always going to strengthen the moral or political backdrop which restricts Parliament's freedom and ability to undermine human rights.[72] A complaint that a stronger political and legal culture now exists offers little support for change unless the limits that are being complained about are significantly different to those that were originally envisaged by the Act's drafters, and the evidence simply does not bear this out. The likely consequences of the HRA's enactment were clearly and repeatedly recognised in the debates that surrounded its enactment, and as much as the Act may have suffered from various teething problems since its enactment,[73] and there may have been a few questionable decisions along the way,[74] it is simply untrue that the HRA is currently operating in some entirely unforeseen manner. There will always be some scope for debate about how the courts should approach a particular case when the decision turns on a subtle statutory divide of one sort or another, but it is not the case that the HRA has led to some sort of illegitimate judicial power grab[75] or that the delicate balance which the Act attempts to strike has entirely collapsed, and our elected representatives now need assistance.[76]

Even if, just for the sake of argument, we accept that the elected branches of government are now subjected to far stronger limits than were originally envisaged, it is not clear why major reform would be thought necessary unless the main motivating concern is not the Act itself, and how it operates, but an ideological scepticism about the legal protection of human rights. Scope for debate about the legitimacy of the HRA's impact on Parliament exists, at least, in part, because the

72 For the extent of this backdrop prior to the HRA, see Hickman (n.10) ch. 2.

73 Bingham (n.24) 570.

74 For instance, see *R v A* (n.48). For critical discussion, see Danny Nicol 'Law and Politics after the Human Rights Act' (2006) *PL* 722, 739.

75 cf Allan (n.45).

76 For instance, see Bingham (n.24) 570–73; Bellamy (n.25) 102; Dickson (n.46) ch. 3; O'Cinneide *Human Rights and the UK Constitution* (n.11) 24; Phillipson (n.32) 32ff.

Act's phrasing has left open a range of possible interpretations.[77] While linguistic ambiguity in acts of Parliament may often be seen as a negative, in this case it has given the courts some room to develop their approach to the HRA over time in line with both other institutional actors and broader constitutional and political considerations. If unforeseen limits have been placed on Parliament through, for instance, the judiciary's approach to "take into account" under section 2,[78] or the increasingly contextual way in which they approach the balance between their section 3 and section 4 powers,[79] then this inbuilt flexibility will allow for adjustments to take place without the need for full-scale reform of the kind that some pursue. All that is necessary is a little action on the part of those political actors, too many of whom seek to lay blame solely at the door of the judiciary.[80]

Those who believe that the three challenges are fundamentally flawed might think that any attempt to see them in their best light is either unnecessary or overly generous. If the principle of parliamentary sovereignty has been misunderstood, or misrepresented, and mistakenly used to try to justify the need for some sort of human rights reform, surely it is enough to point out whatever mistakes have been made? While there is undoubtedly some logic to this approach, there are still a number of good reasons to take that extra step, especially for those concerned about the HRA's future. Perhaps most important, it is worth trying to tackle the arguments of those who agitate for reform as directly as possible, and a response to arguments which are essentially about Parliament's power under the HRA focused principally on the correct way to understand parliamentary sovereignty, the irrelevance of much of the material which they take into account and the difference between parliamentary sovereignty and Parliament being all-powerful fails to do this.

It might be tempting to think that all such concerns are a waste of time because ultimately HRA reform is never likely to come to fruition, whether because the proposals to date have been of a low quality and littered with errors[81] or because the practical barriers to meaningful reform would be so difficult to navigate.[82]

77 Janet Hiebert 'The Human Rights Act: Ambiguity about Parliamentary Sovereignty' (2013) 14 *German Law Journal* 2253.

78 Roger Masterman 'Deconstructing the Mirror Principle' from Roger Masterman and Ian Leigh (eds.) *The United Kingdom's Statutory Bill of Rights: Constitutional and Comparative Perspectives* (OUP 2013).

79 For instance, see Bellamy (n.25) 102; Dickson (n.46) ch. 3; Phillipson (n.32) 32ff.

80 For some suggestions as to how to adapt the operation of the current system from a strong critic of the HRA, see Morgan 'Amateur Operatics' (n.45).

81 On the Conservative Party's proposals for reform, see Alison Young 'HRA Howlers: The Conservative Party and Reform of the Human Rights Act 1998' *UK Constitutional Law Association* (7 October 2014) available at <https://ukconstitutionallaw.org/2014/10/07/alison-young-hra-howlers-the-conservative-party-and-reform-of-the-human-rights-act-1998/> accessed October 1 2016; Dimelow and Young '"Common Sense" or Confusion? The Human Rights Act and the Conservative Party' (The Constitution Society 2015) available at <http://consoc.org.uk/publications/common-sense-or-confusion-the-human-rights-act-and-the-conservative-party/> accessed October 1 2016.

82 Kavanagh, *Constitutional Review* (n.8) 303–7.

However, if the regret which many feel following the referendum on UK membership of the European Union is anything to go by, it is important to take such threats seriously.[83] The HRA might have struggled to generate public enthusiasm for human rights in the way that many had hoped,[84] and it may not be perfect,[85] but who knows what might take its place if too many fail to take the threat of reform seriously until it is too late.

Conclusion

The focus of this chapter has been on the debate that surrounds the HRA and its relationship to the principle of parliamentary sovereignty. I have argued that much of the disagreement in this area is caused by a difference of opinion over parliamentary sovereignty's nature and requirements, and what should be considered an intrusion on Parliament's legislative power. Rather than raise questions about the Act, and how its provisions interact with the constitutional principle, the three challenges outlined earlier all seek to question the approach we take to parliamentary sovereignty itself through their emphasis on a much broader range of material than would normally be considered relevant.

More often than not, this disagreement over the principle's requirements is implicit in either the reasoning or conclusions of those who have doubts about the HRA – parliamentary sovereignty relationship. As a result, it is not always clear that a large part of what might appear to be a direct debate actually takes place at cross-purposes. Once this is recognised, not only is the stark divide in some of the literature cast in a different light; we are also warned against too readily dismissing the arguments of those who doubt reconciliation is possible and believe this justifies reform of some sort, whether through repealing the HRA or replacing it with some form of British Bill of Rights and Responsibilities.

Even if the balance of power under the HRA needs to be addressed, which is itself difficult to accept, it is highly questionable whether change would best be achieved by repealing or replacing the HRA. It would certainly not be the only way to adjust the legal and political culture that surrounds human rights protection in the UK, and could easily have other, more serious, ramifications. Those who believe otherwise will not be easily dissuaded, though. The extraction of the UK from the European Union may serve to distract the current government for the foreseeable future, but it is a question of when, not if, those seeking to defend the status quo will be called into action.

83 Adam Tucker 'Parliamentary Sovereignty and the Human Rights Act' (2012) 3 *Juris* 307, 314.

84 Roger Masterman and Ian Leigh 'The United Kingdom's Human Rights Project in Constitutional and Comparative Perspective' from Roger Masterman and Ian Leigh (eds.) *The United Kingdom's Statutory Bill of Rights: Constitutional and Comparative Perspectives* (OUP 2013) 2; McHarg (n.44) 133.

85 See generally Merris Amos 'Problems with the Human Rights Act 1998 and How to Remedy Them: Is a Bill of Rights the Answer?' (2009) 72 *MLR* 883.

Chapter 5

Dialogue or diktat?

The nature of the interaction between national courts and the European Court of Human Rights and how it influences criticism of the Human Rights Act

Kanstantsin Dzehtsiarou

Introduction

The 1998 Human Rights Act (HRA) has never established that English courts are subordinate to the European Court of Human Rights in Strasbourg (ECtHR) as is sometimes claimed by UK media and politicians.[1] The judgments of the ECtHR are binding and have to be implemented by states party to the European Convention on Human Rights (ECHR). However, this was the case long before the HRA came into force. Moreover, the HRA has not made the Westminster parliament subordinate to Strasbourg; it remains sovereign within the jurisdiction of the UK. The first section of this chapter briefly discusses the impact of the HRA within the UK and argues that Parliament is still sovereign and the powers given to courts and other institutions in order to implement the ECHR are fairly weak. The key achievement of the HRA is that it has created an important mode of dialogue between British courts, especially the Supreme Court, and the ECtHR. Repealing the HRA would not remove the UK from the influence of the ECtHR but rather prevent British courts from directly, promptly and forcefully responding to the Strasbourg court's arguments.

This chapter analyses legal effects of the ECtHR on domestic law and politics in the UK, and the role of the HRA in this regard. Although in 2017 the government temporarily shelved its plans to repeal the HRA and withdraw from the

1 See, for example, Iain Martin 'British justice should not be over-ruled by the European Court of Human Rights' *The Telegraph* (2 January 2012) available at <www.telegraph.co.uk/news/uknews/terrorism-in-the-uk/9029711/British-justice-should-not-be-over-ruled-by-the-European-Court-of-Human-Rights.html> accessed 28 November 2016 as are all subsequent links unless stated otherwise. Jason Groves 'Europe's human rights court is out of control . . . we must pull out: Call by top British judge after ruling that prisoners should get the vote' *The Daily Mail* (7 February 2011) available at <www.dailymail.co.uk/news/article-1354362/Europes-human-rights-court-control—pull-Call-British-judge-ruling-prisoners-vote.html#ixzz4J6w5iXaC>.

ECHR, this chapter explores the consequences of both steps in the event that a future government is minded to pursue such a course of action. Even if the HRA is repealed the UK will still be under obligation to comply with the ECtHR judgments where the UK is a respondent party. A future British Bill of Rights will do nothing to remove this international obligation but might lead to an increased number of successful applications in Strasbourg, fewer avenues for dialogue between the ECtHR and British courts and a greater impact of the Strasbourg court on UK law. As the second section of this chapter notes a British Bill of Rights would be unable to shield the UK from the Strasbourg court. This chapter draws parallels with Russia, Italy and Germany, where constitutional rights cannot replace an international obligation to comply with the ECtHR judgments. There are two ways to avoid any legal obligations coming from the ECtHR: amending the ECHR or denouncing it. Amending the ECHR is not a politically plausible option as it would be extremely hard to persuade 46 other contracting parties to agree on the changes. Denouncing the ECHR is not that complicated legally and would free the UK from any obligations under the Convention but can have detrimental political and reputational consequences, which are discussed in the third section of this chapter.

(1) The Human Rights Act: Does it undermine parliamentary sovereignty?

The UK is a dualist state; this means that international law does not form a part of the internal legal order.[2] To be directly applicable by the domestic courts an international treaty needs to be implemented through a special domestic Act of Parliament. Hence, UK law clearly distinguishes between actions of its government as a sovereign on an international stage and as a sovereign within its jurisdiction. The HRA has neither increased nor decreased the scope of the UK's international legal obligations as its aim was to translate the ECHR into internal legal language and to make it directly applicable in UK law. This means that if the government repeals the HRA the UK's international legal obligations will remain the same. The repeal of the HRA will change the scope of domestic courts' competences as it empowered them to assess compatibility of the authorities' administrative actions with the ECHR. Therefore, arguments for the repeal of the HRA have often focused on how British courts are interpreting the ECHR rather than the substance of the Convention itself.

According to the HRA the Westminster parliament possesses the ultimate power of decision-making and gives national courts an avenue to express their legal concerns about the alleged incompatibility of primary legislation with

2 See Samantha Besson 'The Reception Process in Ireland and the United Kingdom' from Helen Keller and Alec Stone Sweet (eds.) *A Europe of Rights The Impact of the ECHR on National Legal Systems* (OUP 2008) 33.

human rights norms. This arguably mitigates the so-called anti-majoritarian difficulty which occurs when unelected judges have the power to strike down pieces of legislation adopted by a democratically legitimate parliament.[3] This issue is widely discussed in legal literature in relation to the US Supreme Court which can declare laws unconstitutional and proclaim them legally void.[4] The HRA avoids this tension by leaving the sovereign decision-making power with Parliament while providing national courts with an instrument that would allow them to highlight problematic pieces of legislation by issuing declarations of incompatibility. This gives Parliament an opportunity to pre-empt violations of human rights and avoid possible Strasbourg judgments by addressing these issues domestically. This helps to harmonise national and international legal systems without unnecessary tensions. The HRA has also empowered the national courts to take the case law of the ECtHR into account.[5] Here, the HRA is not premised on imperative subordination of national institutions under the ECtHR; it allows the national courts to interpret national legislation in light of the case law of the ECtHR but does not oblige them to automatically follow ECtHR case law. This provision of the HRA has been interpreted using the 'mirror principle'. Lord Bingham defined the mirror principle in *Ullah*, arguing that the national courts should do "no more but certainly no less" than their colleagues in Strasbourg.[6] Although, this principle has been widely criticised[7] it shows that the case law of the ECtHR provides some degree of human rights protection in the UK, allowing national courts to align case law with national particularities.

Some media outlets and politicians present the HRA and the ECtHR as phenomena that can undermine British sovereignty and democracy.[8] A lot of political

3 See, for example, Steven Croley 'The Majoritarian Difficulty: Elective Judiciaries and the Rule of Law' (1995) 62 *University of Chicago Law Review* 689.

4 Adrienne Stone 'Judicial Review without Rights: Some Problems for the Democratic Legitimacy of Structural Judicial Review' (2008) 28 *Oxford Journal of Legal Studies* 1, 1–2. See also Jeremy Waldron 'Deliberation, Disagreement and Voting' from Harold H Koh and Ronald Slye (eds.) *Deliberative Democracy and Human Right* (Yale University Press 1999); Robert Bork 'Neutral Principles and Some First Amendment Problems' (1971) 74 *Indiana Law Journal*, 10; Jeremy Waldron 'The Core of the Case Against Judicial Review' (2006) 115 *Yale Law Journal* 1346.

5 Human Rights Act, s 2(1a).

6 *R (Ullah) v Special Adjudicator* (2004) *UKHL* 26.

7 See, for example, Roger Masterman 'Deconstructing the Mirror Principle' in Masterman and Ian Leigh (eds.) *The United Kingdom's Statutory Bill of Rights: Constitutional and Comparative Perspectives* (OUP 2013); John Laws *The Common Law Constitution* (Cambridge University Press 2014) 75–76.

8 The most popular British newspaper, *The Daily Mail*, is known for its anti-European rhetoric and providing dubious statements about the ECtHR's activities. As an example, the correspondent of *The Daily Mail* wrote,

'How absurd that the question of whether or not prisoners should get the vote rests on a decision by a supra-national court comprised of judges for whom no one has ever had the

discussion surrounding the HRA is based on the false premise that it represents a threat to British democracy.

The HRA did not create a particularly wide avenue for Strasbourg to impact the national legal order in the UK. The HRA does not force the Westminster parliament or national courts to follow every judgment of the ECtHR by the letter. If that was the case the prisoner voting case law would have been implemented ten years ago. In 2005 the ECtHR delivered a judgment in the case of *Hirst v the United Kingdom (No 2)* and stated that the blanket disenfranchisement of convicted prisoners violated the requirement under Article 3, Protocol 1 that the contracting parties to the ECHR had to hold free elections.[9] Since then, this line of the ECtHR's jurisprudence has grown considerably.[10] In 2010 the Strasbourg court delivered a judgment in the pilot case of *Greens and MT v the United Kingdom*[11] which gave the UK six months to introduce legislative proposals to ensure compatibility with the ECHR. In 2011, the UK House of Commons overwhelmingly voted against changing legislation in this area.[12] Yet, at the time of writing, no convicted prisoner is permitted to vote in the UK, which shows that the HRA cannot actually bind the Westminster parliament *stricto sensu*. It is noteworthy that the *Hirst* saga shows that the UK does not need any additional mechanisms, such as a bill of rights, to resist the implementation of ECtHR judgments.

Moreover, the HRA helps UK courts to translate their disagreements with the ECtHR into legal language that the Strasbourg court can easily understand

---

chance to vote. We may kid ourselves that we live in a parliamentary democracy, but the reality is that we are ultimately governed by a judicial dictatorship, accountable to no-one, with its power base in Strasbourg'. Richard Littlejohn, 'Democracy? No, Britain's now a judicial dictatorship – and it's time for revolution' *The Daily Mail* (10 October 2014) available at <www.dailymail.co.uk/debate/article-2723472/Democracy-No-Britain-s-judicial-dictatorship-s-time-revolution-writes-RICHARD-LITTLEJOHN.html>.

Similar rhetoric is known to the House of Commons. Philip Hollobone, MP, during the backbenchers' debate on prisoner voting rights, pointed out that "we are dealing with a court [ECtHR] that has gone wrong. It is clearly not functioning properly. It has a backlog of tens of thousands of unresolved cases. Many of its so-called judges have no legal training at all; they are probably less qualified than me to make judgments on these things. How has it come about that we, in a sovereign Parliament, have let these decisions be taken by a kangaroo court in Strasbourg, the judgments of which do not enjoy the respect of our constituents?", Hansard HC Deb 10 Feb 2011 Vol 523 Col 537.

9 *Hirst v the United Kingdom (no. 2) [GC]*, no. 74025/01, ECHR 2005-IX.

10 See the following cases *Frodl v Austria*, no. 20201/04, 8 April 2010; *Scoppola v Italy (no. 3) [GC]*, no. 126/05, 22 May 2012; *Anchugov and Gladkov v Russia*, nos. 11157/04 and 15162/05, 4 July 2013; *Söyler v Turkey*, no. 29411/07, 17 September 2013.

11 *Greens and M.T. v the United Kingdom*, nos. 60041/08 and 60054/08, ECHR 2010.

12 The Backbench Parliamentary Debates 'Prisoners' right to vote' available at <www.publications.parliament.uk/pa/cm201011/cmhansrd/cm110210/debtext/110210-0002.htm.>

because both their judgments rely on the ECHR.[13] This helps to ensure that the ECtHR will take the position of the UK courts seriously, and a good example of this dialogue is the line of cases on the admission of hearsay evidence in criminal procedure.

Central to this line of cases was the ECtHR's 'sole and decisive test', which means that when the testimony of an absent witness is the sole and decisive reason for a conviction then a violation of Article 6 of the ECHR will almost automatically be established.[14] In *Al-Khawaja and Tahery v the United Kingdom* this test was used and the case was then referred to the Grand Chamber of the ECtHR.[15] In the meantime, the UK Supreme Court had an opportunity to present its legal position on the same issue in the case of *R v Horncastle*.[16] The Supreme Court explained that the 'sole and decisive' test was too rigid and inflexible and did not take into account various safeguards in the UK's national law. The Supreme Court examined ECtHR case law, going so far as to request a more detailed analysis of the ECtHR jurisprudence from the parties, scrutinising details of cases where Article 6(3)(d) had been considered prior to the decision in *Al-Khawaja*.[17] Even though Lord Phillips's judgment in this case was to a large extent based on the analysis of the ECtHR case law, this did not stop the Supreme Court from expressing its disagreement with the ruling of the ECtHR in *Al-Khawaja*. By delivering such a detailed analysis of the ECtHR case law the Supreme Court persuaded the Strasbourg court that the chamber went too far in imposing the sole and decisive test. When the case came to the Grand Chamber of the ECtHR, they considered the arguments provided by the Supreme Court in *Horncastle* and reassessed the 'sole and decisive test', making it more flexible to reflect the safeguards in UK law pointed out by the Supreme Court. Judge Bratza, in his concurring opinion, called this exchange of legal opinions "a good example of the judicial dialogue".[18] Arguably, had the HRA not introduced the ECHR into UK law the Supreme Court would have had to be less explicit in its consideration

13 The ECHR provides a common language of understanding human rights. Torres Pérez points out that "there is a common way of talking about fundamental rights prompted by the European Convention as interpreted by the ECtHR". Aida Torres Pérez *Conflicts of Rights in the European Union: A Theory of Supranational Adjudication* (OUP 2009) 123; see also Lize Glas *The Theory, Potential and Practice of Procedural Dialogue in the European Convention on Human Rights System* (Intersentia 2016) 146.

14 *Doorson v the Netherlands* (26 March 1996) Reports of Judgments and Decisions 1996-II; D Harris et al. *Harris, O'Boyle and Warbrick Law of the European Convention on Human Rights* (3rd ed. OUP 2014) 485–486

15 *Al-Khawaja and Tahery v the United Kingdom* (20 January 2009) nos. 26766/05 and 22228/06.

16 *R v Horncastle* [2009] UKSC 14.

17 Ibid. 30.

18 *Al-Khawaja and Tahery v the United Kingdom* [GC], nos. 26766/05 and 22228/06 (ECHR 2011) Concurring Opinion of Judge Bratza.

of the position of the Strasbourg court, and this would have diminished the impact of the UK courts on the ECtHR.

To sum up, the HRA does not decisively limit the sovereignty of the Westminster parliament as it remains the ultimate decision-maker of human rights related issues on the national level. The HRA provides an avenue for national courts to voice their concerns to Parliament and avoid embarrassment in Strasbourg and creates the conditions for constructive dialogue between the national legal order of the UK and the ECtHR.

(2) A bill of rights: Will it return sovereignty to the Westminster parliament?

It is a common although incorrect view, that a British Bill of Rights will free the UK from the imaginary dictates of Strasbourg.[19] For the purposes of this chapter I call this assumption the 'shield argument'. With or without a new bill of rights the UK, as a state, is bound by the Convention, and pursuant to Article 46 ECHR it is also bound by the judgments of the ECtHR. The Committee of Ministers of the Council of Europe will continue to supervise the UK's compliance with the ECtHR's judgments irrespective of whether the HRA is repealed. No internal legislation can affect the obligations of the UK internationally. The only effective way to avoid international obligations under the Convention would be to denounce it. This possibility will be discussed in more detail in section 3 of this chapter. Alternatively, the UK might try to persuade all other contracting parties to amend the ECHR and make the judgments of the ECtHR merely advisory. On a number of occasions the contracting parties have confirmed their commitment to human rights and the right to individual petition,[20] and it seems hardly possible to secure agreement from all 47 contracting parties to amend Article 46 to ensure that ECtHR judgments are merely advisory. For these reasons, this option is not considered further in this chapter.

Before turning to a discussion of a UK Bill of Rights it is important to highlight why the 'shield argument' is not capable of being effective internationally. The idea is that British courts would operate under a doctrine akin to the one that the German,[21]

19 See for example Telegraph View 'A British Bill of Rights should be welcomed' *The Telegraph* (3 October 2014) available at <www.telegraph.co.uk/news/politics/conservative/11136146/A-British-Bill-of-Rights-should-be-welcomed.html > accessed 6 June 2016.

20 See, for example, the Brighton Declaration para. 1 and 2, available at <www.echr.coe.int/Documents/2012_Brighton_FinalDeclaration_ENG.pdf> accessed 6 June 2016.

21 In the famous judgment of the German Constitutional Court in Görgülü the supremacy of the German Constitution over the ECHR was established. Having said that, the German Constitutional Court encouraged the national courts to interpret national legislation in harmony with the ECHR as it is understood by the ECtHR. *Görgülü* BVerfGE 111, 307, 315.

Italian[22] or Russian courts[23] use in their constitutional interpretation, which maintains that their respective national constitutions are superior to the ECHR at the national level. It is perhaps expected that a bill of rights would have a priority over the judgments of the ECtHR within the UK. The Russian Constitutional Court has developed the doctrine of national constitutional supremacy in its recent case law on prisoner voting rights which is strikingly similar to the prisoner voting rights challenge that the UK is facing.[24] The Constitutional Court of Russia has been on the frontline of Russian resistance to the ECtHR regarding prisoner voting rights, holding that the ECtHR's judgment in *Anchugov and Gladkov v Russia* (a Russian *Hirst No 2*) cannot be executed in Russia.[25] It has been argued that this judgment resulted in a deadlock between the ECtHR and Russia, but the judgment of the Constitutional Court of Russia cannot void the international legal obligation to enforce *Anchugov and Gladkov*.[26] The doctrine of the legal supremacy of national constitutions is possibly valid on the national level, but this does not alter international legal obligations. Moreover, the contracting parties to the ECHR cannot use

22 The Italian Constitutional Court has also identified that the legal status of the ECHR is subordinate to the Italian Constitution. See Judgment nos. 348 and 349 of 2007, Corte Costituzionale; Francesca Biondi and Filippo Fontanelli 'The Decisions No. 348 and 349/2007 of the Italian Constitutional Court: The Efficacy of the European Convention in the Italian Legal System' (2008) 9 *German Law Journal* 889.

23 In its judgment of 14 July 2015 the Constitutional Court of Russia posited that the judgments of the ECtHR should be executed by the national authorities but indicated that they can depart from international obligations established in such judgments in exceptional situations when the execution would lead to breaches of the foundational principles and norms of the Russian Constitution. Judgment of the Constitutional Court of the Russian Federation from 14 July 2015 N 21-П "*in the case of verification of constitutionality of Article 1 of the Federal Law 'On Ratification of the Convention For the Protection of Human Rights and Fundamental Freedoms and Its Protocols', sections 1 and 2 of Article 32 of the Federal Law 'On International Treaties of the Russian Federation', sections 1 and 4 of Article 11, subsection 4 of section 4 of Article 392 of the Civil Procedural Code of the Russian Federation', Sections 1 and 4 of Article 13, subsection 4 of section 3 of Article 311 of the Arbitration Procedural Code of the Russian Federation, sections 1 and 4 of Article 15, subsection 4 of section 1 of Article 350 of the Administrative Court Proceedings Code of the Russian Federation, and subsection 2 of Section 4 of Article 413 of the Criminal Procedural Code of the Russian Federation in relation to the request of the group of the members of state Duma (parliament)*" available at <http://rg.ru/2015/07/27/ks-dok.html> (in Russian) 13.

24 See Judgment of 19 April 2016, no. 12-П/2016 on the case "*concerning the resolution of the question of the possibility to execute in accordance with the Constitution of the Russian Federation the Judgment of the European Court of Human Rights*" (4 July 2013) *Anchugov and Gladkov v. Russia in connection with the request of the Ministry of Justice of the Russian Federation* available at <www.ksrf.ru/en/Decision/Judgments/Documents/2016_April_19_12-P.pdf.>

25 Ibid. 38–39.

26 Kanstantsin Dzehtsiarou, Sergey Golubok and Maxim Timofeev 'Imaginary Dialogue and Fictitious Collaboration: Russian Response to the Prisoner Voting Judgment' *ECHR blog* (29 April 2016) available at <http://echrblog.blogspot.co.uk/2016/04/the-russian-response-to-prisoner-voting.htmlb> accessed 4 June 2016.

these doctrines to justify their failure to implement ECtHR judgments.[27] Under Article 26 of the Vienna Convention on Law of Treaties a party to a treaty cannot use national law to justify its failure to perform a treaty.[28] Although these situations have happened before in international law they are not desirable. Therefore, the 'shield argument' is highly doubtful. Even contracting parties which have national constitutions that list and define human rights, the judgments of the ECtHR still need to be executed.

This section is based on the premise that a bill of rights would lead to repealing the HRA without denouncing the ECHR. In this case the content of a bill of rights would only be able to indirectly affect the relationship between the UK and the ECtHR. It seems plausible to suggest that such a bill would either reflect the rights enshrined in the Convention (a less probable option) or significantly reformulate and curtail them (a more probable option).[29] In the latter case the influence of a bill of rights would be more significant, whereas if the rights enshrined in the bill are the same as in the Convention then it would be likely that British courts take ECtHR jurisprudence into account even if there is no explicit provision in the bill to that effect. Thus, there is a high chance that the mirror principle will *de facto* continue to operate in UK courts. If the rights provided by a bill are significantly narrower than the Convention rights, then the link between the ECtHR and the domestic judiciary might be undermined.

Human rights instruments are almost always the product of heated and protracted negotiations. Even curtailed human rights provisions under a bill of rights would be the result of an inter-party compromise in Parliament. Such a compromise might not be easily reached. It is more likely that a compromise would be achieved at a very abstract level. For example, it is easier to agree that children's rights need to be properly protected than to agree on what exactly this protection should include. Therefore, the rights enshrined in the bill might be broad and abstract. In this case, the national courts will be able to develop their jurisprudence in line with the ECtHR. Although this option is plausible, this chapter focuses on the scenario which is less beneficial to human rights protection – namely, if a future bill of rights provides precise and narrowly defined human rights provisions. In this case the national courts will have to divert from the jurisprudence of the ECtHR.

The gap between the case law of national courts and the ECtHR might lead to an increase in the number of successful applications in Strasbourg originating from the UK. There are examples of this from the pre-HRA times such as the

27 Vienna Convention on the Law of Treaties (23 May 1969) U.N. Doc. A/ CONF.39/27, at 289 (1969), 1155 U.T.S. 331, Article 26.

28 Ibid. Article 46.

29 It is highly doubtful that the Conservative government will be prepared to substantively expand the scope of human rights enshrined in the ECHR. Perhaps this bill will reflect some of the rights enshrined in the Convention while somewhat curtailing others.

ECtHR's judgment in the case of *Smith and Grady v the United Kingdom*.[30] In this case the applicants complained that their dismissal from the army on the basis of their sexual orientation violated their right to private and family life under the ECHR. In this case, the UK Court of Appeal pointed out that it is not empowered to use the test of proportionality adopted by the ECtHR.[31] Instead the Court of Appeal considered if the measure was unreasonable using the test in *Wednesbury*,[32] concluding that it was not unreasonable in public law. This case went to Strasbourg and the ECtHR unsurprisingly found a violation of Article 8 of the ECHR.[33] As a result of this judgment the UK had to introduce *The Armed Forces Code of Social Conduct Policy Statement* lifting the ban on lesbian, gay, bisexual and transgender personnel serving in the military.[34] If the national court could have applied ECtHR case law directly then this case would never have reached Strasbourg. This means that further divergence in interpretation of human rights could generate more adverse judgments against the UK at the ECtHR. As a matter of international law these judgments will have to be executed. More successful applications originating from the UK in Strasbourg will cause delays in the protection of human rights, monetary compensation that the UK will have to pay and embarrassment at the European level. Additionally, in order to have the kind of dialogue described earlier, the ECtHR and UK courts need to operate within compatible legal systems. If these systems are significantly diverse it will be too easy to dismiss each other's arguments as inapplicable in either the context of the ECHR or a bill of rights.

Finally, it seems that the UK government sees a British Bill of Rights and the HRA as mutually exclusive concepts, the expectation being that adoption of the bill should lead to the repeal of the HRA. However, the presence of a codified set of rights in national legislation does not necessarily preclude a state from implementing the ECHR and the case law of the ECtHR. Ireland provides an appropriate comparable example as its constitution contains a set of fundamental rights.[35] In 2003 the Irish Parliament adopted the European Convention on Human Rights Act (ECHR Act) which incorporated the rights enshrined in the ECHR into national law.[36] The ECHR Act is very similar to the HRA both in terms of its structure and the language it uses.[37] When the ECHR Act was

30 *Smith and Grady v the United Kingdom* nos. 33985/96 and 33986/96, ECHR 1999-VI.

31 R *v Ministry of Defence, ex parte Smith and Others* 2 WLR 305.

32 *Associated Provincial Picture Houses Ltd. v Wednesbury Corporation* [1948] 1 KB 223.

33 *Smith and Grady* (n.30).

34 Resolution ResDH (2002) 35 concerning the judgments of the ECtHR on 27 September 1999 (final on 27 December 1999) and 25 July 2000 (final on 25 October 2000); Article 41 in the case of *Smith and Grady v the United Kingdom*, adopted by the Committee of Ministers on 30 April 2002 at the 792nd meeting of the Ministers' Deputies.

35 Constitution of Ireland – Bunreacht na hÉireann, Articles 38–44.

36 Ronagh McQuigg 'The European Convention on Human Rights Act 2003 – Ten Years On' (2014) 3 *International Human Rights Law Review* 61, 61.

37 Ibid. 62.

adopted it was argued that it would have little impact on the reasoning of Irish judges.[38] Although this Act did not dramatically change the way Irish courts dealt with human rights issues it was argued that "for the plaintiffs in the cases where convention-based arguments did impact upon the outcomes, the 2003 legislation acted as a further and effective safeguard for their rights, beyond that of the Constitution".[39] This shows that the presence of a national bill of rights does not necessarily fully replace an Act that implements the ECHR.

(3) Denouncing the European Convention on Human Rights: A pyrrhic victory?

Denouncing the ECHR and withdrawing from it would free the UK from future legal obligations under the ECHR, although it would still have to implement all adverse judgments delivered by the ECtHR including the prisoner voting cases discussed previously. Legally speaking these obligations would continue to exist but the Committee of Ministers would be able to impose very little political pressure on an outgoing member state. The process of denouncing the ECHR is relatively straightforward. Under Article 58 of the Convention the UK government could notify the Secretary General of the Council of Europe, and after six months the Convention would be denunciated. Alternatively, the UK might decide to cease its membership of the Council of Europe, and in this case the Convention would be denunciated automatically. Article 7 of the Statute of the Council of Europe regulates this procedure.[40] Technically and legally it is very simple; it is, however, much more complex politically.

From the rhetoric surrounding the bill-of-rights proposals it seems that the UK government would like the ECHR and the ECtHR not to bind the Westminster parliament. The former home secretary and current prime minister Theresa May pointed out that "[t]he ECHR can bind the hands of Parliament, adds nothing to our prosperity, makes us less secure by preventing the deportation of dangerous foreign nationals – and does nothing to change the attitudes of governments like Russia's when it comes to human rights".[41] Seemingly, the key point of concern here is that the ECHR can 'bind the hands of Parliament'; however, the ECHR does not bind Parliament more than any other international commitment that the UK has undertaken. The only difference is that other international treaties often do not have enforcement mechanisms like those of the ECtHR or do not address serious and sensitive social problems like the ECHR. The International

38 Ray Murphy 'The incorporation of the ECHR into Irish domestic law' (2002) *European Human Rights Law Review* 640, 655.

39 McQuigg (n.36) 95.

40 Statute of the Council of Europe (1949) ETS No.001, Article 7.

41 Theresa May 'Theresa May's speech on Brexit' *Conservative Home* (25 April 2016) available at <www.conservativehome.com/parliament/2016/04/theresa-mays-speech-on-brexit-full-text.html> accessed 6 June 2016.

Covenant on Civil and Political Rights (ICCPR) is no less binding from the perspective of international law than the ECHR. However, the key difference between the ICCPR and the ECHR is that the latter was implemented domestically through the HRA.

The Strasbourg court's influence on Parliament is often grossly exaggerated by the media and politicians. Every year the ECtHR delivers only a few judgments in which it finds violations of the ECHR by the UK. Equally the Strasbourg court declares the vast majority of applications originating from the UK inadmissible.[42] Most of the judgments that are delivered are not particularly controversial and are executed through the normal bureaucratic channels. There are only a handful of problematic judgments, often highlighted by the media. Even in these controversial cases the ECtHR does not demand the UK to significantly change its legal system and is open to a constructive dialogue.[43] Moreover, the contracting parties are left with a significant leeway of how to implement such changes.

At the time of writing perhaps the most controversial cases that the UK has to execute are the prisoner voting cases and the cases where the ECtHR has declared that life imprisonment without any prospect of release is a violation of Article 3.[44] As pointed out earlier, in the prisoner voting cases the Strasbourg court has established the principle that automatic bans violate the ECHR.[45] Subsequently, the court tightened this ruling so that only cases where disenfranchisement is applied by a judge on an assessment of the crime that was committed comply with the Convention.[46] The court then quickly realised this was difficult to enforce and in *Scoppola No 3* lowered the standard, holding that automatic disenfranchisement complies with the Convention provided there was not a blanket ban.[47] In Italy those who were serving sentences of three years or less could vote, which the ECtHR held did not violate the Convention. In the UK legislative proposals to allow those to vote who are in prison 12 months or less, or alternatively four years or less, were presented before Parliament but have not yet been acted on.[48]

42 In 2015 the court found a violation of the ECHR in 13 cases against the United Kingdom. See <http://echr.coe. int/Documents/Stats_violation_2015_ENG.pdf> accessed 6 June 2016. In the same year 575 applications were allocated to a judicial formation or, in other words, submitted to the ECtHR. See 'Analysis of statistics 2015' available at <www.echr.coe.int/Documents/Stats_analysis_2015_ENG.pdf> accessed 6 June 2016.

43 The reaction of the ECtHR to the case of *R v Horncastle* discussed above clearly shows its willingness to engage in a reasonable and constructive dialogue.

44 *Vinter and Others v the United Kingdom* [GC], nos. 66069/09, 130/10 and 3896/10 (ECHR 2013).

45 *Hirst v the United Kingdom (no. 2), supra* note 9.

46 *Frodl* (n.10).

47 *Scoppola* (n.10).

48 See 'Joint Committee on the Draft Voting Eligibility (Prisoners) Bill – First Report; Draft Voting Eligibility (Prisoners) Bill' available at <www.publications.parliament.uk/pa/jt201314/jtselect/jtdraftvoting/103/10302.htm,> accessed 7 June 2016.

In a case about life sentences with no possibility of parole, *Vinter v the United Kingdom*, the ECtHR stated that such sentences are incompatible with Article 3 of the ECHR.[49] The court was careful to point out that their ruling did not require the UK to release the applicants immediately but there should be a possibility (however remote) for release and the judges were willing to allow the UK authorities a significant margin of appreciation. In the case of *Hutchinson v the United Kingdom* the Strasbourg court held that the administration of whole life sentences was now compatible with the requirements of Article 3 after changes to the law following *Vinter*.[50] Given the relatively minor measures required to comply with ECtHR judgments in both types of cases, withdrawal from the Convention seems a grossly disproportionate measure.

As previous chapters in this book have noted, evolutive interpretation of the ECHR by the Strasbourg court has often been raised as a justification for denouncing the Convention,[51] but this would be a disproportionate response to judicial activism because the states have other means of putting pressure on the court. For example, Protocol 15 will amend the preamble to the ECHR by including references to subsidiarity and the margin of appreciation.[52] Moreover, the contracting parties can draft a new protocol which would clearly and unambiguously prohibit the ECtHR from using an evolutive interpretation. Although it has not been done and unlikely to be done, the states have certain tools to restrict the court's 'inadequate activism'.[53]

The ECtHR does not go beyond its mandate given by the ECHR. The court has to ensure an effective protection of human rights and it is almost impossible without an evolutive interpretation of the Convention. The court has not changed its approach to evolutive interpretation dramatically since at least the early 1990s. It is also not clear that the ECtHR has actually gone significantly beyond its mandate since the changes instigated by Protocol 12 in 1998.[54]

This would mean that the UK's withdrawal would not be a response to any particular illegitimate action of the ECtHR but a sign of a momentary political dissatisfaction with Europe, in general, and the ECtHR, in particular. The benefits that the UK would obtain from ECHR withdrawal are also highly uncertain. It is highly possible that if the UK denounces the Convention it would have to

49 *Vinter* (n.44).

50 Grand Chamber judgment *Hutchinson v the United Kingdom* no. 57592/08 (17 January 2017).

51 See Chapter 1.

52 Protocol No. 15 to the ECHR (2013), CETS 213.

53 On a number of occasions the ECtHR was accused of inadequate judicial activism. Lord Hoffmann pointed out that "[t]he proposition that the Convention is a 'living instrument' is the banner under which the Strasbourg Court has assumed power to legislate what they consider to be required by 'European public order'." Lord Hoffmann 'The Universality of Human Rights' (2009) 125 *Law Quarterly Review* 416, 438.

54 Protocol No. 12 to the ECHR (2000).

leave the Council of Europe, of which it is a founding member.[55] Although ratification of the ECHR is not a precondition of membership, because the Statute of the Council of Europe came into existence before the Convention, it now is not possible to become a member without ratification of the ECHR.[56] Moreover, under Article 3 of the statute member states are required to engage in sincere and effective collaboration to protect the human rights of all persons within their jurisdiction and denunciation falls well short of this. According to Article 8 of the statute violation of the obligation to collaborate in human rights protection is a reason for suspension and expulsion from the Council.[57]

Withdrawal from the Council of Europe would significantly undermine the reputation of the UK as a state that cares about human rights protection. The UK would be only the second country in Europe which is not a member of the Council of Europe, the other being Belarus with its very poor human rights record.[58] UK withdrawal would also have the potential to trigger further withdrawals from states such as Russia and Azerbaijan, for whom it would be a perfect excuse to get rid of the ECtHR, and there is some evidence that existing UK backlash against the court has encouraged these countries to take a more hostile attitude towards the ECtHR.[59] The debate about repealing the HRA and denouncing the ECHR has impact beyond Europe. Kenyan president Uhuru Kenyatta who, at the time, was facing criminal charges at the International Criminal Court (ICC) referred to the rhetoric of UK political leaders about the ECtHR to question the ICC's authority.[60] The UK would also become only the second state in Europe to leave the Convention system: during the regime of the Colonels, Greece left the Council to return a few years later when the democratic government was

55 Founding members of the Council of Europe are Denmark, Belgium, Republic of Ireland, Luxembourg, Italy, Netherlands, Sweden and the United Kingdom.

56 Usually signing and ratifying the ECHR is the first step in the accession procedure to the Council of Europe. See, for example, the accession agreement with the Republic of Moldova available at <http://assembly.coe.int/nw/xml/XRef/Xref-XML2HTML-EN.asp?fileid=13927&lang=en> accessed 7 June 2016

57 Statute of the Council of Europe Article 8 (n.40).

58 Belarus remains the only fully recognised country in Europe which is not a party to the ECHR and not a member of the Council of Europe. It is also the only country in Europe still using capital punishment. The US Department of State has called Belarus an authoritarian state where citizens are unable to change their government through elections. Poor prison conditions and abuses by security forces are among other human rights problems in Belarus. See 'Country Reports Human Rights Practices for 2015' available at <www.state.gov/j/drl/rls/hrrpt/humanrightsreport/#wrapper.>.

59 Phillip Leach and Alice Donald 'Russia Defies Strasbourg: Is Contagion Spreading?' *EJIL Talk* (19 December 2015) available at <www.ejiltalk.org/author/leachdonald> accessed 6 June 2016.

60 Adam Wagner 'Kenyan President uses Tory human rights plans to defend war crimes charges' *UK Human Rights Blog* (24 October 2014), available at <https://ukhumanrightsblog.com/2014/10/24/kenyan-president-uses-tory-human-rights-plans-to-defend-war-crimes-charges>.

reinstalled.[61] In the Americas, Trinidad and Tobago and Venezuela – countries with significant problems in the area of human rights – have denounced the American Convention on Human Rights.[62] The UK could potentially be the first Western democracy to denounce a fundamental human rights treaty. Protection and promotion of human rights have traditionally been priorities of the UK's foreign policy. It currently assists newly established and transitional democracies to enhance human rights safeguards and often condemns human rights violations by less democratic nations.[63] It is not at all clear how these existing policy positions can be reconciled with the denunciation of the most successful human rights treaty in the world.

Human rights in the UK are well protected: the courts and police are independent, there is a very little chance that someone is arrested or persecuted for his or her political views and discrimination is prohibited. The UK is not Belarus, Trinidad and Tobago or Venezuela. However, when the ECHR was drafted it was assumed that it would not need to be applied in the UK.[64] The Convention was instead seen principally as an aspirational instrument for the repressed Eastern Bloc. However, over the years the ECtHR has helped the UK to improve human rights protection in various areas. They include non-discrimination of homosexual and heterosexual people,[65] prohibition of corporal punishment,[66] improved access to justice,[67] protection of transsexual people[68] and many others. It would be very short-sighted if the UK authorities were to sacrifice the system of human rights protection in Europe to gain some immediate political benefits, especially since the benefits of doing so are grossly exaggerated. The recent vote in favour of leaving the European Union has already undermined the UK's political position in Europe. A potential denunciation of the Convention would further highlight its attitude to European values – although the Convention was essentially

61 William Schabas *The European Convention on Human Rights. A Commentary* (OUP 2015) 943.

62 See 'Venezuela Denounces American Convention on Human Rights as IACHR Faces Reform' available at <www.ijrcenter.org/2012/09/19/venezuela-denounces-american-convention-on-human-rights-as-iachr-faces-reform/> accessed 7 June 2016.

63 Human Rights are mentioned at least three times in the description of purposes of the Foreign and Commonwealth Office for 2014–2015 FCO 'Our Purpose' (2014) available at <www.gov.uk/government/uploads/system/uploads/attachment_data/file/305461/FCO_priorities_14-15.pdf> accessed 7 June 2016.

64 Lord Hoffmann claimed that "[w]hen we joined, indeed, took the lead in the negotiation of the European Convention, it was not because we thought it would affect our own law, but because we thought it right to set an example for others and to help to ensure that all the Member States respected those basic human rights which were not culturally determined but reflected our common humanity". Lord Hoffmann 'Human Rights and the House of Lords' (1999) 62 *Modern Law Review* 159, 159.

65 *Dudgeon v the United Kingdom*, 22 October 1981, Series A no. 45.

66 *Tyrer v the United Kingdom*, 25 April 1978, Series A no. 26.

67 *Golder v the United Kingdom*, 21 February 1975, Series A no. 18.

68 *Christine Goodwin v the United Kingdom* [GC], no. 28957/95, ECHR 2002-VI.

built around values honoured in the UK. The reputation of the UK would suffer and its voice would become much quieter.

Conclusion

Who has the last word in human rights disputes? The UK authorities claim that the ECtHR binds the Westminster parliament and that this should be changed. This chapter argued that the UK still has the last word in human rights matters. The HRA did not change this and its replacement with a Bill of Right would not change this either. With or without the HRA the UK will be under international obligation to comply with the judgments of the ECtHR. The obligation to comply would only be removed if the UK were to denounce the ECHR. However, the benefits of this would be minimal and the drawbacks considerable.

Chapter 6

Taking sovereignty seriously

*Adam Tucker**

Introduction

Concerns about sovereignty have been, and still are, central to the case against the Human Rights Act (HRA).[1] However, they have not always been taken seriously by defenders of the Act. Indeed, a constitutional orthodoxy has emerged according to which arguments against the Act which target its impact on sovereignty are not just mistaken but also wholly misconceived. Such arguments should not, or so the dominant position among defenders of the Act tells us, be taken seriously.[2]

In this chapter, I argue that there are genuine sovereignty-based reasons to object to the HRA, and whilst they do not ultimately amount to reasons to repeal the Act, their proponents deserve to have their arguments taken seriously. An ongoing failure to do this has left important reasons to preserve the Act absent from public debate. In the previous two chapters, different issues of sovereignty were discussed. Stephen Dimelow's overview of parliamentary sovereignty and Kanstantsin Dzehtsiarou's analysis of the role sovereignty in relation to the European Court of Human Rights both point to the difficult relationship that the HRA has with existing conceptions of sovereignty. The conclusion I reach in this chapter is that the refusal of defenders of the Act to take criticisms in relation to sovereignty seriously has contributed to deepening the pathologies of an (already) unhealthy public controversy.

* I would like to thank Mike Gordon, Graham Gee and Frederick Cowell for helpful advice and constructive criticism of a previous draft of this chapter.

1 They featured, for example, in the debate on the act at second reading in the House of Commons (see below, n.24 and accompanying text) and they are prominent in the Conservatives' 2014 policy paper on Human Rights reform (see below, n.3, and the discussion accompanying n.9).

2 For succinct example of this position, see *Liberty*'s response to some criticism of the Human Rights Act by David Cameron during Prime Minister's Questions in June 2015 available at <www.liberty-human-rights.org.uk/news/press-releases-and-statements/liberty-responds-david-camerons-pmqs-comments-human-rights-act> accessed 12 December 2016 (discussed below, n.34 and accompanying text).

I am conscious that both the 'case against' and the 'defence' of the HRA are nebulous notions. Neither has an identifiable or organised core, and each consists of a variety of positions, arguments and motivations which are not necessarily internally consistent (and, in a pluralist democracy, rightly so). In 2015, however, the government was elected on a general election manifesto promise to repeal the Act, itself preceded by several years of sustained criticism of the Act and, latterly, by the publication of a fairly detailed policy document outlining their case against the Act. I have treated this as the core of the case against.[3] The defence of the Act is harder still to pin down. I focus on academic commentary intended (as I understand it) to respond to the case against the HRA and to the arguments that feature in the case against. In particular, I refer throughout to Conor Gearty's book *On Fantasy Island* (a book which has many virtues which, alas, I do not mention here). I do this not because it is constitutive of the case defending the HRA (although now it is, at least partly) but because the position it defends (with unprecedented care and rigour) is reflective of an attitude towards the constitutional position of the HRA which seems to have become entrenched as a kind of orthodoxy among constitutional scholars, consistently with other positions I discuss here.[4]

The chapter unfolds as follows: First, I distinguish two senses of sovereignty, national sovereignty and parliamentary sovereignty. I show that both of these senses of sovereignty ground identifiable, publicly articulated objections to the HRA. Next, I tackle each in turn. I argue that each sense of sovereignty grounds cogent concerns about the Act. The HRA compromises both national sovereignty and parliamentary sovereignty, and arguments which begin from either foundation deserve to be treated seriously and engaged with rather than dismissed. I conclude by suggesting that a failure to do so has imperilled the future of the HRA and has contributed to a degradation in the quality of constitutional discourse in the UK.

(1) Two (relevant) senses of sovereignty

Sovereignty is a multifaceted and flexible term.[5] Its essence is the idea of independent authority or supremacy; a sovereign authority is one with the power to

3 Conservative Party 'Protecting Human Rights in the UK: The Conservatives Proposals for Changing Britain's Human Rights Laws' (2014) available at <file:///C:/Users/ubfcow01/Downloads/HUMAN_RIGHTS%20(3).pdf> accessed 12 December 2016.

4 For the view from outside this orthodoxy, see Graham Gee and Grégoire Webber 'HRA Watch: Reform, Repeal, Replace? Conventional Wisdom and the Human Rights Act' *UK Constitutional Law Blog* (15 June 2015) available at <https://ukconstitutionallaw.org/2015/06/15/hra-watch-reform-repeal-replace-graham-gee-and-gregoire-webber-conventional-wisdom-and-the-human-rights-act/> accessed 20 November 2016.

5 As Robert Jackson recently observed, it is a "big idea" which "defies academic attempts to pin it down and fit it into tidy analytical categories" Robert Jackson *Sovereignty: The Evolution of an Idea.* (Wiley 2013) xi. For an important attempt at systematic categorisation see Stephen Krasner *Sovereignty: organized hypocrisy* (Princeton University Press 1999).

make decisions free from outside interference and without the risk that those decisions will be overridden by a different or competing decision-maker. But different authorities can be supreme or independent in different ways, and arguments about sovereignty accordingly take different forms and can invoke different meanings of the term. Two different aspects of sovereignty must be distinguished in the case against the HRA. First, it features appeals to the idea of *national sovereignty*. This is a moral-political concept which is also prominent in international legal doctrines. Here, I understand it as the idea that political communities ought to be empowered to make their own decisions without outside interference or override. In particular, it requires that the community of the UK can use its domestic political institutions to make its own decisions, without fear of interference from external institutions. Any arrangement which empowers outside institutions to override domestic decisions is thus a threat to national sovereignty. Note, however, that the principle of national sovereignty makes no particular claims about how our domestic political institutions are organised, so long as they are (collectively) independent from outside interference. This is where our second sense of sovereignty enters the picture. This is the idea of *parliamentary sovereignty*. This is a domestic legal concept about the allocation of political power between the institutions of the government of the United Kingdom.[6] In Dicey's famous formulation it requires (asserts, even) that

> Parliament . . . has, under the English constitution, the right to make or unmake any law whatever; and, further . . . no person or body is recognised by the law of England as having a right to override or set aside the legislation of Parliament.[7]

Accordingly, Parliament is sovereign to the extent that it can legislate without risk of its decisions being overridden, in particular by the courts, and any judicial power to override legislation is a violation of that sovereignty. The case against the HRA relies, separately, on each of these senses of sovereignty. It alleges that different features of the scheme put in place by the Act violate both national and parliamentary sovereignty and that these violations count as reasons to contemplate repeal or reform of the Act. My argument in the rest of this chapter is that those arguments have not been taken as seriously as they ought to have been and that the position of the HRA is weakened as a result of that neglect.

6 Note that it also channels, albeit imperfectly, yet another (moral-political) sense of sovereignty: *popular sovereignty*, the idea that the people are the masters of their own destiny. This third sense does not feature in my analysis here, but it should be kept in mind that it lurks in the background of many of the arguments that I discuss (and many that I do not!).

7 A.V Dicey *Introduction to the Study of the Law of the Constitution* (10th ed. Macmillan 1961) 39–40.

(2) National sovereignty in the case against the Human Rights Act

A concern with national sovereignty has always been implicit in the (vague but long-standing) proposal that the HRA be replaced with a British or *UK* Bill of Rights.[8] This particular concern is more explicitly articulated in the policy document published by the Conservative Party in late 2014 in preparation for the 2015 general election. The first of its four objections to the HRA included the following claim:

> There is mounting concern at Strasbourg's attempts to overrule decisions of our democratically elected Parliament and overturn the UK courts' careful applications of Convention rights.[9]

And the second of those four objections opened as follows:

> [The] Human Rights Act undermines the role of UK courts in deciding on human rights issues in this country. Section 2 of the HRA requires UK courts to "take into account" rulings of the Strasbourg Court when they are interpreting Convention rights. This means problematic Strasbourg jurisprudence is often being applied in UK law.[10]

These themes were echoed in the Conservatives' 2015 general election manifesto, which included (distinct) promises to "scrap the Human Rights Act and curtail the role of the European Court of Human Rights" and to "[b]reak the formal link between British courts and the European Court of Human Rights, and make our own Supreme Court the ultimate arbiter of human rights matters in the UK".[11]

This particular thread of opposition to the HRA is based on concern that a foreign court (the European Court of Human Rights in Strasbourg) is exercising excessive authority over domestic institutions, both Parliament and the courts. These arguments are thus grounded in an appeal to the value of national sovereignty. In legal terms the key provision of the Act here is section 2, which provides (in the relevant part) as follows:

> A court or tribunal determining a question which has arisen in connection with a Convention right must take into account . . . any judgment, decision,

8 David Cameron advocated a *British* Bill of Rights in 2006, the Conservatives promised in 2010 and the Commission on a Bill of Rights assessed in 2012 the possibility of a *UK* Bill of Rights and the Conservatives promised in 2015 a *British* Bill of Rights in 2015 (my emphasis).

9 *The Conservatives' Proposals* (n.3).

10 Ibid. 4.

11 *The Conservative Party Manifesto 2015* available at <www.bond.org.uk/data/files/Blog/ConservativeManifesto2015.pdf> 58 accessed 1 November 2016.

> declaration or advisory opinion of the European Court of Human Rights . . . so far as, in the opinion of the court or tribunal, it is relevant to the proceedings in which that question has arisen.[12]

The cogency of the argument from a national sovereignty perspective will thus depend on the extent to which section 2 compromises or violates national sovereignty. More specifically, it will depend on the intensity with which the courts understand their obligation to "take into account" the jurisprudence of the Strasbourg court. At first sight, then, the argument from a national sovereignty perspective is likely to appear weak. There is, after all, no threat to sovereignty in (merely) taking into account what outsiders are doing and, furthermore, that looks like the kind of thing that a responsible sovereign would consider doing anyway. Accordingly, the dominant response to this line of argument has been to deny it has any purchase at all rather than to engage with it. This line of argument is common to the defences of the HRA or responses to the government's proposals proposed by Conor Gearty, Mark Elliott and Alison Young and Stephen Dimelow.[13] Elliott criticises the Conservatives for "the implication that there is presently a 'link' that requires UK Courts to *apply* ECtHR interpretations of the Convention". This, he argues, is not (or at least is no longer) the case: "Although UK courts did . . . come close to reading such an obligation into . . . it is clear that they now conceive of their relationship with Strasbourg in more flexible terms."[14]

Gearty unpacks this line of thought in greater detail. One of the fantasies around which his book is constructed is that which has come to surround the operation of section 2, namely the fantasy of the 'supremacy of Strasbourg'. In summary, Gearty's argument runs as follows. There was a problem, he concedes, with "how the courts initially approached" their task, as they "allowed the permissive language of section 2 to harden into an unavoidable obligation".[15] The foundation of this hardening was Lord Bingham's speech in *Ullah*, where he articulated what is now commonly known as the "mirror principle":

> . . . the Convention is an international instrument, the correct interpretation of which can be authoritatively expounded only by the Strasbourg court. From this it follows that a national court subject to a duty such as that imposed by section 2 should not without strong reason dilute or weaken the

12 Human Rights Act 1998, section 2.

13 Conor Gearty *On fantasy island: Britain, Strasbourg, and human rights* (OUP 2016); Mark Elliott 'My analysis of the Conservative Party's proposals for a British Bill of Rights' (3 October 2014) available at <https://publiclawforeveryone.com/2014/10/03/my-analysis-of-the-conservative-partys-proposals-for-a-british-bill-of-rights/> accessed 20 November 2016; Alison Young and Stephen Dimelow *Common Sense or Confusion: The Human Rights Act and the Conservative Party* (The Constitution Society 2015).

14 Ibid. Elliott.

15 Gearty (n.13) 104–5.

> effect of the Strasbourg case law . . . since the meaning of the Convention should be uniform throughout the states party to it. The duty of national courts is to keep pace with the Strasbourg jurisprudence as it evolves over time: no more, but certainly no less.[16]

Resistance to the mirror principle, driven (as Gearty notes) by the fact that it "simply did not accord with the intention of section 2" led to a judicial retreat to a new position of "calm co-responsibility" and a "new, more equal partnership" with the Strasbourg court.[17] Accordingly, Gearty rejects the fantasy of the supremacy of Strasbourg.

This narrative is compelling, not least because Gearty's and Elliott's accounts of what Lord Wilson once called the "retreat from the *Ullah* Principle" are legally accurate.[18] But it is important to note that this does not entail that the argument from national sovereignty is misguided. Consider the passage on which Gearty relies to characterise the ("calm", "more equal", "flexible") position to which the courts have now retreated. In *Horncastle*, Lord Phillips characterised the duty of the court under section 2 as follows:

> The requirement to 'take into account' the Strasbourg jurisprudence will normally result in the domestic court applying principles that are clearly established by the Strasbourg court. There will, however, be rare occasions where the domestic court has concerns as to whether a decision of the Strasbourg court sufficiently appreciates or accommodates particular aspects of our domestic process. In such circumstances it is open to the domestic court to decline to follow the Strasbourg decision, giving reasons for adopting this course. This is likely to give the Strasbourg court the opportunity to reconsider the particular aspect of the decision that is in issue, so that there takes place what may prove to be a valuable dialogue between the domestic court and the Strasbourg court. This is such a case.[19]

Even on this approach, the domestic court's power to resist Strasbourg jurisprudence is limited to cases where the Strasbourg court has not "sufficiently appreciated or accommodated particular aspects of our domestic process". The same basic position has more recently been outlined, in slightly different language, in *Chester*.[20] Lord Mance described the domestic courts' ability to defy

16 *R (Ullah) v Special Adjudicator* [2004] UKHL 26, [2004] 2 AC 323 [20].
17 Gearty (n.13) 108–9. Gearty traces the story through the following line of cases: *Horncastle*, *Al Khawaja* and *Tahery*, *Hanney*, *Kaiyam*, *Massey*, *Robinson* and *Vinter*.
18 *Moohan v Lord Advocate* [2014] UKSC 67, [104].
19 *R v Horncastle and others* [2009] UKSC 14, [2010] 2 AC 373 [11]. Following Gearty, I have reproduced the relevant passage (almost) in full. Gearty (n.13) 107.
20 *Chester v Secretary of State for Justice* [2013] UKSC 63, [2014] AC 271.

Strasbourg as being limited to situations "involv[ing] some truly fundamental principle of our law or some most egregious oversight", and Lord Sumption restricted the domestic courts' room for manoeuvre to "altogether exceptional cases", specifically where the Strasbourg court "has misunderstood or overlooked some significant feature of English law".[21]

So something more than mere disagreement is needed before the domestic courts can resist Strasbourg jurisprudence. In the absence of special circumstances, of the kind which Lord Phillips, Lord Mance and Lord Sumption each try to capture in the words quoted above the domestic courts' duty under section 2 – even in its recent, more modest form – requires the court to defer to Strasbourg's authority even if it disagrees with its position. The current position is exemplified by Lord Sumption's speech in Chester (which, although he was not writing for the majority in the case, gets the process demanded of him by the law exactly right). He made clear that he was constrained to follow a line of Strasbourg jurisprudence with which he disagreed:

> Without the decisions in *Hirst (No 2)* and *Scoppola*, I would have held that the question how serious an offence has to be to warrant temporary disenfranchisement is a classic matter for political and legislative judgment, and that the United Kingdom rule is well within any reasonable assessment of a Convention state's margin of appreciation. However, the contrary view has now been upheld twice by the Grand Chamber of the European Court of Human Rights, and is firmly established in the court's case law.[22]

So whilst the retreat from *Ullah* does markedly reduce the conflict between the demands of the HRA and the requirements of national sovereignty, it does not eliminate it altogether. After *Horncastle* and *Chester*, there are caveats on the power of the courts to resist Strasbourg, caveats which conflict with the national sovereignty of the United Kingdom. So Alison Young and Stephen Dimelow slightly misconceive the case against the Act when they argue that

> the portrayal of the current situation in domestic law as being that UK courts will always apply decisions against it . . . is highly misleading.[23]

Any claim that the courts *always* defer to Strasbourg would, of course, be wrong. But that is not part of the case against the HRA. The fact that courts *sometimes* do so would be enough for the argument from national sovereignty to get off the ground. They sometimes do because there are caveats on their authority to depart from Strasbourg jurisprudence. As those caveats originate

21 *Chester* [27], [121].
22 *Chester* [137].
23 Young and Dimelow (n.13) 36.

in section 2 of the HRA, it is cogent for the Act's opponents to attack it for its impact on national sovereignty and to agitate for reform to reduce, or even to eliminate, that impact. Such criticisms neither misunderstand nor misrepresent the law. As such, the appropriate response is not to deny their cogency but to engage with their merits.

(3) Parliamentary sovereignty in the case against the Human Rights Act

Doubts about the HRA have been grounded in concerns about its impact on parliamentary sovereignty since the Act's inception. Theresa May, then an opposition MP, opposed the bill which became the HRA during its second reading in the House of Commons in 1998 on the grounds that it would "reduce parliamentary sovereignty" and criticised the government for being "not . . . able to understand or accept" those ramifications of the Bill.[24] In an intervention in the House of Commons early in his parliamentary career, David Cameron complained that "the Human Rights Act has resulted in . . . Parliament sometimes being unable to do things that all reasonable people accept are the right things to do".[25] Perhaps most famously, as prime minister he reacted angrily to the decision in *R (F) v. Home Secretary*[26]:

> My hon. Friend speaks for many people in saying how completely offensive it is, once again, to have a ruling by a court that flies in the face of common sense . . . I am appalled by the Supreme Court ruling . . . I can also tell my hon. Friend that a commission will be established imminently to look at a British Bill of Rights, because it is about time we ensured that decisions are made in this Parliament rather than in the courts.[27]

But these concerns always ran counter to the conventional and academic wisdom about the Human Rights Act.[28] Jack Straw, the then home secretary, piloting the Act through the House of Commons, had insisted (at the third reading) that "[o]ne of the Bill's many strengths is . . . maintaining the sovereignty of Parliament".[29] Lord Steyn, in a celebrated passage in *Kebilene*, said it was "crystal

24 Theresa May HC Deb 16 February 1998 vol. 306, col. 848.

25 David Cameron HC Deb 30 October 2001 vol. 373, col. 824.

26 [2011] 1 AC 331. The Supreme Court issued a declaration of incompatibility regarding the absence of any provision in the Sexual Offences Act 2003 for the eventual lifting of duties imposed "indefinitely" on certain categories of sex offenders to keep the police notified of where they are living and of plans to travel abroad.

27 Cameron HC Deb 16 February 2011 vol. 523, col. 955. Despite the prime minister's distaste for the decision, his government prepared remedial secondary legislation, The Sexual Offences Act 2003 (Remedial) Order 2012.

28 For a rare example of an academic attack on the Act grounded in concerns about parliamentary sovereignty, see David Campbell, '"Catgate" and the challenge to parliamentary sovereignty in immigration law' (2015) *Public law* 426.

29 Jack Straw HC Deb 21 October 1998 vol. 317, col. 1358.

clear that the carefully and subtly drafted Human Rights Act 1998 preserves the principle of parliamentary sovereignty".[30] Tom Hickman captured this orthodoxy precisely, when he described it as a "cardinal, and uncontroversial" feature of the Act that it "ultimately preserved parliamentary sovereignty".[31]

Nevertheless, the third of the four objections in the Conservatives' 2014 policy document focused on the Act's implications for parliamentary sovereignty:

> Labour's Human Rights Act undermines the sovereignty of Parliament, and democratic accountability to the public. Although, the HRA affirms the sovereignty of the UK Parliament over human rights matters, Section 3(1) undermines Parliamentary sovereignty in practice. This provision requires UK courts to read and to give effect to legislation in a way which is compatible with Convention rights, "so far as it is possible to do so". There are cases in which, due to this rule, UK courts have gone to artificial lengths to change the meaning of legislation so that it complies with their interpretation of Convention rights, most often following Strasbourg's interpretation, even if this is inconsistent with Parliament's intention when enacting the relevant legislation.[32]

This passage contains a (reasonably) clearly articulated legal argument about section 3 of the Act, the relevant part of which reads,

> So far as it is possible to do so, primary legislation . . . must be read and given effect in a way which is compatible with the Convention rights.[33]

In particular, it alleges that in applying this section, the Courts have understood it to be "possible" to read legislation in ways which violate parliamentary sovereignty. Consistently with the conventional wisdom outlined earlier, this has not been taken seriously in evaluations of the reform proposals. For example, Shami Chakrabarti (then director of Liberty, now Baroness Chakrabarti) suggested in 2015 that these arguments revealed the prime minister to be in need of "an urgent lesson in constitutional and legal literacy" as "[u]nder the Human Rights Act . . . parliamentary sovereignty is perfectly preserved".[34]

This is unfortunate, because it is true that section 3 of the HRA has compromised parliamentary sovereignty. Whilst this is not obvious from the text of the provision itself, which uses the language of the 'possible', it is clear from a famous

30 *R v DPP ex parte Kebilene* [2000] 2 AC 326, 367.

31 Tom Hickman *Public Law after the Human Rights* Act (Hart Publishing, Oxford 2010) 63, emphasis added.

32 Conservative Pary (n.3).

33 Human Rights Act 1998, section 3.

34 Press Statement 'Liberty responds to David Cameron's PMQs comments on the Human Rights Act' *Liberty* (3 June 2015) available at <www.liberty-human-rights.org.uk/news/press-releases-and-statements/liberty-responds-david-camerons-pmqs-comments-human-rights-act> accessed 11 November 2016.

dictum in the leading case on the limits of section 3, *R v A*, where Lord Steyn memorably outlined the judicial power created by that section:

> the interpretative obligation under section 3 of the 1998 Act is a strong one. It applies even if there is no ambiguity in the language in the sense of the language being capable of two different meanings . . . it will sometimes be necessary to adopt an interpretation which linguistically may appear strained. The techniques to be used will not only involve the reading down of express language in a statute but also the implication of provisions.[35]

On this reading, section 3 equips the courts with two ways to construct (unambiguous) legislation in order to make it comply with Convention rights: reading down and the implication of provisions. These techniques only come into play when the interpretation they make possible is contrary to the intention of parliament in passing the legislation to be interpreted. If the interpretation arrived at was consistent with Parliament's intention, there would be no need for recourse to section 3 in the first place. In other words, section 3 provides a way for the courts to override primary legislation. It is therefore a violation of parliamentary sovereignty.

Conor Gearty dedicates a chapter of *On Fantasy Island* to defending the conventional wisdom (that the Act respects and preserves parliamentary sovereignty) against this account of section 3.[36] He begins by conceding that section 3 requires the judges to "engage in a fresh way" and characterises Lord Steyn's dictum in *R v A* (cited above) as "heady stuff indeed".[37] But, he argues, this approach to the judiciary's task under section 3 was "manifestly not what the Human Rights Act had intended" and therefore "did not take off". He claims that Lord Steyn's "colleagues on the bench were not nearly so robust" and that following "an almost immediate hostile reaction . . . the final nail in this activist adventure was nailed in" by Lord Bingham in *Anderson*.[38] The problem with this riposte to the critics of the HRA is that Lord Steyn's approach to section 3 *did* take off. Indeed, it is today still a sound statement of the courts' duty under that section and of the way it creates powers to override legislation. In particular, it is still the case that section 3 empowers the courts to contradict parliamentary intention and that they can do so both by reading down statutory words and by implying extra terms into statutes. As the following cases show, both practices are now well established.

The significance of the judicial power to read down statutes is highlighted by the decision in *Sheldrake v DPP*.[39] Here, the House of Lords read section 11(2)

35 *R v A* [2001] UKHL 25, [2002] 1 AC 45, 68.
36 Gearty (n.13) ch. 6.
37 Ibid. 81, 85.
38 *R v Anderson* [2002] UKHL 46, [2003] 1 AC 837.
39 *Sheldrake v Director of Public Prosecutions* [2004] UKHL 43, [2005] 1 AC 264. See also *DPP v Wright* [2009] EWHC 105 (Admin), [2010] QB 224 (applying *Sheldrake* to

of the Terrorism Act 2000 as imposing an evidential rather than a legal burden.[40] This was done, explicitly, contrary to Parliament's intention in enacting the provision. Giving judgment for the majority, Lord Bingham confirmed that, in principle, the interpretative obligation in section 3 of the HRA "may require the court to depart from the legislative intention of Parliament".[41] He stressed that in the case at hand, there could be "no doubt that Parliament intended section 11(2) to impose a legal burden on the defendant".[42] The court's task, he said was to assess "whether a burden enacted by Parliament unjustifiably infringes the presumption of innocence."[43] The court found that it did, and the legislation was read down with the burden on the defendant transformed, accordingly.

The significance of the power to imply extra terms is highlighted in *Waya*, *Secretary of State for the Home Department v MB* and *Pomiechowski*.[44] *Waya* concerned the confiscation regime under the Proceeds of Crime Act 2002.[45] That regime required the court to assess the amount recoverable through confiscation orders using a systematic, three-stage test: the identification of the benefit obtained by the defendant, the valuation of that benefit and the valuation of the defendant's recoverable assets (to set a cap on the recoverable amount).[46] Section 6(5) of the Act obliged the court to make an order requiring the payment of that amount. The court held that the systematic nature of the test combined with the obligation to order payment of the full amount it yielded created a risk (realised, the court found, in this case) that such an order would violate a defendant's right to the peaceful enjoyment of his possessions, guaranteed by Protocol 1, Article 1 of the Convention. Accordingly, and in exercise of its powers under section 3 of the HRA, the court inserted a qualification as to proportionality into the Act:

> It is plainly possible to read paragraph (b) as subject to the qualification: "except in so far as such an order would be disproportionate and thus a breach of article 1, Protocol 1." . . . in order to ensure that the statute remains Convention-compliant.[47]

---

an analogous burden of proof in the Hunting Act 2004 and *R v Lambert* [2001] UKHL 37 (which is cited, on this point, in the Conservative's reform proposals, discussed earlier).

40 Terrorism Act 2000, section 11(2). Section 11(1) made it an offence to belong or profess to belong to a proscribed organisation; Section 11(2) made it a defence to "prove" that the organisation was proscribed when the member became a member or began to profess membership or that the member had not participated in the organisation's activities while it was proscribed.

41 *Sheldrake* (n.39) [28].

42 Ibid. [50].

43 Ibid. [31].

44 *R v Waya* [2012] UKSC 51, [2013] 1 AC 294; *Pomiechowski v District Court of Legnica, Poland* [2012] UKSC 20, [2012] 1 WLR 1604; *Secretary of State for the Home Department v MB* [2007] UKHL 46, [2008] 1 AC 440.

45 Proceeds of Crime Act 2002.

46 *Waya* applying *R v May* [2008] UKHL 28, [2008] AC 1028.

47 *Waya* (n.44) [16].

The court took a similar approach in *MB*. The Prevention of Terrorism Act 2005 included a provision for the courts to supervise the imposition of control orders by the home secretary.[48] The Act also required that the rules of court in such proceedings obliged the court to refuse permission to disclose information where disclosure would be contrary to the public interest.[49] This requirement to refuse disclosure created a conflict with Article 6 of the Convention in cases involving material whose disclosure was contrary to the public interest but which was also essential to a fair hearing. Accordingly, the court implied a qualification into the relevant sections of the statute:

> paragraph 4(3)(d) of the Schedule to the 2005 Act, should be read and given effect "except where to do so would be incompatible with the right of the controlled person to a fair trial". Paragraph 4(2)(a) . . . would have to be read in the same way.[50]

Pomiechowski concerned the strict time limits for appeals under the Extradition Act 2003. The court found that the statutory scheme infringed Article 6 of the Convention, and remedied the infringement by implying a qualification into the statute:

> the statutory provisions concerning appeals can and should all be read subject to the qualification that the court must have a discretion in exceptional circumstances to extend time for both filing and service, where such statutory provisions would otherwise operate to prevent an appeal in a manner conflicting with the right of access to an appeal process . . . under article 6 . . . The High Court must have power in any individual case to determine whether the operation of the time limits would have this effect. If and to the extent that it would do so, it must have power to permit and hear an out of time appeal which a litigant personally has done all he can to bring and notify timeously.[51]

In each case, the court altered legislation contrary to parliamentary intention in order to bring it into line with the demands of Convention rights. Any and all of these cases show the conflict between the interpretive obligation in section 3 of the HRA and the doctrine of parliamentary sovereignty. But these cases (and others like them) and the literature do feature three potential responses to this line of argument. Each seeks, in a different way, to reconcile the operation of section 3 with the doctrine of parliamentary sovereignty.

48 Prevention of Terrorism Act 2005, section 3.
49 Prevention of Terrorism Act 2005, para. 4 of the Schedule.
50 *MB* (n.44) [72].
51 *Pomiechowski* (n.44) [39].

The first is implausible. It suggests that, since the HRA, Parliament is taken to have a standing intention that legislation be compatible with Convention rights. The use of section 3 is sometimes justified in this way. For example, in *Pomiechowski*, Lord Mance suggests that his decision to imply a judicial discretion to extend time limits into the statute was compatible with Parliament's intention in enacting the Extradition Act:

> In the present case, there is no reason to believe that Parliament either foresaw or intended the potential injustice which can result from absolute and inflexible time limits for appeals. It intended short and firm time limits, but can only have done so on the basis that this would in practice suffice to enable anyone wishing to appeal to do so without difficulty in time.[52]

But this line of argument contradicts the pervasive dicta scattered throughout the line of cases discussed earlier which acknowledge that the use of section 3 goes against rather than honours Parliament's intention. Indeed, this is often the source of judicial misgivings. For example, Lord Bingham was tempted to dissent in *MB* from a decision which he recognised "would very clearly fly in the face of Parliament's intention".[53] Similarly, Lord Phillips articulates some misgivings about the conflict between interpretation under section 3 and parliamentary intention in his 2010 Weedon lecture.[54]

A second, subtler, line of argument gives priority to Parliament's intention in 1998. Gearty, for example, notes of the section 3 duty that the judges "had it thrust upon them by Parliament" and that these cases involve the courts "squaring two statutory purposes".[55] Richard Bellamy notes the argument, which he attributes to the court itself, that "post-HRA rights-based review of legislation has legitimacy because it accords with the express will of Parliament that [the court] interpret the law with regard to these norms".[56] And, in Paul Roberts' elegant explanation of the decision in *Sheldrake*,

> [t]his approach was calculated to serve parliamentary sovereignty in the deeper, richer sense, previously elaborated by Lord Steyn in *R. v. A (No. 2)* . . . by giving effect to Parliament's contextualising second order directive for broad compliance with the HRA in all aspects of legislation and

52 Ibid. [39].
53 *MB* (n.44) [44].
54 Lord Phillips 'The Art of the Possible: statutory interpretation and human rights' (27 April 2010) available at <www.supremecourt.uk/docs/speech_100419.pdf> accessed 20 November 2016.
55 Gearty (n.13) 83, 89.
56 Richard Bellamy 'Political constitutionalism and the Human Rights Act' (2011) 9 *International Journal of Constitutional Law* 86, 105.

law enforcement – including judicial interpretation of Parliament's own first-order legislative intentions.[57]

A third line of argument denies the contradiction between section 3 and parliamentary sovereignty by pointing to the limits of the powers that it gives to the courts. In *Anderson*, Lord Bingham emphasised that section 3 does not go so far as to empower the courts to adopt interpretations which are "contrary to express statutory words or . . . by implication necessarily contradicted by the statute".[58] In *Re S*, Lord Nicholls said that courts cannot depart "substantially from a fundamental feature of an Act".[59] In *Ghaidan*, Lord Nicholls denied that the courts cannot remove "the very core and essence, the 'pith and substance' " of legislation.[60] The courts' own articulation of these limits is a little inconsistent, but the underlying idea is clear. This aspect of section 3 jurisprudence is an important part of Gearty's dismissal of the argument of supporters of parliamentary sovereignty; the courts cannot override, he notes, "what the statute was really about".[61]

These second and third responses are true. Section 3 does rely on Parliament's intention in enacting the 1998 Act for its legitimacy and the powers it grants to the court are not plenary or unlimited. But neither of those facts is enough to counter the argument from parliamentary sovereignty. In each of the cases described above, the court deployed the tools described by Lord Steyn in *R v A* to alter legislation contrary to Parliament's intention. In *Sheldrake*, the court made the defence less onerous than Parliament intended. The decision in *Waya* resulted in confiscation orders being issued for lower sums than Parliament intended. The decision in *MB* meant that the home secretary was unable to rely on material which Parliament intended her to be able to rely on. And in *Pomiechowski* the court arrogated to itself a discretion to extend time limits which Parliament had intended to be short and inflexible. This is enough to establish a conflict with parliamentary sovereignty. Section 3 is a modest, self-imposed restraint on parliamentary sovereignty. But, a modest, self-imposed restraint is still a restraint. And, for that reason, the argument from parliamentary sovereignty is cogent. It should be taken more seriously when it is deployed by critics of the HRA.

57 Paul Roberts 'Criminal procedure, the presumption of innocence and judicial reasoning under the Human Rights Act' from Helen Fenwick, Gavin Phillipson and Paul Masterman (eds.) *Judicial reasoning under the UK Human Rights Act* (Cambridge University Press 2007) 410.

58 *Anderson* (n.38) [59].

59 *Re S and others* [2002] UKHL 10 [40].

60 *Ghaidan v Godin Mendoza* [2004] UKHL 30, [2004] 2 AC 557 [111] (The internal quote, 'pith and essence' is to Lord Watson [in a different context] in *Union Colliery Co of British Columbia Ltd v Bryden* [1899] AC 580,587).

61 Gearty (n.13) 92.

Conclusion: Sovereignty and the case against the HRA

So far, then, I have argued that the arguments from national sovereignty and from parliamentary sovereignty are cogent, in the sense that it is true that the Human Rights Act compromises sovereignty in both senses. I have also suggested that it follows that those arguments ought to have been (and ought to be) taken more seriously by defenders of the Act. But (perhaps belatedly) I should stress that none of this has been intended to constitute an endorsement of these elements of the case against the Act, at least not *qua* arguments against the Act. It simply does not follow from the facts that because the HRA compromises national and parliamentary sovereignty that it ought to be repealed. On the contrary, both of these features of the Act strike me as eminently justifiable. In fact, in my view, they are justified. There are good reasons for cooperating in an international, partly judicial, effort to settle the concrete demands of our collective abstract commitment to the rights declared (in fairly abstract fashion) in the ECHR. There are good reasons for that cooperation to involve the acknowledgement of a certain degree of authority (even in domestic law) for the decisions of the European Court of Human Rights. And there are also good reasons for giving the courts a limited (and reversible) but real power to override parliamentary violations of those rights to which we as a community have announced (and continue to profess) our commitment. As it happens, those good reasons are captured reasonably well by the subtle and nuanced scheme put in place by the HRA – even when, as it is fair to argue happened in the lines of cases discussed earlier, it has been developed in ways which go beyond Parliament's intention in 1998. These various reasons have been explored, tested and developed in a rich tradition of academic literature, predating, abstracted from and focused on the HRA. Furthermore, many of those reasons feature in the judicial decisions discussed earlier about the appropriate scope of the Act's provisions. These reasons ought to be at the heart of the controversy about the Act's future. But they have been effectively obscured from public debate by the emergence of a constitutional orthodoxy, which denies the Act's impacts on sovereignty, characterises the arguments from sovereignty as misconceived and treats their advocates as constitutional illiterates. The debate about the HRA is not an example of healthy constitutional debate. Unfortunately, some of the positions defended by the Act's critics *are* fundamentally misconceived in ways which do point to constitutionally illiteracy or bad faith.[62] But the arguments from sovereignty are not among them.

62 The most famous example is, of course, Catgate, where the current prime minister (then home secretary) said, "We all know the stories about the Human Rights Act . . . the illegal immigrant who cannot be deported because – and I am not making this up – because he had a pet cat". The speech has not, as far as I know, been officially published. It is however, widely available. A full text of the speech is available at <www.politics.co.uk/comment-analysis/2011/10/04/theresa-may-speech-in-full> accessed 20 November 2016. For a sympathetic analysis (which nevertheless characterises the speech as "impossible to justify", see Campbell, above, (n.28).

I want to close by suggesting that the debate is not just substantively impoverished by the absence of arguments which ought to be at its heart. The refusal to take seriously and engage with the arguments from sovereignty has contributed in its own way to the degradation in the quality of our national discourse. Dismissing cogent arguments is frustrating for and disrespectful to those who espouse them. Sovereignty provides rational (albeit, in my view, ultimately mistaken) reasons to oppose the HRA. But those reasons do not, by themselves, amount to reasons to hate or dislike human rights as a concept. However, by failing to take that rational opposition seriously, and by rhetorically banishing its proponents from an important arena of constitutional controversy, defenders of the Act risk weakening rather than strengthening the Act's place in the UK Constitution. By their refusal to engage in honest rational debate, they may even be giving the Act's opponents a reason to hate human rights.

Part III

Controversial claimants under the Human Rights Act

Chapter 7

Terrorist threats, antiterrorism and the case against the Human Rights Act

Conor Gearty

Introduction

There is surely no field of public discourse that has challenged human rights law more seriously than that of counterterrorism. All of these fields share the same roots in liberal democracy but push such polities in radical different directions. Terrorism, 'the weapon of the weak' to use that 'oft-repeated dictum',[1] uses violence against civilian actors as a means of communicating a message to power rather than as a way of scoring a military success against it. This sort of action thrives in open societies because there it finds the freedom necessary for the successful execution of its violence, the insecure transport system, the open sporting and cultural venues, the (relative) absence of state surveillance and the tolerance of radical speech.[2] With its indiscriminate reach, its invariable suddenness, its calculated brutality and its disregard of traditional laws of war, this violence terrorises not only those unlucky enough to be subject to it but those who – witnessing what has happened – fear they might be next. It is this randomness that drives a horror of such violence into the heart of liberal society.[3] Somehow we think that we can, by our own careful actions, avoid the car accident, or the armed robber, or the burglar, but who can plan to avoid a terrorist assault on a movie theatre, hotel or concert venue? Those in positions of responsibility making them the intended recipients of the message so bloodily communicated – our political leaders and police chiefs – take particular umbrage at the perpetrators requiring them to glean the intended meaning of such deliberate carnage. Why should they, when the message has been so violently delivered? Surely the right response is to

1 Paul D'Anieri *International Politics. Power and Purpose in Global Affairs* (3rd ed. Wadsworth 2013) 280. For two very perceptive studies see Louise Richardson *What Terrorists Want. Understanding the Enemy; Containing the Threat* (John Murray 2006) and Richard English *Does Terrorism Work* (Oxford 2016).

2 Paul Wilkinson *Terrorism versus Democracy: The Liberal State's Response* (3rd ed. Routledge 2011). On free speech aspects see Ian Cram *Terror and the War on Dissent. Freedom of Expression in the Age of Al-Qaeda* (Springer 2009).

3 Richard English *Terrorism: How to Respond* (OUP 2009), especially chapter 1.

crack down hard on those responsible, not to listen sympathetically to what they say? And whilst pursuing past wrongdoers those same leaders feel compelled to prevent further atrocities: there are other stable doors that can be locked even if this one, violent horse has bolted.

Seeming to stand in the way of the robust action so often demanded in response to terrorist atrocities are the very principles of liberal democratic society that make such assaults logistically possible. Indeed, some terrorist campaigns deliberately seek to destroy these principles: the 'pluralism, tolerance and broad-mindedness' celebrated as a strength of all such societies[4] and the requirements of fairness, due process and individuated justice that are integral parts of open societies. At the core of these principles are human rights which are invariably embedded not only in liberal democracy's political discourse but also in local, regional and international law. The essence of such rights is captured in their insistence on taking the individual seriously – respect for human dignity is often taken as the basis of our rights culture.[5] This demand should not buckle under utilitarian pressure. Nor should it blink when confronted by the 'enemy within' or 'the enemy without' – human rights are as blind to ethnic and national origin as they are to gender and (in most contemporary forms) sexual orientation. These rights are the clearest manifestation in law of the global dream: that to be 'a citizen of nowhere'[6] is not an insult to be suffered but a badge to be proudly worn, that the world is composed of individual, free people rather than various (nationally defined) peoples.

Conceived and enacted in the last years of the 1990s, the Human Rights Act (HRA) entered a counterterrorism arena in which commitments to human rights had already proved controversial. The European Court of Human Rights (ECtHR) in Strasbourg caused extreme controversy in 1978 when it found that the British treatment of selected internees in Northern Ireland breached the prohibition on inhuman and degrading treatment under Article 3 of the European Convention on Human Rights (ECHR).[7] A decade later, the finding that a pre-charge detention period of up to seven days for terrorist suspects breached the right to a hearing before a judge under Article 5(3) of the ECHR enraged Margaret Thatcher's administration and provoked a limited derogation under Article 15 (afterwards upheld by the Strasbourg court).[8] In the years running

4 Echoing here of course the frequently expressed phraseology of the European Court of Human Rights; for an early and influential conceptualisation see *Lingens v Austria* (1986) 8 EHRR 407 [41].

5 Chris McCrudden (ed.) *Understanding Human Dignity* (OUP 2013).

6 Theresa May's speech at the Conservative Party Conference 2016 available at <www.telegraph.co.uk/news/2016/10/05/theresa-mays-conference-speech-in-full> accessed 14 November 2016.

7 *Ireland v United Kingdom* [1978] 2 EHRR 25.

8 *Brogan v United Kingdom* [1988] 11 EHRR 117; *Brannigan and McBride v United Kingdom* [1993] 17 EHRR 539.

up to the HRA two further interventions caused particular uproar. In 1995 the Strasbourg court ruled (albeit by the narrowest of margins, ten votes to nine) that the United Kingdom breached the Article 2 rights of three acknowledged IRA members who the Special Air Service shot dead in Gibraltar, where the three had been planning a major bombing.[9] The following year the same court insisted that foreigners suspected of terrorism could not simply be deported to a country if there was a serious risk that their rights would be violated, in particular, their right not to be tortured or killed, or be subjected to inhuman or degrading treatment or punishment.[10] The home secretary who had to deal with both of these cases was Michael Howard, and even though the judgment in each case was accepted, it was accepted in ways that were as begrudging and minimalist as possible. Howard went on to be leader of the Conservative opposition to Tony Blair's New Labour government during its second term, and David Cameron, who had been Howard's political adviser when he was home secretary, went on to succeed Howard as Conservative Party leader in 2005.

The terrorist-related arguments mustered against the HRA have never been phantoms dreamt up by opponents whose hostility has got the better of their reason. They flow from a radically different view of what liberal democracy ought to be allowed to do in its own defence. This was a view that, as some of the preceding cases remind us, already underscored decades of hostility to rights when Northern Ireland related political violence was the problem and the Strasbourg court (rather than any local tribunal) the human-rights-irritant.[11] The commitment to universal human rights has not implausibly seemed to impede the 'struggle' (or, in wilder renditions, the 'war') against terrorism. Why shouldn't the safety of the state be taken into account when decisions about the removal of dangerous foreign nationals are being made? Is not the (lengthy if need be) detention of suspected terrorists entirely appropriate in cases where there is evidence of their involvement in terrorist acts, even if this cannot be proved in court? Why should the obligations of due process be blind to the fact that the individual in the dock is committed not only to his or her own freedom but to the destruction of all of ours as well?[12] These sorts of questions were asked even during passage of the Human Rights Bill and in the immediate aftermath (pre-implementation of the Act in October 2000) by Labour government ministers as well as opposition spokespersons.[13] The events of 11 September 2001 gave them fresh strength and

9 *McCann v United Kingdom* [1995] 21 EHRR 97.

10 *Chahal v United Kingdom* [1996] 23 EHRR 413.

11 Aileen McColgan, 'Lessons from the Past: Northern Ireland Terrorism Now and Then, and the Human Rights Act' from Tom Campbell, Keith Ewing and Adam Tomkins (eds.) *The Legal Protection of Human Rights: Sceptical Essays* (OUP 2011).

12 On an attempt to reconcile human rights and terrorism-prevention see Michael Ignatieff *The Lesser Evil. Political Ethics in an Age of Terror* (Edinburgh University Press 2004).

13 See the thoughts of the Home Secretary responsible for the Act, Jack Straw *Aspects of Law Reform. An Insider's Perspective* (CUP 2013) ch. 2.

sense of urgency. Even without the Al-Qaeda attacks of that day counterterrorism could well have been an important component in the critique of human rights that had already begun and was certain to grow. But the actions of Osama Bin Laden and his cohort of suicide killers have ensured that in the years that followed, it was the demands of counterterrorism that led the attack on the HRA.[14] The front line has been fought over detention and deportation, and it is to each of these I turn first before moving on to discuss the role of the criminal law in managing the tensions that are revealed in these two arenas of dispute.

(1) Detention and control

The 1996 decision of the ECtHR in *Chahal v United Kingdom*, referred to in passing earlier,[15] concerned a Sikh terrorist whose return to India had been successfully resisted. There was no suggestion that he was inclined or likely to engage in political violence within the United Kingdom, nor was there any complaint about the government's entitlement to expel him. The problem was a practical one; no jurisdiction would take him (or could be obliged to take him) except the one where it was plausible that he was at risk of having his Article 3 rights violated. In the immediate aftermath of the September 11 attacks the Secretary of State for the Home Department David Blunkett found himself unable to expel a number of non-British residents about whom there were (to put it at its lowest) concerns that they might be involved with Al-Qaeda and/or organisations associated with it. At the same time, it was thought impossible to proceed against them under existing criminal law. Although the substance of the law had been greatly expanded by the permanent and comprehensive 2000 Terrorism Act (on which more shortly), inchoate offences still required admissible evidence by way of proof, and in these cases none could be guaranteed.

Mr Blunkett decided to introduce a system of administrative detention for those persons not of British origins who were suspected of being terrorists and whose expulsion was impossible for *Chahal*-based reasons. When the 2001 Anti-Terrorism Crime and Security Act received Royal Assent, seventeen men were certified under section 21 of the Act as persons reasonably believed by the home secretary to be terrorists whose presence in the United Kingdom constituted a 'risk to national security' as a result of which – given they could not be removed – their (indefinite) detention was to be legally sanctioned. After early unsuccessful challenges, nine of the detainees found themselves before the Appellate Committee of the House of Lords, then the UK's most senior judicial body. To the surprise of many, and the indignation of ministers, they scored an unequivocal victory.[16]

14 For an early overview of the post-2011 tensions see Conor Gearty '11 September 2001, counter-terrorism and the Human Rights Act' (2005) 32 *Journal of Law and Society* 18.

15 See (n.10).

16 *A v Secretary of State for the Home Department* [2004] UKHL 56, [2005] 2 AC 68. For a detailed review of the case see Conor Gearty 'Human rights in an age of counter-terrorism: Injurious, irrelevant or indispensable?' (2005) 58 *Current Legal Problems* 25–46.

Because the detention was so obviously in breach of the right to liberty under Article 5 of the ECHR, with there being next to no prospect of this being merely a preliminary move in deportation proceedings (allowed under Article 5(1)(f)), the government felt obliged to suspend the effect of Article 5, as they were entitled to do under the derogation provisions of Article 15 of the ECHR. This derogation provision could be used so long as the government showed that the country faced 'a public emergency threatening the life of the nation'. The law lords were, on the whole, willing to give the authorities the benefit of the doubt on this, not without a few wobbles it is true, but the majority were clear that the selective detention without trial of foreign suspects was not 'strictly required by the exigencies of the situation' as required under Article 15.

Here we see the first practical example of how the idea of human rights rears up against assumptions rooted in national security. It was precisely the aspect of the detention scheme that had made it politically feasible – the limiting of its application to foreign nationals – that made it suspect under a human rights law that is ever (and from its perspective rightly) on the lookout for discrimination on grounds of nationality.[17] When asked to defend this discriminatory distinction, lawyers for the home secretary could not answer honestly along these lines because to do so would be to lose the case: the hierarchy of the laws under scrutiny placed human rights at the top. They therefore had no answer to the sort of unsettling analogies that were on the majority of the judge's minds, perhaps best expressed by Lady Hale:

> No one has the right to be an international terrorist. But substitute 'black', 'disabled', 'female', 'gay', or any other similar adjective for 'foreign' before 'suspected international terrorist' and ask whether it would be justifiable to take power to lock up the group but not the 'white', 'able-bodied', 'male' or 'straight' suspected international terrorists. The answer is clear.[18]

The political reaction to the case was predictable, albeit diluted to some extent by the shock of Mr Blunkett's shock resignation – the day before it was delivered – brought on by an unrelated, personal matter.[19] His successor, Charles Clarke, had the task of deciding how to respond to the judgment. This was important because the form of the relief granted had been a declaration of incompatibility under section 4 of the HRA which meant that it could have simply been ignored by the authorities, pleading an overriding necessity to defend the state. This would have been a somewhat awkward manoeuvre from the Labour Party that had, after all, only a short while before introduced the HRA, and this would have also

17 See in particular the prohibition on discrimination in Article 14 ECHR.

18 *A v Secretary of State for the Home Department* (n.16) [238].

19 Tom Happold and Sarah Left 'Blunkett Resigns' *The Guardian* (15 December 2004) available at <www.theguardian.com/uk/2004/dec/15/davidblunkett.immigrationpolicy1> accessed 15 November 2016.

necessitated an unattractive disregard of the rational arguments on the issue in favour of suspiciously broad appeals to security (necessary because justifying discrimination against non-nationals simply on that basis was still a political taboo in the mid-2000s). Nor would such a robust disregard of the rights protected by the ECHR have solved anything in the medium term, as this would almost certainly have attracted the censorious oversight of the Strasbourg court.[20]

Accordingly, in the spring of 2005 the government introduced a new set of antiterrorism laws, eventually encapsulated in the Prevention of Terrorism Act 2005 but only after a huge parliamentary struggle, particularly in the House of Lords.[21] For the purposes of this chapter it is not necessary to go into great detail about the complex system of 'control orders' that replaced the detention provisions, other than to note how central human rights were both to the framing of the original bill and to the parliamentary debate on their details. Key features of the new approach made this clear. The administrative constraints under which subjects of control orders could be placed fell short of detention but could nonetheless be extremely restrictive.[22] Crucially, these orders could be applied to British as well as non-British suspects alike. Additional safeguards were required to kick in where the planned restrictions on particular individuals were so severe as to warrant derogation from Article 5 under Article 15 (as opposed to when they did not, in which case oversight was milder).[23]

The new law anticipated – indeed even required – judicial oversight for human rights compatibility, with the executive seeking to draw the courts into a near co-planning role with regard to what would and would not 'work' under the ECHR. This produces our second practical example of the tension between those tasked with protecting security and thinking of the common good and judges who have to view the case in front of them. True to the manner in which the Act had been constructed, a series of disputes arose early on about the legitimacy of various control orders. The central initial issue was the extent to which the right to due process was being eroded through the way these orders were being made.[24] In earlier proceedings, *Secretary of State for the Home Department v MB and AF*, the law lords had already dealt with one such case.[25] The issue common to all these applications was the degree to which non-derogating control orders needed to have their conditions altered to make them compatible

20 See the Strasbourg ruling on those issues that remained open after the Belmarsh decision: *A v United Kingdom* (2009) 49 EHRR 29.

21 See Meg Russell and Maria Sciara, 'Parliament and the House of Lords: A More Representative and Assertive Chamber?' from Michael Rush and Philip Giddings (eds.) *The Palgrave Review of British Politics 2005* (Palgrave Macmillan 2006) 128–129.

22 Prevention of Terrorism Act 2005, sections 1–3.

23 Ibid. See section 4.

24 *Secretary of State for the Home Department v AF, AE and AN* [2009] UKSC 28, [2010] 2 AC 269.

25 [2007] UKHL 46, [2008] 1 AC 440.

with the right to a fair trial provisions under Article 6 of the ECHR. In the first *AF* case Lord Bingham spoke of the 'core irreducible minimum of procedural protection'[26] that was in his view absent in both cases then before him. But the other four of the five on the bench took different views about what was required, Lord Hoffman holding that the chosen statutory framework of closed hearings and special advocates was probably consistent with the Convention while Lady Hale, Lord Carswell and Lord Brown were more inclined to root their decisions in the specific facts of the cases before them. The upshot of it all was by no means self-evident: where the government had wanted a general rule their lordships seemed to be offering endless judicial red tape. Hence, the second *AF* case, with *AE* and *AN* on this occasion, just two years later, with nine judges instead of the usual five, and a recent decision in Strasbourg to contend with which had (as it happens) proved Lord Hoffmann's earlier optimism on behalf the scheme unfounded.[27] The lords now sought in a series of carefully crafted speeches to be clear about what the Convention required and how this could be achieved by reading down the 2005 Act rather than embarking on a new round of declarations of incompatibility. But it looked obstructive to those with security and speedy decisions uppermost on their minds as it appeared to interfere with a vital national interest.

These two House of Lords decisions were, however, merely the tip of the iceberg so far as litigation was concerned. At the time of the hearing of *AF, AE and AN* there were 38 persons subject to control orders, and apart from the seven who had absconded, it did seem as though all the remaining 31 had been shrouded in a fog of litigation: AF's second visit to the House of Lords represented no less that the eighth substantive hearing of his challenge.[28] Procedure was not the only basis of attack: the rights to privacy and to liberty, and even on occasion the right to be protected from inhuman and degrading treatment, were thrown into the mix by lawyers keen (not unreasonably) to do the very best for their clients. One would not have to be a particularly authoritarian home secretary to be frustrated by such legal suffocation, and one would need to have been a saintly holder of that office to see that none of these entanglements with human rights were the fault of the judges as opposed to the parliamentary legislation that they were being required to interpret. So why not get the judges to be clearer about what they expect, thereby helping lawmakers by offering informal advice on what might pass muster? This may appear a reasonable question, but it was one to which the judges took grave exception. Here was a third great tension between the executive and judicial branches, flowing out of the way in which separation of powers is arranged between the three branches of government, as irritating to ministers as it was constitutionally inevitable.

26 Ibid. at 43.
27 *A v United Kingdom* (n.20).
28 See the details set out in the case itself [2009] UKSC 28, at 6–7 (Lord Phillips).

An early control order case to reach the House of Lords, *Secretary of State for the Home Department v JJ*, revolved around the question of how severe the imposition of a home curfew needed to be to breach the Convention, in particular, Article 5 but with Article 8 playing a role as well.[29] The secretary of state looked for specifics (e.g. would 16 hours confinement a day breach Article 5?) and in doing so was encouraged by judicial suggestions of a possible precise rule along these lines, from Lord Brown.[30] This necessitated yet another trip back to an enlarged appellate tribunal, this time the newly established Supreme Court sitting as a bench of seven. In *Secretary of State for the Home Department v AP* the justices unanimously reiterated that all the circumstances needed to be taken into account, that no bright-line rule was possible.[31] Showing an enthusiasm to escape the miasma of litigation into which at this point even the court itself felt it was at risk of submerging, they held that henceforth appeal courts would embrace "the wisdom of generally not interfering with [first instance] decisions in control order cases".[32] While these various cases were being brought, the senior judges' reluctance to engage in behind the scenes discussions had begun to exasperate Charles Clarke, the then home secretary, further widening the divide between the executive and the judiciary on matters related to counterterrorism.[33] Of course the judges could not risk pre-empting hearings on specific cases by having been involved openly or (worse) behind closed doors in deliberations about abstract rules which would then apply to individuals before them. But the indignation of ministers engaged in good faith efforts to resolve the (as they saw it) havoc wreaked by human rights adjudication was also entirely understandable. The issue became moot with the disappearance of the control order scheme (and its replacement by a milder framework of Terrorist Prevention and Investigation Measures [TPIMs][34]), a casualty of hostility from the Liberal Democrat part of the new coalition government that emerged after the 2010 election. This change of administration also brought to power a Conservative Party by now dedicated

29 *Secretary of State for the Home Department v JJ* [2007] UKHL 45, [2008] 1 AC 385.

30 ". . .[R]ather than leave the Secretary of State guessing as to the precise point at which control orders will be held vulnerable to article 5 challenges, . . . for my part I would regard the acceptable limit to be 16 hours, leaving the suspect with 8 hours (admittedly in various respects controlled) liberty a day. Such a regime, in my opinion, can and should properly be characterised as one which restricts the suspect's liberty of movement rather than actually deprives him of his liberty"; ibid. at 105.

31 [2010] UKSC 24, [2011] 2 AC 1 at [3] (Lord Brown – with whom Lords Phillips, Saville, Walker and Clarke agreed).

32 Ibid. [20] (Lord Brown).

33 House of Lords, Select Committee on the Constitution, 6th report Session 2006–7 (11 July 2007), paras. 93–97 have the details of the controversy surrounding the issue, available at <www.publications.parliament.uk/pa/ld200607/ldselect/ldconst/151/15104.htm> accessed 15 November 2016.

34 Terrorism Prevention and Investigations Measures Act 2011.

to waging war on the HRA, and it was not long before a particular terrorism-related *casus belli* presented itself.[35]

(2) Deportation

The problem exposed by *Chahal*, which the scheme of administrative detention developed under the 2001 Act attempted to address, did not disappear with its collapse following the 2004 decision in *A v Home Secretary*.[36] Nor did control orders or TPIMs solve the problem of dangerous foreign nationals whose lack of criminal activity in the United Kingdom meant little when compared with their capacity for mischief abroad. Here is our fourth practical tension: Why should a terrorist suspect's personal inviolability be put before the safety of the state? This was a particular issue with one individual, the Palestinian-Jordanian Abu Qatada (or, to give him his original name, Omar Othman). Long a thorn in the side of successive governments on account of his high public profile as a radical preacher in north London, Abu Qatada was successfully able to resist efforts to remove him for nearly a decade, relying on a combination of UK and Strasbourg human rights law to avoid deportation. Especially irksome to ministers was the way in which ECHR rights appeared to be constantly expanding via new litigation to embrace fresh fears concerning his proposed forced return to Jordan. Over several years of appeals the focus shifted from the risk of his being ill-treated to the possible denial of justice at his trial in Jordon because it would rely on evidence obtained by torture. Eventually, after much toing-and-froing between Whitehall, the Royal Courts of Justice and Strasbourg, and even a visit to Jordan by Theresa May, the then home secretary, in July 2013 Abu Qatada was flown out of the United Kingdom.[37]

The long-running litigation was as damaging to the public perception of the HRA as the John Hirst prisoners' voting decision was damaging to the public perception of the ECHR.[38] In both cases the applicant appeared to have been drawn from a 'central casting' parade of villains, with each being as friendly to the media as they were alienating to the audiences who had the chance to see them. The judgments have each been more a saga than a simple case, ensuring

35 Conservative Manifesto 2010 *Invitation to join the Government of Britain* available at <www.google.co.uk/url?sa=t&rct=j&q=&esrc=s&source=web&cd=1&cad=rja&uact=8&ved=0ahUKEwiNzdfX-77QAhXpK8AKHa34AdkQFggbMAA&url=https%3A%2F%2www.conservatives.com%2F~%2Fmedia%2FFiles%2FManifesto2010&usg=AFQjCNHip2u7D2bu9dJpCVeTfOP0CXiJzQ&sig2=PTeA9AVmQXtgSbnAhR_wUQ&bvm=bv.139782543,d.d2> 4 accessed 20 November 2016, p. 79.

36 Gearty (n.16).

37 See BBC News 'Abu Qatada deported from UK to stand trial in Jordan' *BBC News UK* (7 July 2013) available at <www.bbc.co.uk/news/uk-23213740> accessed 14 November 2016.

38 *Hirst v United Kingdom (No 2)* (2005) 42 EHRR 849.

there was no protection in the temporary nature of their impact. With *Hirst* there were numerous copycat actions by other prisoners and frequent efforts by the Council of Europe (through its Committee of Ministers) to secure UK compliance.[39] With Abu Qatada there was a seemingly endless round of applications for different forms of relief as the case slowly inched its way to its 2013 denouement. Even as early as the premiership of Tony Blair, home secretary John Reid had been calling for modifications of the Act to allow deportation of foreigners deemed undesirable.[40] In 2006 Blair had rejected the suggestion of a possible veto on court judgments after a decision to block deportation of nine Afghan hijackers to their country was described by him as an "abuse of common sense".[41] So much had the Abu Qatada case commanded public attention that the success enjoyed by Mrs May in finally having him removed under her watch was frequently mentioned by supporters in the course of her short but successful campaign to succeed David Cameron as prime minister in 2016.[42] Rarely, if ever, are the successes enjoyed by the authorities in deporting terrorist suspects factored into the discussion on human rights, the successful extradition of Babar Ahmad, for example, shows how the authorities were able to deport individuals deemed to be a security threat to the US despite claims of an Article 3 violation.[43] Instead, the common perception created by the media coverage of antiterrorism cases is that the government repeatedly loses such cases. Part of this is because of factors discussed in later chapters in this book, such as the way that legal arguments are presented in the media and social perceptions of those using the HRA; however, this contributes to the perception that the balance is tipped against the security services when it comes to antiterrorism cases.

(3) The criminal law

Opponents of human rights who got stuck into the Abu Qatada saga rarely noted that the case depended on evidence obtained by torture involving a man who was in due course acquitted by Jordan's State Security Court of charges of conspiracy

39 For a summary of these activities and a full update of recent developments see House of Commons Library Briefing Paper *Prisoners' Voting Rights: Developments since May 2015* (CPB 7461 12 January 2016).

40 Brendan Carlin 'John Reid calls for human rights law reform' *The Telegraph* (17 September 2007) available at <www.telegraph.co.uk/news/uknews/1563347/John-Reid-calls-for-human-rights-law-reform.html> accessed 16 November 2016.

41 BBC News 'Blair to amend human rights law' *BBC News* (14 May 2006) available at <http://news.bbc.co.uk/1/hi/uk/4770231.stm> accessed 15 November 2016.

42 See, for example, this article by Mrs May's supporter and Employment Minister Priti Patel in *The Sun* (8 July 2016) available at <www.thesun.co.uk/news/1410048/theresa-may-has-the-vision-determination-and-experience-to-be-our-next-prime-minister-and-is-the-strongest-candidate-for-the-job/> accessed 15 November 2016.

43 *Ahmad v United Kingdom* (2013) 56 EHRR 1.

to carry out terrorist acts.[44] In the field of terrorism and human rights, the availability of the criminal law is the great dog that does not bark, the unmentioned option that critics may not even be aware of or chose to ignore when they launch their attacks. Human rights law requires a proper criminal law system and an adequate enforcement of it – the state's positive obligation to protect rights (including the right to life in Article 2) makes such demands inevitable. The word *proper* does a great deal of work here – the ECHR (and therefore the HRA) insists that the criminal trials of terrorist suspects be fairly conducted – and Article 6 goes into great detail about what this entails in practice. As to the substance of criminal law, the Strasbourg system is relaxed to the point of near-civil-libertarian carelessness – countries can create whatever substantive criminal law they desire so long as the basics of a fair trial are observed.[45] Thus, there was no serious objection to the charge against Abu Qatada being one of 'conspiracy' (rather than any specific action).

The medley of provisions that were available in the Terrorism Act 2000, as an alternative to the subsequently disgraced detention power in the 2001 Act, were (all with a very wide definition of terrorism[46]) to be found in no fewer than 23 of the 64 sections scattered across the first six parts of the Act. These included instruction or training in firearms or explosives (at home or abroad) or inviting someone to take part in such training,[47] collecting information 'of a kind likely to be useful to a person committing or preparing an Act of terrorism' or merely possessing this kind of information[48] and directing "at any level, the activities of an organisation which is concerned in the commission of acts of terrorism" (with a punishment of up to life in prison).[49] There was even the double-thought crime of possessing "an article in circumstances which give rise to a reasonable suspicion that [the] possession is for a purpose connected with the commission, preparation or instigation of an Act of terrorism".[50] The 2000 Act contained an offence of inciting terrorism overseas. This allowed the authorities to proceed against residents of the United Kingdom and punish them as though the Act which they had incited (murder, offences against the person, criminal damage) actually occurred even though the acts incited would have been committed abroad so that it was "immaterial whether or not the person incited [was] in the United Kingdom at the time of the incitement."[51] Later antiterrorism legislation in 2001,[52]

44 See BBC News 'Abu Qatada cleared of terror charges' *BBC News* (24 September 2014) available at <www.bbc.co.uk/news/world-29340656> accessed 15 November 2016.

45 See *Beghal v Director of Public Prosecutions* [2015] UKSC 49, [2015] AC 49 where the challenge is as usual to powers rather than the substance of the criminal law itself.

46 Terrorism Act 2000, s 1.

47 Ibid. s.54.

48 Ibid. s.58

49 Ibid. s.56.

50 Ibid. s.57.

51 Ibid. s.59(4).

52 Anti-terrorism, Crime and Security Act 2001.

2006[53] and 2008[54] added more powers to support these criminal laws as well as enhancing aspects of ordinary criminal law.

Why is this criminal model of law enforcement not enough for the proponents of a tough line on terrorism? If it were, there would be no conflict with the ECHR except insofar as its enforcement via the exercise of police discretion (e.g. in stop and search) might attract the critical attention of a Strasbourg court vigilant in preventing undue invasions of privacy and/or discriminatory action against vulnerable groups.[55] This would be – and has been – irritating to the authorities but would hardly constitute in itself a basis for the sort of hostility that defenders of antiterrorism law have meted out to human rights lawyers and activists. There is a deeper explanation, a fifth and final practical example of the way in which the 1998 Act challenges assumptions about national security that are deeply embedded within the state.

For much of the twentieth century the United Kingdom had to deal with an enemy that challenged the integrity of the state's political institutions, both from without and (more relevantly for our purposes) from within. The Soviet Union and its satellite states had sympathetic Communist Party members operating lawfully within Britain who were judged as dangerous and whose actions did not have to fall within the criminal sphere before close scrutiny of them could be justified. Over time a grand system of state security grew up, staffed by intelligence services whose job it was to be vigilant against this external and internal threat and to Act decisively when needed in the interests of national security.[56] None of this system operated in accordance with any transparent law.[57] Criminal prosecution was the exception rather than the rule.[58] Executive discretion and secrecy ruled. Intelligence was gathered to assist in executive decision-making, not the prosecution of crimes. With the collapse of the Soviet Union in the late 1980s this large-scale institutional framework lost the enemy whose existence had been its rationale. At the same time, and under pressure from the ECtHR which found that to the extent that these security activities invaded rights their lack of legal basis took them outside the ECHR,[59] legislation was introduced to place the various security services on a statutory basis: MI5 in 1989[60] and MI6 and GCHQ

53 Terrorism Act 2006.

54 Counter-Terrorism Act 2008.

55 *Gillan and Quinton v United Kingdom* (2010) 50 EHRR 1105; *Beghal* (n.45).

56 For legal dimensions to this covering much of the twentieth century see Keith Ewing and Conor Gearty *The Struggle for Civil Liberties. Political Freedom and the Rule of Law in Britain, 1914–1945* (OUP 2000); Keith Ewing and Conor Gearty *Freedom under Thatcher. Civil Liberties in Modern Britain* (OUP 1990).

57 Keith Ewing, Joan Mahoney and Andrew Moretta '*Surveillance and the Liberal State*' *UK Constitutional Law Blog* (16 June 2013) available at <https://ukconstitutionallaw.org/2013/06/16/keith-ewing-joan-mahoney-and-andrew-moretta-surveillance-and-the-liberal-state/> accessed 16 November 2016.

58 For example see *Chandler v Director of Public Prosecutions* [1964] AC 763.

59 For example see *Malone v United Kingdom* (1984) 7 EHRR 14.

60 Security Service Act 1989.

in 1994.[61] In the spring of 1992, after a series of mishaps in the policing of terrorism in the UK, primacy in the field of counterterrorism (then mainly against the Irish Republican Army, of course) was handed from the police over to the security services.[62] Since then there has been a strong momentum towards reconfiguring counterterrorism along a 'Cold War' rather than a policing model. With their emphasis on executive discretion based on secret intelligence, the detention and control order powers discussed earlier fit the bill very well, as do the wider powers in legislation which allow detention before charge of such a long duration that it can easily begin to look like short-term internment.[63]

When it came into force in 2000 the HRA posed a direct challenge to this growing edifice of administrative control. We have already seen how human-rights-based hostility forced changes to the antiterrorism powers taken in reaction to the 11 September 2001 attacks. A further example of the same point that came before that day is the power of proscription. In pre-legislative plans for what became the Terrorism Act 2000 and following earlier statutory precedents[64] the power to ban 'terrorist' organisations had been reposed entirely in the home secretary, subject only to what was confidently expected would be the lightest of light touch judicial review. But before that Act took its final shape, ECtHR decisions made it clear that more safeguards would be needed if the powers were to survive the protections of freedom of association found in Article 11 of the ECHR.[65] A new tribunal was duly created, where those facing such bans could take their cases, the Proscribed Organisations Appeals Commission (POAC), and it has proved surprisingly effective.[66]

Here we see a pattern; the security and human rights regimes have played out a score draw, with neither winning triumphantly but each avoiding defeat. Crimes continue to be prosecuted and security services maintain their secret activities and intelligence gathering. Where the activities of the latter require action that impacts on human rights, it is not directly prevented by the HRA. Rather, it is channelled into quasi-judicial realms, places that mimic traditional judicial proceedings without quite being the full deal. Here is the battleground that has thrown the tension between human rights and security into sharp relief:

61 Intelligence Services Act 1994.

62 See the statement by the Home Secretary Kenneth Clarke at House of Commons Parliamentary Debates (8 May 1992) cc 297–306.

63 In the autumn of 2005, the then prime minister Tony Blair was defeated in the Commons on his initiative to extend detention before charge to 90 days: BBC News 'Blair defeated over terror laws' *BBC Online* (9 November 2005) available at <http://news.bbc.co.uk/1/hi/uk_politics/4422086.stm> accessed 16 November 2016.

64 In Great Britain starting with the Prevention of Terrorism (Temporary Provisions) Act 1974, s 1. (Northern Ireland had, unsurprisingly, a separate legal code for anti-terrorism.)

65 See in particular *Socialist Party v Turkey* (1998) 27 EHRR 51.

66 See now Part Two of the Terrorism Act 2000, and for how the provisions operate, albeit in a case where the proscription was upheld, *R (Lord Carlile of Berriew and Others) v Secretary of State for the Home Department* [2014] UKSC 60, [2015] 1 AC 945.

how much should the former yield to the latter, how much 'judicial' should there be and how much be left at the merely 'quasi'? In *A v United Kingdom*, the sequel to the *Belmarsh* case at the ECtHR,[67] the Strasbourg judges demanded that those affected by secret proceedings should at least be informed of the gist of the case against them, a ruling that was reluctantly accepted by the Supreme Court.[68] The easiest way to cut through to a human-rights-sensitive solution in these and other cases would be to allow evidence against suspects in criminal proceedings that had been secured via lawfully obtained material from the interception of their communications. Domestic law currently prohibits this, and the security services and the police have resisted any change in this area.[69] Where court cases threaten to reveal too much, the prevailing view has been that it is better to go fully into secret sessions or that the case should be allowed to collapse rather than, by virtue of criminal procedure, disclosing any evidence gained through surveillance.[70]

Conclusion

No case encapsulates the pressure placed on human rights law by the demands of anti-terrorism more than that of Moazzam Begg. Held in Guantanamo and before that in Bagram jail in Afghanistan for three years and then subjected to close police scrutiny on his return to the United Kingdom, he was charged with serious terrorist offences in 2014, leading to his being remanded without custody in Belmarsh prison for seven months. However, on the day that the criminal proceedings against him were scheduled to start the Crown withdrew the charges and suddenly he was free to go.[71] Mr Begg was never convicted of any crime, and yet his life was severely affected by the application of various administrative powers derived from decisions made on the basis of national security. The insistence on equality and on individual dignity in human rights law requires that the information behind these sorts of decisions should be exposed in a fair trial. The utilitarian demands of antiterrorism strategy condemn such scrupulousness as reckless and misguided. Stuck with a statutory insistence to respect the former, in the face of strong calls for the latter from both political leaders of all parties and the media, the courts do their best to deliver judgments in line with legislation in

67 *A* (n.20).

68 *AF, AE and AN* (n.24).

69 For a glimpse of the rear-guard actions fought to prevent the use of such evidence, see the response to the *Report of the Privy Council Review of Intercept as Evidence* Cm 7324 (30 January 2008); Home Office, *Intercept as Evidence. A Report* Cm 7760 (December 2009).

70 See Justice and Security Act 2013, Part Two.

71 Richard Norton-Taylor 'The strange case of Moazzam Begg' *The Guardian* (7 October 2014) available at <www.theguardian.com/world/defence-and-security-blog/2014/oct/07/moazzam-begg-mi5-syria> accessed 19 November 2016.

which the legislature appears no longer to believe. If the powers of the HRA are fatally diluted by a new bill of rights (long in the wings but not yet centre stage[72]) those who believe in equality of respect and individual freedom may look back on the HRA with nostalgic sadness. If the Act is destroyed, one of the forces that will have greatly weakened it for that kill will have been the counterterrorist critique.

72 *Protecting Human Rights in the UK. The Conservatives' Proposals for Changing Britain's Human Rights Laws* (October 2014) available at <http://news.bbc.co.uk/1/shared/bsp/hi/pdfs/03_10_14_humanrights.pdf, accessed 19 November 2016> accessed 19 November 2016.

Chapter 8

Deportation and the Human Rights Act 1998

Debunking the myths

Siobhán Lloyd

> The ECHR can bind the hands of parliament, adds nothing to our prosperity, makes us less secure by preventing the deportation of dangerous foreign nationals – and does nothing to change the attitudes of governments like Russia's when it comes to human rights.
>
> —Theresa May, MP (then home secretary), 25 April 2016[1]

Introduction

An article published in the *Daily Telegraph* in 2009 claimed that a man who was about to be deported was allowed to remain because he and his partner had bought a pet cat.[2] Although the claim was nonsense, it was repeated by Theresa May, the then home secretary, at the Conservative Party conference in 2011.[3] The case involved a Bolivian national who had been living with his partner for four years. The immigration judge found that he was able to rely on a Home Office policy concerning those who had been living in the UK with a settled partner for over two years, without enforcement action having been taken against them.[4] The appeal was also allowed under Article 8,[5] but the Home Office requested a

1 Theresa May MP *Home Secretary's speech on the UK, EU and our place in the world* (25 April 2016) available at <www.gov.uk/government/speeches/home-secretarys-speech-on-the-uk-eu-and-our-place-in-the-world> accessed 17 September 2016.

2 David Barrett 'Immigrant allowed to stay because of pet cat' *The Telegraph* (17 October 2010) available at <www.telegraph.co.uk/news/newstopics/howaboutthat/6360116/Immigrant-allowed-to-stay-because-of-pet-cat.html> accessed 17 September 2016.

3 Theresa May MP, speech at the Conservative Party Conference (4 October 2011) available at <www.politics.co.uk/comment-analysis/2011/10/04/theresa-may-speech-in-full> accessed 18 September 2016.

4 Home Office's Enforcement Instructions and Guidance (in force at the time), DP3/96, para. 53.4.1.

5 Francesca Klug 'Deportation and the right to respect for private and family life under Article 8' (*LSE Human Rights Futures Project* 2013), available at <http://image.guardian.co.uk/sys-files/Guardian/documents/2011/10/04/KlugDeportation.pdf> accessed 17 September 2016.

reconsideration of the case on the grounds that inappropriate weight had been attached to the partner and the pet cat. The senior immigration judge upheld the original determination on the basis that there was no material error because the appellant was entitled to rely on the policy but joked that "the cat. . . . need no longer fear having to adapt to Bolivian mice".[6]

This story serves to illustrate how myths around deportation are used to undermine the Human Rights Act 1998 (HRA) and indeed the European Convention on Human Rights (ECHR) itself. This chapter explores how the law on deportation and human rights has evolved since the HRA entered into force in October 2000 and assesses whether there is any truth in the claims that the HRA prevents the government from deporting dangerous foreign nationals. It starts by explaining the home secretary's powers to deport before going on to consider how the courts have dealt with cases involving Articles 3, 6 and 8 of the ECHR.

(1) The power to deport individuals under UK law

The home secretary has wide-ranging powers under the Immigration Act 1971, and subsequent acts of Parliament, to regulate and control the entry, stay and departure of non-British citizens from the United Kingdom.[7] She is responsible for laying before Parliament statements of rules that are to be applied when exercising those powers.[8] These statements are known as the Immigration Rules and are regularly updated and amended. Under the Immigration Act, non-British citizens are liable to deportation if the home secretary deems their deportation to be conducive to the public good[9] or where a court recommends deportation.[10] There is also power to deport a non-British national where another person in the family to which he or she belongs has been made subject to a deportation order.[11] Part 13 of the Immigration Rules sets out the criteria that the home secretary and her officials will take into consideration when deciding whether or not to make a deportation order.

6 IA/14578/2008 Determination and Reasons of Senior Immigration Judge Gleeson (10 December 2008) available at <http://t.co/civ1CLa> accessed 17 September 2016; Adam Wagner 'Catgate: another myth used to trash human rights' *The Guardian* (4 October 2011) available at <www.theguardian.com/law/2011/oct/04/theresa-may-wrong-cat-deportation> accessed 17 September 2016; Adam Wagner 'Cat had nothing to do with failure to deport man' *UK Human Rights Blog* (4 October 2011) available at <https://ukhumanrightsblog.com/2011/10/04/cat-had-nothing-to-do-with-failure-to-deport-man/> accessed 17 September 2016.

7 Immigration Act 1971, s 1(2), s 4(1).

8 Ibid. s 1(4) & s 3(2).

9 Ibid. s.3(5)(a).

10 Ibid. s 3(6).

11 Ibid. s 3(5)(b).

The Immigration Rules do not apply to nationals of the European Economic Area (EEA).[12] Separate provisions are contained within Articles 27 through 33 of the Citizenship Directive[13] and are partly transposed into domestic law through Part IV of the Immigration (European Economic Area) Regulations 2016/1052. EEA nationals can only be excluded from another member state on the grounds of public policy, public security or public health.[14] Any exclusion measure must comply with the principle of proportionality, be based exclusively on the personal conduct of the person concerned and that conduct must represent a genuine, present and sufficiently serious threat affecting one of the fundamental interests of society.[15] This makes it more difficult to expel an EEA national.

Following the enactment of the HRA, the Immigration Rules were amended to require immigration officials and the Home Office to carry out their duties in a manner that is compliant with the ECHR.[16] Since October 2000, a person alleging that a decision under the Immigration acts had breached their Convention rights has been able to appeal that decision.[17]

Automatic deportation provisions were introduced in 2007 following revelations in newspapers that hundreds of foreign national prisoners had been released without having been considered for deportation.[18] The UK Borders Act 2007 requires the home secretary to make a deportation order in circumstances where a foreign national has been sentenced to at least 12 months' imprisonment[19] or where the offence is specified by an order made by the home secretary and the person has been sentenced to a period of imprisonment.[20] There are a number of exceptions to this rule including where deportation would breach a person's

12 *R (Nouazli) v Secretary of State for the Home Department* [2016] UKSC 16 [48]-[49]. Articles 27–33 govern the principles to be applied when deciding whether to expel a citizen of the European Economic Area. These provisions have been transposed into domestic law through Part IV of the Immigration (European Economic Area) Regulations 2006/1003.

13 Directive 2004/38/EC (29 April 2004) on the rights of citizens of the Union and their family members to move and reside freely within the territory of the member states.

14 Immigration (EEA) Regs 2006/1003, Article 27(1) and Article 19(3).

15 Citizenship Directive and Regulation 21(5) of the Immigration (EEA) Regulations, art 27(2).

16 See paras. 9–10 of Lord Bingham of Cornhill's judgment in *Huang v Secretary of State for the Home Department* [2007] UKHL 11; [2007] 2 AC 167.

17 Immigration Act 1999, s 65, which entered into force on 2 October 2000, allowed a person to appeal to an adjudicator. This provision was repealed on 1 January 2003. Since that date a person has been able to appeal an immigration decision to the tribunal on the same grounds by virtue of the Nationality, Immigration and Asylum Act 2002, s 82–84. These provisions have been amended on numerous occasions but since 20 October 2014, s 82(1) has provided that "[a] person ('P') may appeal to the Tribunal where . . . (b) the Secretary of State has decided to refuse a human rights claim made by P".

18 BBC NEWS 'Clarke is fired in Cabinet Purge' *BBC News UK* (5 May 2006) available at <http://news.bbc.co.uk/1/hi/uk_politics/4975938.stm> accessed 11 June 2016.

19 UK Borders Act 2007, s 32(2) and (5).

20 Ibid. s 32(3) and (5).

ECHR rights[21] or a right under the EU Treaties.[22] In 2015, over 40,000 people were either removed or left voluntarily after the initiation of removal. Around 5,600 foreign nationals who had committed offences were removed.[23]

(2) Deportation and the prevention of torture

The European Court of Human Rights in Strasbourg (ECtHR) has recognised that states are entitled, subject to existing obligations in international law, "to control the entry, residence and expulsion of aliens".[24] In the seminal case of *Soering v the United Kingdom*,[25] the ECtHR considered whether a German national applicant's rights under Article 3 of the ECHR (the prohibition of torture) would be violated if he were extradited to Virginia, in the United States, where he might be convicted of murder and face the death penalty. The ECtHR found that a decision by a state to extradite a fugitive "where substantial grounds have been shown for believing that the person concerned, if extradited, faces a real risk of being subjected to torture or to inhuman or degrading treatment or punishment in the requesting country", would violate Article 3.[26]The conditions on death row coupled with the applicant's individual circumstances meant that there would be a violation of Article 3, if the UK implemented the US authorities' request for extradition.[27]

To a certain extent, Article 3 overlaps with the UK's obligations under the Refugee Convention[28] Article 33(1), which prohibits the expulsion or return (refoulement) of a refugee to another state where his life or freedom would be threatened. The principle of non-refoulement does not apply where there are reasonable grounds for holding that the person concerned is a danger to the security of their host country or, having been convicted of a particular serious crime, they

21 Ibid. s 33(1) and 33(2)(a).

22 Ibid. s 33(1) and (4).

23 Scott Blinder 'Migration Observatory Briefing: Deportations, Removals and Voluntary Departures from the UK' *The Migration Observatory at the University of Oxford* (18 August 2016) available at <www.migrationobservatory.ox.ac.uk/wp-content/uploads/2016/04/Briefing-Deportations-1.pdf> accessed 1 November 2016.

24 *Abdulaziz v the United Kingdom* [1985] 7 EHRR 471 [67]; *Chahal v the United Kingdom* [1997] 23 EHRR 413 [73]; *Saadi v Italy* [2009] 49 EHRR 30 [124].

25 *Soering v the United Kingdom* [1989] 11 EHRR 439.

26 Ibid. [88] and [91].

27 Ibid. [111].

28 United Nations Convention and Protocol relating to the Status of Refugees (1951 and 1967). Article 1(A)(2) of the Convention defines a refugee as a person who "[o]wing to well-founded fear of being persecuted for reasons of race, religion, nationality, membership of a particular social group or political opinion is outside the country of his nationality and is unable or owing to such fear, is unwilling to avail himself to the protection of that country; or who, not having a nationality and being outside the country of his former habitual residence is unable or, owing to such fear, unwilling to return to it".

constitute a danger to the community of that country.[29] This was the issue that the Court of Appeal was confronted with in the case *R v Secretary of State for the Home Department ex parte Chahal*,[30] which concerned the decision to deport an Indian national who it was alleged had been involved in terrorist activity in support of the Sikh separatist movement in India.[31] The Court of Appeal held that the combined effect of the Immigration Rules at the time and the Refugee Convention required the secretary of state to balance the risks to national security in the UK against the risks to the applicant's personal safety in the country to which he was to be returned.[32] Although the ECtHR recognised in *Chahal v United Kingdom* the difficulties faced by states in protecting their citizens from terrorist violence, it emphasised the absolute nature of the prohibition on torture and reiterated the real risk test in prohibiting expulsion on Article 3 grounds.[33] This applied "however undesirable or dangerous" an individual is.[34]

The United Kingdom invited the ECtHR to reconsider these principles in *Saadi v Italy*,[35] complaining that the rigidity of the principle had caused contracting states problems by preventing them from enforcing expulsion measures in national security cases. The UK argued that states should be able to weigh up the rights secured by the applicant under Article 3 against those secured by all other members of the community, such as Article 2 (right to life). Additionally, where it is proved that an applicant presents a threat to national security, stronger evidence must be adduced by the applicant to prove that there is a risk of ill treatment. The ECtHR rejected these arguments reiterating that protection against ill treatment is absolute.[36] The court refused to modify the standard of proof as it could lead to national courts accepting more readily a real risk of ill treatment to the individual.[37] David Bonner notes that since 2005 the UK government has been attempting to find ways around *Chahal* because of the perceived risk to national security but has not considered non-compliance, the option sometimes pursued by the Italian government.[38] It is this element of the obligation under Article 3 that is at the root of claims, such as the "Human Rights Act has helped

29 Ibid. Article 33(2). Article 1F excludes from the protection of the Convention those persons who have committed crimes against peace, a war crime or a crime against humanity as well those who have committed a serious non-political crime outside the country of refuge prior to his admission to that country.

30 [1995] 1 W.L.R. 526.

31 *Chahal v the United Kingdom* [1997] 23 EHRR 413 [12–43].

32 Staughton LJ at 533 and Nolan LJ at 537. See *Chahal* (n.31), [41] for a summary of the Court of Appeal's judgment.

33 *Chahal* (n.31).

34 Ibid. [80].

35 [2009] 49 EHRR 30.

36 Ibid. [138]. See also *Othman v the United Kingdom* [2012] 55 EHRR 1 [185].

37 Ibid. [140].

38 David Bonner 'If you cannot change the rules of the game, adapt to them: United Kingdom responses to the restrictions set by Article 3 ECHR on 'national security'

28 Terrorists to Stay in the UK".[39] The article making this claim, which appeared in the *Daily Telegraph*, noted that in many of the cases the individuals concerned claimed they could not be deported because there was a risk of torture.

(3) A 'crazy interpretation': Contesting the scope of the duty under Article 3

The ECtHR has interpreted the Convention as a 'living instrument' and this has often been the focus of criticism of the HRA. The infamous case of *Othman v United Kingdom* concerning the deportation of Abu Qatada became the focus of this line of criticism in relation to deportation. Abu Qatada, a cleric of Jordanian nationality, was alleged to have been involved in terrorist activities and had been convicted in Jordan, after a trial conducted in absentia using evidence obtained through torture of his co-accused. The UK government recognised that Article 3 of the ECHR initially precluded the deportation of terrorist suspects to Jordan so both countries' governments signed a Memorandum of Understanding (MoU) in 2005 in which the Jordanian authorities committed to abiding by human rights standards, including ensuring that Abu Qatada would not be subjected to the death penalty. Following the signing of the MoU, the home secretary served him with a notice of intention to deport him to Jordan. Abu Qatada appealed to the Special Immigration Appeals Chamber (SIAC), which deals with cases concerning national security. He argued that deportation would violate, among other things, Article 3 and his right to a fair trial protected by Article 6 of the Convention because if deported, he would face a retrial and the Jordanian authorities would use the evidence obtained under torture. SIAC dismissed his appeal, holding that the MoU was likely to ensure that he was not subjected to ill treatment.[40]

The case was subsequently heard by the Court of Appeal, the House of Lords and the ECtHR. What is interesting about the ECtHR judgment in *Othman v the United Kingdom*[41] is that it agreed with most of the domestic courts' conclusions. It recognised the difficulties states faced in protecting their populations from terrorist violence and considered it legitimate for them to take a firm stand against those contributing to terrorist acts, concluding that they should be able

deportations' from Rob Dkickinson, Elena Katselli, Colin Murray and Ole Pedersen (eds.) *Examining Critical Perspectives on Human Rights* (Cambridge University Press 2012).

39 Robert Mendick 'Human Rights Act has helped 28 terrorists to stay in UK' *The Daily Telegraph* (London 31 January 2015).

40 See para. 52 of Lord Phillips judgment. The facts are taken from paras [40]–[59] of Lord Phillips of Worth Matravers judgment in *RB (Algeria) v Secretary of State for the Home Department* [2010] 2 AC 110 and *Othman v the United Kingdom* [2012] 55 EHRR 1 [7]-[25].

41 [2012] 55 EHRR 1.

to deport non-nationals whom they consider to be threats to national security.[42] Article 3 did not preclude Contracting States from seeking diplomatic assurances from states where there is a systematic problem of torture and ill treatment and because of the MoU in this case, there was no violation of Article 3 were he to be deported.[43] The point of divergence however, came in relation to the right to a fair trial. In *Soering*, the ECtHR had held that Article 6 could only be raised exceptionally in expulsion or extradition cases where the person concerned had suffered or was at risk of suffering a flagrant denial of justice in the requesting country.[44] In *Othman*, the House of Lords found that there was no authority to say that the risk of the use of evidence obtained under torture amounted to a flagrant denial of justice.[45] Lord Philips held that for a breach of Article 6 there must be substantial grounds for believing that there would be a fundamental breach of the principles of a fair trial guaranteed by Article 6 and that this failure would lead to a miscarriage of justice that itself constitutes a flagrant violation of the victim's fundamental rights[46] – which Abu Qatada was not able to show. The ECtHR disagreed, finding that the admission of evidence obtained under torture would make the whole trial not only immoral and illegal but also entirely unreliable in its outcome. It would therefore amount to a flagrant denial of justice if such evidence were admitted in a criminal trial.[47] Abu Qatada had produced compelling evidence that his co-defendants in his Jordanian trial were tortured. In these circumstances, deportation to Jordan would have amounted to a violation of Article 6 of the Convention.

Abu Qatada was eventually deported the following year, after the UK and Jordanian parliaments ratified a mutual legal assistance agreement in which the Jordanian authorities guaranteed that evidence obtained under torture would not be used against him.[48] The following day, Theresa May, the then home secretary, told Parliament that he would have been deported a long time ago but that the ECtHR had "moved the goalposts by establishing new, unprecedented legal grounds" and declared that something had to be done about the ECtHR's "crazy interpretation" of the law and mooted the possibility of repealing the

42 Ibid. [183–4].
43 Ibid. [193] and [207].
44 *Soering v the United Kingdom* [1989] 11 EHRR 439, [113].
45 *Othman v Secretary of State for the Home Department* [2010] 2 AC 110, [201] (Lord Hoffman).
46 Ibid. [141] (Lord Phillips of Worth Matravers).
47 *Othman* (n.45) [267].
48 SIAC and the Court of Appeal had considered the case again *Othman v Secretary of State for the Home Department* [2013] EWCA Civ 277. Although both found that Article 6 would be breached if Abu Qatada was deported, he consented to his own deportation after the agreement was ratified. He was eventually acquitted of the charges against him in Jordan. See Shiv Malik 'Abu Qatada cleared of terror charges by Jordan court and released from jail' *The Guardian* (24 September 2014) available at <www.theguardian.com/world/2014/sep/24/abu-qatada-cleared-terror-charges-jordan-court> accessed 18 September 2016.

HRA.[49] Nevertheless, it is simply not the case that the ECtHR had established unprecedented legal grounds in *Othman*. Whilst it is true that in the 22 years between *Soering* and *Othman* the ECtHR never found that an expulsion or extradition would breach Article 6,[50] the Court of Appeal had allowed Abu Qatada's appeal on the basis that the use of evidence obtained under torture is prohibited not just because it compromises the right to a fair trial, violating Article 6, but also because of its connection to Article 3 which contains a "fundamental, unconditional and non-derogable prohibition against torture".[51] Even though the House of Lords overturned the Court of Appeal's decision it is incorrect to say that the ECtHR had shifted the goalposts.

In any event, the ECtHR does not operate within a vacuum, and the UK is party to a number of international instruments that either prohibit or seek to prevent torture. These include the International Covenant on Civil and Political Rights,[52] the European Convention for the Prevention of Torture and Inhuman or Degrading Treatment or Punishment and the Rome Statute of the International Criminal Court,[53] as well as the UN Convention against Torture and Other, Cruel, Inhuman and Degrading Treatment or Punishment 1984 (UNCAT).[54] Article 3 of the latter prohibits the refoulement or extradition of a person to another state where they would be subject to torture and Article 15 requires states to prohibit any evidence extracted under torture from being used in court proceedings. In *Othman*, the ECtHR considered jurisprudence of the UN Committee against Torture, UNCAT's monitoring body, where it was indicated that Article 15 applied to extradition cases in circumstances where testimonies had been extracted under torture.[55] It also considered jurisprudence relating to Article 15 from courts in France, Germany and Canada, where it had been held that extradition requests should be refused because of risks that evidence in the requesting country was obtained from third parties under torture.[56]

49 Theresa May HC Deb 8 July 2013 vol.566, col. 23–24.

50 *Othman* (n.36) [260].

51 *OO (Jordan) v Secretary of State for the Home Department* [2008] 3 W.L.R. 798 [48].

52 International Covenant on Civil and Political Rights (adopted 16 December 1966, entered into force 23 March 1976) 999 UNTS 171, Art. 7.

53 Torture is considered to be a crime against humanity under Article 7(f) of the Rome Statute of the International Criminal Court.

54 Convention against Torture and Other, Cruel, Inhuman and Degrading Treatment or Punishment (adopted 10 December 1984) 1465 UNTS 85.

55 [125] – [131] in which it referred to the cases of *PE v France* [2003] 10 I.H.R.R. 421 and *GK v Switzerland* [2003] 10 I.H.R.R. 962 as well as the Committee's concluding observations on France and the United States and a report on Mexico. Although the UK does not recognise the competence of the Committee against Torture to receive individual complaints under Article 22 UNCAT, it is obliged under Article 18 of the Vienna Convention on the law of treaties to refrain from acts which would defeat the object and purpose of a treaty.

56 Ibid. [132] – [134], [139].

The ECtHR's conclusions were hardly the 'crazy' unprecedented interpretation of Article 6 that the ECtHR's detractors claimed.

Whilst there is some truth in the *Daily Telegraph*'s assertion[57] that some foreign national offenders cannot be deported because of Article 3 and the HRA, the reality is that the repeal of the latter may not lead to a different outcome. Britain, after all, contributed to the drafting of Article 3 with one of its representatives wanting to make clear that torture should be prohibited in all circumstances, declaring that it would "be better for society to perish than to permit this relic of barbarism to remain".[58] Significantly, neither the Coalition government's advisory Commission on a Bill of Rights nor the Conservative Party's 2015 manifesto suggested that the text of Article 3 itself should be changed.[59]

Additionally, the pre-HRA domestic jurisprudence also showed that the courts were willing to look for international guidance on the interpretation of the prohibition of torture.[60] Shortly before the ECtHR's judgment in *Chahal*, the Court of Appeal recognised that expelling or returning someone to his or her country of origin where there were substantial grounds for believing that the person would be in danger of torture, loss of life or inhuman or degrading treatment would not only breach Articles 2 and 3 of the ECHR but also Article 3 of UNCAT.

(4) Deportation and Article 8: Accusations of absolutism

Article 8 provides that everyone has the right to respect for his private and family life, his home and his correspondence. The courts' interpretation of Article 8 has come under intense criticism from elements of the media as well as politicians since the enactment of the HRA. An illustrative headline in the *Daily Express* contained the headline "Killers, Rapists and Perverts STAY in UK under Human Rights Act"[61] and complained that many foreign national criminals had won the

57 Robert Mendick 'Human Rights Act has helped 28 terrorists to stay in UK' *The Daily Telegraph* (London 31 Jan 2015).

58 *Preparatory Work on Article 3 of the European Convention on Human Rights* Memorandum prepared by the Secretariat of the European Commission on Human Rights DH (56) 5, available at <www.echr.coe.int/LibraryDocs/Travaux/ECHRTravaux-ART3-DH(56)5-EN1674940.pdf> accessed 7 September 2016, p 3. Seymour Cocks MP presented his amendments to the Consultative Assembly of the Council of Europe on 7 September 1949.

59 The Commission on a Bill of Rights 'A UK Bill of Rights' (December 2012) available at <http://webarchive.nationalarchives.gov.uk/20130128112038/http:/www.justice.gov.uk/downloads/about/cbr/uk-bill-rights-vol-1.pdf> accessed 8 September 2016, para. 12.9; The Conservative Party '*The Conservative Party Manifesto 2015: Strong Leadership. A Clear Economic Plan. A Brighter, More Secure Future*' (2015) available at <www.conservatives.com/manifesto> accessed 8 September 2016, p 73.

60 *R v Bow Street Metropolitan Stipendiary Magistrate ex parte Pinochet Ugarte (No.3)* [2000] 1 A.C. 147, at 197–201.

61 Matthew Davis 'Killers, rapists and perverts STAY in UK under Human Rights Act' *The Daily Express* (18 January 2016) available at <www.express.co.uk/news/

right to stay by claiming that that deportation would breach their right to a family life. In her speech at the Conservative Party Conference in 2011, the then home secretary, Theresa May denounced the use of Article 8 to prevent deportation in the following terms:

> We all know the stories about the Human Rights Act. The violent drug dealer who cannot be sent home because his daughter – for whom he pays no maintenance – lives here. The robber who cannot be removed because he has a girlfriend.[62]

She argued that the problem was not the way in which the Article 8 had been framed by its drafters; rather, it was the British courts which had 'perverted' its meaning by construing the right to a family life as "an almost absolute right".[63] In an article titled "Why Our Rights Must Trump Those of Foreign Criminals", Dominic Raab, MP, a prominent critic of the HRA, argued that Article 8 had become the "number one way in which dangerous foreign criminals avoid being sent home".[64]

Unlike Article 3, Article 8 is qualified by Article 8(2), which provides that any interference must be in accordance with the law, be necessary in a democratic society and in the interests of a number of listed factors, including national security and the prevention of disorder or crime. As discussed earlier, the ECtHR recognises states' general right to control the entry and residence of non-nationals and does not create a general obligation on contracting states to respect the choice by married couples of their country of residence.[65] It has also recognised on numerous occasions that states have to strike a fair balance between the competing interests of the individual and the community as a whole and are given a wide margin of appreciation in this context.[66] It is clear from this case law that the ECtHR has never treated Article 8 as an absolute right.

The ECtHR set out some general principles on deportation and Article 8 in the case of *Boultif v Switzerland*.[67] For interference with that right to be necessary in a democratic society it must be justified by a pressing social need and be *proportionate* to the legitimate aim pursued.[68] The court recognised that the removal of a person who has close family members in a contracting state could

uk/635509/Killers-rapists-perverts-stay-UK-Human-Rights-Act> accessed 12 September 2016.

62 Theresa May's speech (n.3).

63 Ibid.

64 Dominic Raab 'Why our rights must trump those of foreign criminals' *Daily Mail* (29 January 2011) available at <www.dailymail.co.uk/debate/article-2547729/Why-rights-trump-foreign-criminals-writes-DOMINIC-RAAB.html> accessed 8 September 2016.

65 *Abdulaziz, Cabales and Balkandali v the United Kingdom* [1985] 7 EHRR 471, [68].

66 Ibid. [63]; *Nunez v Norway* [2014] 58 EHRR 17, [68].

67 [2001] 33 EHRR 50.

68 Ibid. [46].

lead to an infringement with the right to respect to a private and family life.[69] It listed a number of factors that the courts should take into account including the time an individual has been living in the country and the nature of their family life, such as the length of a marriage or whether they have children.[70] Where children are concerned, it is important to prioritise their best interests and well-being, as well as the difficulties that they may face in the country to which the applicant is to be deported, and the solidity of any social, cultural and family ties with the host country and the country of destination.[71]

The post-HRA domestic jurisprudence also demonstrates that Article 8 has been treated as a qualified right. In *R (on the application of Razgar) v Secretary of State for the Home Department*, Lord Bingham held that proportionality "must always involve the striking of a fair balance between the rights of the individual and the interests of the community which is inherent in the whole of the Convention".[72] He added in *Huang* that when assessing Article 8(2) there was a "need to discourage non-nationals admitted to the country temporarily from believing that they can commit serious crimes and yet be allowed to remain".[73] The Court of Appeal recognised in *Samaroo*[74] that the home secretary was entitled to attach importance to a general policy of "deporting those convicted of importing Class A drugs in order to protect those resident in the UK from the harmful effects of drugs and, by deterring others, in the interest of preventing crime and disorder".[75] Nor do the courts always allow foreign national criminals to remain just because they have a girlfriend or a tenuous relationship with their children. In *Balogun v the United Kingdom*,[76] the ECtHR found that there would be no violation of Article 8 if the UK deported someone who had twice been convicted of possession of Class A drugs with intent to supply, even though he had been living in the UK since he was eight years old and had a girlfriend. In *Samaroo*, the appellant had his appeal dismissed notwithstanding his marriage to a British citizen and the difficulties that she would have raising his child without him.

But what would be the difference if the HRA was repealed? Prior to its enactment, the home secretary and officials in the Home Office were already under an implicit duty to consider the private and family life of a person who they were considering deporting. Part 13 of the Immigration Rules required the secretary of state *to balance* the public interest against any compassionate circumstances and take into account matters such as the age, length of residence and personal history of the person being deported, which are not so dissimilar to the factors that the ECtHR

69 Ibid.
70 *Boultif v Switzerland* [2001] 33 EHRR 50 [48].
71 *Uner v Netherlands* (2007) 35 EHRR 45 [58].
72 [2004] 2 AC 368 [20].
73 [2007] 2 A.C. 167 [16].
74 [2002] INLR 55.
75 [2002] INLR 55, para. 40.
76 [2013] 56 EHRR 3.

enunciated in *Boultif*.[77] Similarly, since section 55 of the Borders Citizenship and Immigration Act 2009 entered into force, Home Office officials have been under a duty, as a matter of domestic law, to have regard to the need to safeguard and promote the welfare of children. This has been equated to the best interest of the child test contained within Article 3 of the Convention on the Rights of the Child, and it has been held that this requires that in any decision involving a child, the best interests of the child shall be treated as *a* primary consideration.[78] However, it is not to be treated as the only consideration[79] and can be outweighed by other factors including the "need to maintain firm and fair immigration control".[80]

The most significant difference the HRA has made has been the introduction of the proportionality test which requires the reviewing court to assess the balance that the decision-maker in a deportation case has struck between the requirements of immigration policy and the human rights of the individual being deported. It also requires attention to be directed to the relative weight accorded to general interests and considerations.[81] It is the relative weight point that Theresa May played to her advantage as home secretary in 2012 when she amended Part 13 of the Immigration Rules.[82] This was part of a wider reform of the rules which set out the criteria by which cases under Article 8 would be considered – this was justified because of the "public interest" in controlling "immigration and in protecting the public from foreign criminals".[83] The new rules stated that where a person is liable to deportation, the presumption shall be that the public interest requires deportation.[84] Criteria were established to assess claims that deportation would violate the right to a family life with a child or partner for those sentenced to less than four years' imprisonment. Where an individual did not meet these criteria, or had been sentenced to a term of imprisonment of four years or more, it would only be in *exceptional circumstances* that the public interest in deportation would be outweighed by other factors.[85] As Katherine Otto notes, the 2012 rule changes and the Immigration Act 2014 were shaped to specifically respond to public concerns, about both foreign criminals and judges' perceived 'softness' in deportation cases involving Article 8.[86] The Court of Appeal has, for the most part, upheld this approach to deportation,

77 Rule 364 of the Immigration Rules HC395 (Statement of Changes in Immigration Rules laid before Parliament 23 May 1994).

78 *ZH (Tanzania)* [2011] UKSC 4, [23] and [33].

79 *ZP (India)* [2015] EWCA Civ 1197, [29].

80 *ZH (Tanzania)* (n 77), [33] (Lady Hale).

81 *R (Daly) v Secretary of State for the Home Department* [2001] 2 AC 532 547C-F.

82 Statement of Changes to the Immigration Rules (2012) (HC 194).

83 Ibid. Rule 398, 399 and 399A (HC 194), Explanatory Memorandum, [2.1].

84 Ibid. Rule 396.

85 Ibid. Rule 398 and 399 (HC 194).

86 Katherine Otto 'The Foreign National Prisoner's Dilemma in the United Kingdom: The Human Rights Implications of Restricting Article 8 Claims' (2014) 24 *Transnational Law and Contemporary Problems* 432.

finding in *MF (Nigeria)*[87] that the new rules constituted a "complete code".[88] Paragraph 398 expressly contemplates a weighing of "other factors" against the public interest in deporting foreign national criminals,[89] but "in approaching the question of whether removal is a proportionate interference with an individual's Article 8 rights, the scales are very heavily weighted in favour of deportation".[90] It clarified that the *exceptional circumstances* referred to in paragraph 398 were *very compelling reasons.*[91] The Supreme Court held in *Hesham Ali (Iraq)* that whilst the immigration rules are not law, they are "a relevant and important consideration for tribunals determining appeals brought on Convention grounds" assisting the evaluation of whether a deportation is proportionate and in general "only a claim which is very strong indeed" would be likely to succeed.[92]

The rules were subsequently modified in light of the Immigration Act 2014,[93] in which Parliament asserted that the more serious the offence committed, the greater the public interest in deportation.[94] For those sentenced to less than four years' imprisonment, the public interest requires deportation except where the person has a genuine and subsisting relationship with a qualifying partner or child[95] and the effect of deportation would be *unduly harsh* on the partner or child.[96] A further exception is where the person has been lawfully resident in the UK for most of their life or is socially and culturally integrated into the UK, and there would be significant obstacles to the person's integration to the country to which he or she would be deported.[97] For those who do not meet the exceptions, the public interest requires deportation unless there are very compelling circumstances above and beyond those stated previously.[98] Under the new rules little weight is attached to relationships that were formed when the person was in the UK unlawfully or where their immigration status was precarious.[99] This elevates the importance of the legal status of an individual and appears to move away from the ECtHR's position which, as Daniel Thym describes, was to treat "illegal entry and residence status [as] only one, albeit important, element" of

87 [2013] EWCA Civ 1192.
88 Ibid. [44].
89 Ibid. [38].
90 Ibid. [42].
91 Ibid. [43]; See also *the Secretary of State for the Home Department v SS (Congo)* [2015] EWCA Civ 387 [30].
92 [2016] UKSC 60
93 The Immigration Act 2014, s 19 inserted sections 117A-D into the Nationality, Immigration and Asylum Act 2002 (NIAA 2002). Statement of Changes to the Immigration Rules HC 532 (10 July 2014).
94 Nationality, Immigration and Asylum Act 2002, s 117C(1) and (2).
95 Ibid. s 117C(5). S 117D(1) defines a 'qualifying child' as a person under the age of 18 who either is a British citizen or has lived in the UK for seven years or more. To be a 'qualifying partner' the partner must be a British citizen or settled in the UK.
96 Ibid. s 117C(5) and s 117D(1).
97 Ibid. s 117C(4).
98 Ibid. s 117C(6) and rule 398(c).
99 Ibid. s 117B(4)(a) and (5).

a proportionality exercise.[100] Again this illustrates how Article 8, far from posing an absolute barrier to deporting individuals from the UK, in fact, permits a considerable margin of appreciation to states in designing immigration policy.

There are of course cases where foreign national criminals have avoided deportation from the UK relying on Article 8. For example, the appellant in *MF (Nigeria)*, who had been convicted of handling stolen goods and possessing a false passport, was allowed to remain on account of his relationship with his stepdaughter.[101] Nevertheless, the Court of Appeal has held that it will almost always be proportionate to deport those sentenced to at least four years' imprisonment, even taking into account the best interests of any children concerned.[102] Thus, in *LC (China)*,[103] it upheld a decision to deport someone who had been sentenced to five years imprisonment for robbery finding that "neither the fact that the appellant's children enjoy British nationality nor the fact that they may be separated from their father for a long time will be sufficient to constitute exceptional circumstances of a kind which outweigh the public interest in his deportation".[104] Even where the person has been sentenced to a period of less than four years' imprisonment, the Court of Appeal has qualified that assessment whether deportation would be "unduly harsh" on a child or partner requires consideration of the public interests in deportation to be weighed against the impact on their child or partner.[105] Therefore, contrary to what is often reported, the public interest will regularly trump the individual right to a private and family life. The perception of Article 8 as an absolute right seems to have arisen more as a form of populist resistance to the constitutionalisation of human rights in the media, which has made Article 8 look far more powerful in the process of resisting deportation than it actually is. This, Rebecca Hamlin argues, has undermined support for the HRA as a whole even if it does not correspond to the wider legal reality.[106]

Conclusion

It cannot be denied that some foreign national criminals have been able to rely on the HRA to avoid deportation. The absolute prohibition of torture, inhuman or degrading treatment or punishment means that foreign national criminals will not be deported to certain states even if they have committed terrorist related offences or other serious crimes. This may be unpalatable to some, but it reflects the international consensus on torture. The Abu Qatada case demonstrates

100 Daniel Thym 'Respect for Private and Family Life under Article 8 ECHR in Immigration Cases: A Human Right to Regularize Illegal Stay?' (2008) 57 *ICLQ* 87 101.

101 *MF (Nigeria)* [2013].

102 *CT (Vietnam)* [2016] EWCA Civ 488, [19].

103 [2014] EWCA Civ 1310.

104 Ibid. [24].

105 *IT (Jamaica) v the Secretary of State for the Home Department* [2016] EWCA Civ 932, [51]-[57].

106 Rebecca Hamlin 'Foreign Criminals, the Human Rights Act, and the New Constitutional Politics of the United Kingdom' (2016) 4 *Journal of Law and Courts* 437, 440.

however, that contracting states to the ECHR can take steps to militate against the risk of torture or the use of evidence obtained under torture in criminal proceedings so as to be able to deport individuals.

Article 8, on the other hand, is much more nuanced. Although certain politicians and elements of the media, have maintained that the courts treat the right to a family and private life as a trump card, neither the Strasbourg court nor the senior domestic courts view Article 8 as an absolute right. Prior to 2012, the courts were already sensitive to the requirement to weigh the circumstances of the individual concerned against the public interest in deporting criminals who were foreign nationals with Klug estimating that as little as between 2% and 8% of those facing deportation in 2010 won their appeals on Article 8 grounds.[107] Since 2012, however, there has been a detailed framework in place to assess Article 8 claims that the Court of Appeal has interpreted very restrictively. This has made it extremely difficult for those foreign national criminals who are sentenced to at least four years' imprisonment to resist deportation. This is regardless of any relationship they may have with any British children, their spouse, partners or girlfriend, suggesting a significant diluting of the power of Article 8. It is only a little less difficult for those sentenced to less than four years' imprisonment to avoid deportation.

However, persistent claims that the HRA undermines the capacity of the government to deport individuals convicted of a crime have led to the common assumption that human rights law prevents individuals from being deported. This has hardened into an assumption, discussed in later chapters, that the HRA confers specific benefits to individuals facing deportation, leading to common perceptions that the Act is 'unfair' or only applies to non-nationals. It seems that attempts by successive governments to change the law surrounding deportation have had little impact on these perceptions. Yet the reality for many criminals of foreign nationality is perhaps best summed up by the following headline from the *Sunday Express*: "Foreign criminals to be DEPORTED despite human rights: Judges in landmark ruling."[108]

107 Francesca Klug 'Deportation and the right to respect for private and family life under Article 8' *LSE Human Rights Futures Project* (2013) available at <http://image.guardian.co.uk/sys-files/Guardian/documents/2011/10/04/KlugDeportation.pdf> accessed 17 September 2016, p 6.

108 Vickie Oliphant 'Foreign criminals to be DEPORTED despite human rights: Judges in landmark ruling' *The Sunday Express* (26 May 2016) available at <www.express.co.uk/news/uk/673966/Foreign-criminals-migrants-deported-despite-human-rights-Article-8-excuses-judges-rule> accessed 18 September 2016. The article relates to the case of *CT (Vietnam)* [2016] EWCA Civ 488. The subheading states that the judges ruled that foreign national criminals can no longer use their children as an excuse to be deported, which is inaccurate. The Court of Appeal held that it will almost always be proportionate to deport those sentenced to at least four years' imprisonment, even taking into account the best interests of any children concerned, at [19].

Chapter 9

Welfare, anti-austerity and gender

New territory and new sources of hostility for the Human Rights Act

Laura Lammasniemi

Introduction

The aftermath of the global financial crisis has brought about a variety of austerity measures including unprecedented cuts to the existing welfare system in the UK. Simultaneously there has been increased condemnation, if not vilification, of welfare claimants in the tabloid press and a variety of reality TV series such as Channel 4's *Benefits Street*, a TV series set in a street in Birmingham where the majority of residents are said to receive welfare benefits. This has coincided with a series of high profile and controversial challenges to various austerity measures in the courts using the Human Rights Act 1998 (HRA). This chapter shows that benefit claimants are often represented collectively in an overwhelmingly negative light. This representation fails to take into account the gendered nature of the welfare state and the disproportionate impact the cuts have had on women. This chapter argues that the HRA has provided an avenue for women to challenge these discriminatory cuts, but in turn, this led to the claimants in these cases being framed as undeserving and led to the HRA itself attacked.

While rarely acknowledged in mass media, the disproportionate impact of austerity measures enacted since 2010 on women has been recognised by feminist commentators,[1] by leading rights organisations and unions[2] and by even the government's own consultations and equality assessments.[3] Yet, the government

1 Penny Griffin 'Crisis, austerity and gendered governance: a feminist perspective' (2015) 109 *Feminist Review* 190; Rebecca Bramall *The Cultural Politics of Austerity: Past and Present in Austere Times* (Palgrave Macmillan 2013).

2 Trades Union Congress 'The impact on women of recession and austerity' (11 March 2015) available at <www.tuc.org.uk/economic-issues/equality-issues/gender-equality/equal-pay/impact-women-recession-and-austerity> accessed 1 August 2016; Fawcett Society 'Where's the Benefit: an independent inquiry into women and Jobseeker's Allowance' (February 2015) available at <www.fawcettsociety.org.uk/our-work/campaigns/independent-inquiry-women-jobseekers-allowance/> accessed 24 July 2016.

3 Department for Work and Pensions (DWP) 'Benefit cap: Equality Impact Assessment' (July 2012) available at <www.gov.uk/government/uploads/system/uploads/attachment_data/file/220153/eia-benefit-cap-wr2011.pdf> accessed 12 April 2014.

has insisted that these measures were necessary to introduce "long-term positive behaviour change" and reduce dependency on welfare benefits.[4] There have been a number of challenges on human rights and equality grounds of the austerity measures from cuts to services,[5] legal aid cuts[6] and specific welfare benefit cuts such as the bedroom tax[7] and benefit cap.[8] While spending cuts have had a disproportionate impact on women, this chapter focuses on cuts to welfare benefits, the bedroom tax and the benefit cap, in particular, to demonstrate how the European Convention on Human Rights (ECHR) has been used to challenge the recent austerity measures on grounds of gender discrimination. The HRA and the ECHR do not explicitly contain socio-economic rights, but since the enactment of the HRA the courts have had the power to hear judicial review challenges on the decisions of public authorities and scrutinise secondary legislation including those concerning welfare benefits and socio-economic rights more broadly.[9]

In stark contrast to tabloid and conservative press, the left-wing press has focused on the detrimental impact of the cuts to individuals and society more broadly.[10] This chapter, however, focuses mainly on the media sources with widest circulation such as *The Sun* and *Daily Mail* which represent welfare claimants negatively. The chapter draws an explicit link between these negative portrayals and the HRA, situating the HRA as means of facilitating these 'undeserving' claims and claimants. This chapter argues that the media representations and continued attacks on the HRA in the context of welfare, have framed benefit claimants as 'bad'/non-productive citizens who are not as worthy of state protection and the same rights as 'good' citizens are. Although this is often exaggerated, and ignores the legal position and the way that the HRA is used in these cases, it has nevertheless contributed to the perception that the HRA helps 'undeserving individuals', a phenomenon which is examined in Chapters 10 and 11 of this book.

This chapter begins by examining the representation of benefits claimants in the media. It highlights the collective and stereotypically negative representation

4 DWP 'A Welfare State Fit for the 21st Century' (23 January 2014) available at <www.gov.uk/government/speeches/a-welfare-state-fit-for-the-21st-century> accessed 1 August 2016.

5 *R (Rahman) v Birmingham City Council* [2011] EWHC 944 (Admin).

6 See *R (Law Society) v Legal Services Commission* [2010] EWHC 2550 (Admin) (2010) 107(40) LSG 22; *Allan Rutherford LLP v Legal Services Commission* [2010] EWHC 3068 (Admin).

7 *R (Rutherford and others) v SSWP* [2016] UKSC 58.

8 *R (on the application of SG and others (previously JS and others)) v Secretary of State for Work and Pensions)* [2015] UKSC 16.

9 Ellie Palmer *Judicial Review, Socio-Economic Rights and the Human Rights Act* (Hart 2009) 320.

10 Jen Birks 'Moving life stories tell us just why politics matters': Personal narratives in tabloid anti-austerity campaigns' (2016) *Journalism* 1.

of benefit claimants to examine how these representations have constructed the unemployed as unworthy of human rights protection and socio-economic rights as an undesirable extension of the existing human rights framework. It then moves on to discuss the role of the HRA in scrutinising welfare benefits and the judicial challenges on austerity measures under the HRA and how this then feeds into arguments that the HRA should be repealed.

(1) The case against the rights of 'benefit scroungers'

In the UK, national mass-circulation daily newspapers have a privileged political position. Broadcasters are required by law to be politically neutral but the newspapers have historically been quite reactionary enjoying a degree of editorial independence unmatched in Western Europe. From the 1980s onwards new production methods and ownership led to the market in daily newspapers diminishing, but moving more to the right and at the time of writing around 70% of all newspapers are considered right-wing or right-leaning.[11] The newspaper media is a significant political player and is highly instrumental in shaping both other sources of media and public attitudes in general. The conservative press, such as the *Daily Mail* and *The Telegraph*, have long attacked the idea of socio-economic rights and have applauded government efforts to cut welfare spending.[12] The *Daily Mail* has frequently identified "criminals and those who refuse to work" as the main beneficiaries of the HRA[13] whereas *The Telegraph* has attacked "welfare aristocrats" and has voiced their support for welfare cuts.[14]

In 2011, the then prime minister David Cameron set up a Bill of Rights Commission to assess the current human rights framework and explore the idea of creating a domestic bill of rights to replace the HRA. The Bill of Rights Commission did not recommend repeal of the HRA but built on the ECHR to create a stronger human rights framework that would include protections for

11 YouGov Survey, 'British press 'most right-wing' in Europe' (February 2015) available at <https://yougov.co.uk/news/2016/02/07/british-press-most-right-wing-europe/> accessed 20 September 2016. See also Adrian Bingham and Martin Conboy *Tabloid Century: The Popular Press in Britain, 1896 to the Present* (Peter Lang 2015).

12 Telegraph View 'Welfare reforms are sensible and right' *The Telegraph* (24 August 2015) available at <www.telegraph.co.uk/news/politics/11819645/Welfare-reforms-are-sensible-and-right.html> accessed 1 August 2016.

13 James Slack 'The human right to claim benefits: Jobless could sue for better payments under controversial plan' *Daily Mail* (12 July 2012) available at <www.dailymail.co.uk/news/article-2172260/The-human-right-claim-benefits-Jobless-sue-better-payments-controversial-plan.html> accessed 1 August 2016.

14 Bruce Anderson 'Only David Cameron has the guts to tackle the welfare aristocrats' *The Telegraph* (11 April 2010) available at <www.telegraph.co.uk/news/election-2010/7575961/Only-David-Cameron-has-the-guts-to-tackle-the-welfare-aristocrats.html> accessed 1 August 2016.

socio-economic rights.[15] When the Bill of Rights Commission published its 2012 report[16] recommending an expansion of the current human rights framework to include socio-economic rights, the recommendation was widely dubbed ludicrous and different variations of the headline 'spongers/jobless can sue for benefits' featured in the tabloid press.[17] Furthermore, conservative politicians such as Dominic Raab, MP, who later served as parliamentary undersecretary of state for human rights, argued that the commission should have recommended the scaling back of a rights culture, as extending current human rights laws would be undesirable and undemocratic because it would give judges control over social policy.[18] The following year the Labour Party also examined the possibility of expanding the existing human rights framework to include socio-economic rights, and again the tabloid and conservative press including *The Telegraph* dubbed the plans as a "scroungers charter" that would give further rights to those who already have too much.[19]

The representation of benefit claimants in the press has been perhaps even more striking than the direct attacks on their 'human rights'. Talking about an impoverished neighbourhood in Glasgow, Stephen Glower for the *Daily Mail* wrote,

> We might be back in the Depression and the early 1930s, were it not for the baseball caps, tracksuit bottoms and trainers which the inhabitants – all of them white – wear. They shuffle listlessly down the street, or gather to have a smoke outside the numerous pubs. Some of the younger women are grossly fat, but the older men are thin, almost emaciated. Their faces look pallid and unhealthy, and they usually don't have any teeth, false or otherwise.[20]

15 Commission on Bill of Rights 'A UK Bill of Rights: Choice before Us' vol. 1 (December 2012) available at <http://webarchive.nationalarchives.gov.uk/20130128112038/http://justice.gov.uk/about/cbr> accessed 20 July 2016.

16 Ibid.

17 Anil Dawar 'Spongers can sue to claim benefits' *Daily Express* (13 July 2012) available at <www.express.co.uk/news/uk/332520/Spongers-can-sue-to-claim-benefits> accessed 2 August 2016; James Slack 'The human right to claim benefits: Jobless could sue for better payments under controversial plan' *Daily Mail* (12 July 2012) available at <www.dailymail.co.uk/news/article-2172260/The-human-right-claim-benefits-Jobless-sue-better-payments-controversial-plan.html#ixzz4LXjEv2rr> accessed 2 August 2016.

18 Roger Smith 'The Good, the Bad, and the Ugly' *New Law Journal* (12 July 2012) available at <www.newlawjournal.co.uk/content/good-bad-ugly> accessed 24 July 2016.

19 Patrick Hennessy 'Labour's 'secret plan' to make claiming benefits a human right' *The Telegraph* (13 July 2013) available at <www.telegraph.co.uk/news/politics/labour/10178148/Labours-secret-plan-to-make-claiming-benefits-a-human-right.html> accessed 1 August 2016.

20 Stephen Glower 'Is Glasgow East going to be New Labour's graveyard?' *Daily Mail* (23 July 2008) available at <www.dailymail.co.uk/news/article-1037387/Is-Glasgow-East-going-New-Labours-graveyard.html#ixzz4I9Inettp> accessed 1 August 2016.

The 'poor' in such articles are nearly always referred to as 'they', a unified group which is subjected to collective and reproachful representation. The benefit claimants are associated with lack of care for their appearance or health with frequent references to smoking, drinking and overeating or lack of basic (dental) hygiene as demonstrated by the preceding quotation.

If the jobless man is frequently represented as an owner of a Stafford terrier dog, smoking outside a job centre wearing a tracksuit, the jobless woman is represented as a working-class single mother.[21] Most women who are in receipt of welfare benefits or tax credits are in part-time or low-pay employment, yet women in tabloids are presented as jobless, working-class single mothers.[22] Jobless single mothers are rarely represented in a positive way and often described with reference to their implied promiscuity, laziness and questionable parenting skills or values. Talking about underage pregnancies, "a fable for our tragically degraded times", the *Daily Mail* went onto say that "the length and breadth of this country there are many Chantelles, having sex and often getting pregnant while underage".[23] The representation of single mothers frequently highlights their 'inappropriate' sexuality by focusing on teenage pregnancies or children from multiple partners. They are also subject to moral and physical scrutiny that is not applied to other groups, and they are often depicted as overweight or overly sexualised.[24]

Against this backdrop, benefit claimants have a very particular image in the public consciousness. The emergence of reality TV series such as *Benefits Street* and *Fairy Jobmother* reinforced this image and sent out a message that benefit dependency is a choice rather than a necessity. Hannah Ahmad argued that TV series such as *Fairy Jobmother*, a reality series about an employment expert finding employment for the unemployed, reject the notion that any "hurdles cannot be surmounted by individual willpower regardless of any social inequities or power imbalances in play".[25] They brought about a new era of individualism that

21 Hannah Hamad 'Fairy Jobmother to the Rescue: Postfeminism and Recessionary Cultures of Reality TV' from Diane Negra and Yvonne Tasker (eds.) *Gendering the Recession* (Duke University Press 2014) 240.

22 Malgorzata Paprota 'The Chantelles of Benefits Britain: Collective representations of the clients of the welfare state in conservative British press (2008–2012)' (2015) 39(2) *Lublin Studies in Modern Languages and Literature* 179.

23 Melanie Philips 'Alfie, Chantelle and the sheer madness of sex education that teaches nothing about morality' *Daily Mail* (16 February 2009) available at <www.dailymail.co.uk/debate/article-1146083/MELANIE-PHILLIPS-Alfie-Chantelle-sheer-madness-sex-education-teaches-morality.html#ixzz4I9JrZOsq> accessed 1 August 2016.

24 For instance, see Lucy Waterlow 'Single mother on benefits uses her £20K-a-year handouts to fund her dreams of becoming a plus-size burlesque dancer called Chazabelle' *Daily Mail* (25 May 2016) available at <www.dailymail.co.uk/femail/article-3608489/Single-mother-benefits-dreams-new-life-burlesque-dancer.html#ixzz4IFzBYuKW> accessed 1 August 2016.

25 Hamad (n.21), 225.

focuses on the transformative power of paid work. These series and disparaging press articles about benefit claimants, single mothers, in particular, imply that staying home is a lazy choice and that domestic labour is not work. Paid work is traditionally viewed not only as important to individual well-being, but also it is a way for an individual to contribute to society and, in turn, receive social rights and welfare when in need.[26] The representation of benefit claimants changed following the financial crisis in 2008, and in recent years this escalated with paid work being increasingly viewed as an obligation for a good citizen – and failure to engage in paid work as a sign of a bad citizen. A failure to contribute to society through paid work has seen benefit claimants framed as 'scroungers', less-worthy citizens. The press and recession-related reality TV series collaboratively reconstructed negative stereotypes of those on benefits and reinforced class constructions.[27] Simultaneously they have created divisions between good citizens versus bad citizens, those worthy of state protection and human rights and those not worthy.

The welfare state has been deeply gendered from its inception and remains so, but these negative representations do not take into account these gendered dimensions.[28] From 2010 onwards the overhaul of welfare benefits has been at the core of the government's socio-economic policies with the overall aim of reducing the amount of people reliant on welfare benefits. The government's equality impact assessments recognise that women, single mothers, in particular, are the main recipients of housing benefit, and therefore, restrictions to housing benefit and the total amount of welfare benefits households can receive will have a disproportionate impact on women.[29] Despite criticism and mounting judicial challenges, the gender disparity in the administration of these policies has not been sufficiently addressed in subsequent policies.[30] Universal credit, a single monthly payment merging existing benefits and tax credits an individual or a household may be entitled to, will be implemented across the United Kingdom by the end of 2017. This new system has faced criticism, much like previous cuts, particularly from feminist commentators for its failure to take into consideration the disproportionate impact it would have on women.[31] Universal

26 Ruth Lister 'The dilemmas of pendulum politics: balancing paid work, care and citizenship' (2002) 31 *Economy and Society* 520.

27 Laura Paterson et al. 'Negotiating stance within discourses of class: Reactions to *Benefits Street*' (2016) 27 *Discourse & Society* 195.

28 Pat Thane *The Foundations of the Welfare State* (2nd ed. Routledge 1996) ch. 7.

29 DWP (n 3); TUC (n 2); Fawcett Society (n 2); DWP 'Social sector housing under-occupation – equality impact assessment' (June 2012) available at <www.gov.uk/government/publications/social-sector-housing-under-occupation-equality-impact-assessmen> accessed 12 April 2014.

30 Women's Budget Group 'The impact on women of the 2016 Budget: Women paying for the Chancellor's tax cuts' (April 2016) available at <http://wbg.org.uk/budget-analysis/2016-assessments/> accessed 12 November 2016.

31 Griffin (n.1).

credit is payable to a household, rather than individuals, meaning that women, particularly women in migrant communities, might lose or be excluded from financial control within their families because of language barriers and a lack of knowledge on how to access welfare benefits.[32] Universal credit, therefore, seriously undermines women's financial autonomy.

(2) The European Convention on Human Rights and socio-economic rights

Traditionally, the scrutiny of social welfare has been considered to be subject to democratic rather than judicial accountability. Judges have been reluctant to allow judicial review of social and economic policy due to judicial deference – particularly so if the policy was in the manifesto of the governing party, thereby securing some form of democratic endorsement. Lord Scarman summarised the traditional view on courts and review of spending cuts in *R v Secretary of State for the Environment ex p. Nottinghamshire County Council*:

> . . . [I] cannot accept that it is constitutionally appropriate, save in very exceptional circumstances, for the courts to intervene on the ground of 'unreasonableness' to quash guidance framed by the Secretary of State and by necessary implication approved by the House of Commons, the guidance being concerned with the limits of public expenditure by local authorities and the incidence of the tax burden as between taxpayers and ratepayers. Unless and until a statute provides otherwise, or it is established that the Secretary of State has abused his power, these are matters of political judgment for him and for the House of Commons. They are not for the judges or your Lordships' House in its judicial capacity.[33]

This has since been confirmed in various judgments, most recently in the 2015 Supreme Court ruling *R (on the application of SG and others (previously JS and others)) v Secretary of State for Work and Pensions*, discussed in the next section, when Lord Reed rejected arguments for an alternative and more proportionate cap on welfare benefits and said that decisions as to the level and content of the cap were "a matter of political judgment" rather than a question for the judiciary.[34] He held that in applying *Stec v the United Kingdom*[35] the courts should consider that "certain matters are by their nature more suitable for determination

32 Kalwinder Sandhu and Mary-Ann Stephenson 'Layers of inequality – a human rights and equality impact assessment of the public spending cuts on black, Asian and minority ethnic women in Coventry' (2015) 109 *Feminist Review* 109.

33 [1986] AC 240, [247C – H].

34 [2015] UKSC 16, [69].

35 [2006] 43 EHRR 47.

by Government or Parliament [rather] than by the courts".[36] Lady Hale, in contrast, argued that discrimination was a constitutional issue and said that "even in the area of welfare benefits, where the court would normally defer to the decision of the legislature, if that decision results in unjustified discrimination, then it is the duty of the courts to say so".[37] She reiterated this point during the proceedings of *R (A) (AP) (Appellant) v Secretary of State for Work and Pensions*, where she said that discrimination claims, as well as deciding what is a matter for the courts or Parliament, are a matter of constitutional law and, thereby, within the remit of the court.[38] Ellie Palmer further argued that particularly since the enactment of the HRA there has been "a clear disagreement" between senior judges how deference should be exercised but the concept of deference has shifted significantly in cases of social policy, in particular.[39]

Challenges to austerity measures, or to social policy more broadly, on purely economic grounds are still unlikely to succeed but case law from recent years demonstrates cases that can "effectively marshal human rights arguments are more likely to succeed in justifying interference by the courts".[40] It is commonly accepted that welfare benefits fall within the remit of the ECHR. On the face of it, the ECHR does not include a right to social security, yet from the early days of the ECHR individuals have brought challenges dealing with social security rights in front of the European Court of Human Rights (ECtHR) and previously the European Commission on Human Rights.[41] The most frequently invoked Articles of the ECHR in social welfare claims have been Article 8 (the right to respect for private and family life) and Article 1 of the Protocol 1 (A1P1) which provide that

> [e]very natural or legal person is entitled to the peaceful enjoyment of his possessions. No one shall be deprived of his possessions except in the public interest and subject to the conditions provided for by law and by the general principles of international law . . . The preceding provisions shall not, however, in any way impair the right of a State to enforce such laws as it deems necessary to control the use of property in accordance with the general interest or to secure the payment of taxes or other contributions or penalties.

These Articles of the ECHR have been either invoked alone or in conjunction with Article 14 (the prohibition of discrimination). Case law from the ECtHR

36 [2015] UKSC 16 [92].
37 Ibid. [160].
38 Supreme Court hearing (29 Feb 2016, afternoon session), available at <www.supremecourt.uk/cases/uksc-2016-0025.html> accessed 1 April 2016.
39 Palmer (n.9), 175.
40 Thom Dyke 'Judicial Review in an Age of Austerity' (2011) 16 *Judicial Review* 202.
41 Klaus Kapuy 'Social Security and the European Convention on Human Rights: How an Odd Couple Has Become Presentable' (2007) 9 *European Journal of Social Security* 221.

has not always been consistent on the application of A1P1 in relation to welfare benefits but in *Gaygusuz v Austria*,[42] the court held that a social security claim based on contributions constitutes a pecuniary right for the purposes of A1P1. In *Stec* the ECtHR took this further and said that it would be "artificial to hold that only benefits financed by contributions to a specific fund fall within the scope of Article 1 of Protocol No. 1".[43] Furthermore, the court confirmed the role of A1P1 protecting welfare rights and said that where "an individual has an assertable right under domestic law to a welfare benefit, the importance of that interest should also be reflected by holding Article 1 of Protocol No. I to be applicable".[44] While the courts have been reluctant to engage with cases that deal purely with social policy or economic decisions, case law shows that welfare cuts are justiciable because of the human rights implications of the cuts. The HRA has therefore provided a way for individuals most affected by the cuts to welfare benefits to challenge the relevant regulations, and a majority of these challenges, as discussed in the next section, have been based on discrimination claims on the grounds of gender and disability.

(3) Judicial challenges on gender grounds

This section examines the case law on challenges to welfare cuts, particularly the cases on the benefit cap and the bedroom tax, and demonstrates that gender discrimination has become the core of many of the judicial review challenges to cuts to welfare benefits. The case of *SG* was the first Supreme Court ruling to consider the legality of the benefit cap, a limit on the total amount of welfare benefits an individual or a household can receive, and whether it amounted to a violation of the ECHR.[45] The total amount of benefits was fixed under the Benefit Cap (Housing Benefit) Regulations 2012 (the 2012 Regulations) so that it reflected the salary of an average single person/family in the UK, but the cap has since been further reduced and subsequently applied equally to single- and two-parent families, regardless of the size of the family or living costs.[46]

In *SG* it was not argued that the cap itself was a violation of A1P1 per se but, rather, that it constituted a violation when read together with Article 14 as it indirectly discriminated against women. All five Supreme Court judges agreed that the cap put women at a disadvantage but disagreed by a narrow margin whether the discrimination was justified because of legitimate aims. Providing the leading

42 [1996] no. 17371/90.
43 [2006] 43 EHRR 47, [50].
44 Ibid [51].
45 Benefit Cap (Housing Benefit) Regulations 2012 (SI 2012/2994) (the 2012 Regulations) amending the Housing Benefit Regulations 2006 (SI 2006/213) regulations 75B, 75D and 75G. The Regulations list welfare benefits as out-of-work benefits, child benefit, child tax credit and housing benefit.
46 DWP (n.3).

judgment, Lord Reed recognised the gendered implications and disparity but concluded that the secretary of state's aims of ensuring the economic well-being of the country, incentivising work and imposing a reasonable limit on the total amount of welfare benefits per household were legitimate and proportionate.[47] The dissenting rulings from Lady Hale and Lord Kerr argued that the discriminatory impact on women could not be justified, and therefore the measures amounted to a violation of Article 14. Lady Hale also expressed concern over the severity of the measures and stated that

> [t]he prejudicial effect of the cap is obvious and stark. It breaks the link between benefit and need. Claimants affected by the cap will, by definition, not receive the sums of money which the state deems necessary for them adequately to house, feed, clothe and warm themselves and their children.[48]

Both Lady Hale and Lord Kerr discussed the wellbeing of the mother and her children as intertwined, therefore, recognising the importance of caring labour. Decades of feminist scholarship has established and analysed the existence of gendered and caring labour and, arguably, the failure of welfare policy to recognise care of young children as 'productive' undervalues such labour.[49] Under the austerity policies, women are expected to participate in the workforce in a similar way to men, and the cuts to welfare benefits do not take into account that women are more likely to already be participants in unpaid caring and gendered labour. The policies have also not taken into account difficulties in securing quality child care or the desire of some women to care for their young children. The infrastructure of welfare support is often crucial for single parents' entry into the job market and access to paid work.[50] The stigmatisation and marginalisation of jobless single mothers are therefore counterproductive, undermining the aims of the government policies.

The court in *SG* also considered the stigmatisation of benefit claimants in the media, and Lord Reed was of the view that the benefit cap was consistent with government aims to restructure the welfare system and argued that these measures were necessary in order to restore public confidence in the system. The attacks on benefit claimants and media reports stigmatising non-working households have,

47 [2015] UKSC 16 [63–66].

48 Ibid. [180].

49 See Eileen Boris *Home to Work: Motherhood and The Politics of Industrial Homework in the United States* (Cambridge University Press 1994); Eileen Boris and Rhacel Salazar Parreñas (eds.) *Intimate Labors: Care, Sex, and Domestic Work* (Stanford University Press 2010); Abigail Gregory and Jan Windebank *Women's Work in Britain and France: Practice, Theory and Policy Women's* (Palgrave Macmillan 2000); Ruth Lister 'Reforming welfare around the work ethic: new gendered and ethical perspectives on work and care' (1999) 27(2) *Policy & Politics* 233.

50 Jane Lewis (ed.) *Lone Mothers in European Welfare Regimes* (Jessica Kingsley 1997) 141.

as discussed earlier, distorted public perception of the nature and the scope of the welfare system. Lord Reed made reference to the media representations of benefit claimants and said that public confidence in the welfare system has to be restored so that the "recipients are not stigmatised or resented".[51] He further argued that the reform was legitimate to "reflect a political view as to the nature of a fair and healthy society", implying that cuts would give an impression of a less generous, and therefore fairer, welfare system.[52] He framed the benefit system as "the means by which society expresses solidarity with its most vulnerable members".[53] The focus on vulnerability and who is most worthy is similar to the way claimants of human rights claimants are often framed as worthy or unworthy of state protection, which is discussed further in Chapter 11, where Frederick Cowell explores the relationship between undeserving claimants and the structure of the law itself.

Like the benefit cap, the bedroom tax, which involves a reduction of up to 25% in claimants' entitlement to housing benefit if they live in social housing that is deemed to have one or more spare bedrooms, has been challenged in the courts on gendered and disability grounds.[54] In a key ruling on the bedroom tax, *R (MA) v Secretary of State for Work and Pensions*,[55] it was held that the scheme as a whole discriminated against disabled persons, but the policy was not manifestly without valid foundation, and so the discrimination was objectively and reasonably justified. It would, therefore, be necessary to decide on the particular facts of each case whether a claimant had been discriminated against under the provision. Following *MA*, in the joint appeal case of *R (Rutherford and another) v Secretary of State for Work and Pensions; R (A) v Secretary of State for Work and Pensions* the Supreme Court held that the bedroom tax was discriminatory against a family of a severely disabled child who needed a spare bedroom for overnight care and an adult couple who could not share a bedroom because of disabilities.[56] In the earlier stage, the Court of Appeal also upheld a discrimination claim by *A*, a female victim of serious domestic violence who lived in an accommodation adapted to her family's needs under the sanctuary scheme (part of the same proceedings).[57] The claimant, A, had been subject to exceptional levels of violence by her former partner, and after being allocated a three bedroom house, it was adapted to her heightened security needs and included several features, such as a 'safe' room, that were vital for her protection. The Court of Appeal recognised that requiring her to give up an accommodation which met her specific needs and relocate could put the claimant's and her child's well-being at risk and concluded that this constituted a violation of Article 14 as it discriminated against her as a female

51 [2015] UKSC 16, [66].
52 Ibid.
53 Ibid.
54 Introduced under the Housing Benefit (Amendment) Regulations 2012.
55 [2014] EWCA Civ 13.
56 [2016] UKSC 58.
57 [2016] EWCA CIV 29.

victim of domestic violence. On appeal, the majority of Supreme Court judges did not accept this and decided that sanctuary scheme cases should be decided on a case-by-case basis, but no exemption should be made for those who are victims of gender-based violence and living in a sanctuary scheme.[58] In their dissenting judgments, Lady Hale and Lord Carnwarth focused solely on victims of gender-based violence. Lady Hale argued that those living in sanctuary schemes should be exempt from the bedroom tax. Furthermore, she argued that public authorities should take into account the needs of victims of gender-based violence in order to "make better decisions".[59]

Similar to the claimant in *A*, both the claimants in *SG* had been victims of domestic violence and argued that the benefit cap forced them to move to cheaper areas, farther away from their support networks and communities that were essential to them and their children. In *SG*, Lady Hale noted that

> . . . the greater the need, the greater the adverse effect. The more children there are in a family, the less each of them will have to live on. . . . This prejudicial effect has a disproportionate impact upon lone parents, the great majority of whom are women, and is also said to have such an impact upon victims of domestic violence, most of whom are also women.[60]

Victims of domestic violence are often housed in temporary accommodation, which is relatively expensive and so the benefit cap had a disproportionate effect on women who are victims of domestic violence and were attempting to leave abusive partners. The government recognised the impact of the cap on victims of domestic violence after the challenge in *SG* and amended the regulations so that 'specified accommodation', a wide range of accommodation provided for vulnerable people that is exempt from the cap, now also includes women's refuges.[61] Although the Supreme Court ruling in *SG* was disappointing in that it failed to condemn the gender discrimination inherent in the measures, the challenge was still effective as it forced the government to amend the regulations so that women's refuges and temporary accommodation for victims of domestic violence are excluded from its scope. The courts have, therefore, provided an important scrutiny of these measures and merely the right to bring challenges under the HRA has brought about significant changes.

While the negative association between the HRA and benefit claimants in the mass media has been constant, particularly since the financial crisis in 2008, it has not been as forthright as that of foreign criminals or terror suspects. The coverage

58 [2016] UKSC 58 [63–66].
59 [2016] UKSC 58 [80].
60 [2015] UKSC 16, [180].
61 Housing Benefit and Universal Credit (Supported Accommodation) (Amendment) Regulations 2014 (SI 2014/771).

of HRA-related judicial review challenges has also not been consistent and rulings that allow for more controversy have received far more media attention. When the courts have found no violation of the ECHR, such as in *SG*, the rulings were not as widely reported or commented on in the tabloid press. In contrast, successful cases that invoked the HRA to challenge the austerity measures, have been framed largely in a negative light and have been used to directly attack the HRA. In 2012, the Court of Appeal ruled in the case of *R (Reilly) v Secretary of State for Work and Pensions* that the 'back to work' scheme, which required people who were in receipt of jobseekers allowance to work for free, was unlawful as the Department of Work and Pensions (DWP) regulations failed to provide enough detail about the scheme in the wording.[62] The claimants also argued that the scheme was in conflict with Article 4(2) of the ECHR which provides, subject to exceptions, that "no one shall be required to perform forced or compulsory labour". The Court of Appeal, and later Supreme Court, rejected the Article 4 claim yet the case was widely discussed in relation to the HRA, and for instance, the *Daily Express* reported the proceedings as "[y]et another farce from the hated Human Rights Act".[63] Ian Duncan Smith, then secretary of state of work and pensions, accused the claimants of "pathetic" use human rights laws and called them "job snobs".[64] Cait Reilly, the applicant, and her attempt to use the HRA to challenge the scheme came under intense scrutiny and direct attacks by the newspapers hostile to the HRA.[65] Much of the reporting on the case was focused on Reilly as an individual and the seemingly 'inappropriate' use human rights law in a negative way, comparing the claim to 'real' human rights claims such as "like being incarcerated in a Nazi prisoner of war camp".[66]

The *Reilly* case was framed as an example of rights inflation used to describe how both human rights law and welfare provisions had been stretched too far and Reilly herself was described as an undeserving recipient of welfare and human

62 [2013] EWCA Civ 66. The Supreme Court upheld the ruling in *R (Reilly & Anor) v Secretary of State for Work and Pensions* [2013] UKSC 68.

63 Stephen Pollard 'Yet another farce from the hated Human Rights Act' *Daily Express* (13 January 2012) available at <www.express.co.uk/comment/expresscomment/295319/Yet-another-farce-from-the-hated-Human-Rights-Act> accessed 29 August 2016.

64 Ian Duncan Smith 'The delusions of X Factor and sneering job snobs who betray the young' *Daily Mail* (20 February 2012) available at <www.dailymail.co.uk/debate/article-2104022/The-delusions-X-Factor-sneering-job-snobs-betray-young.html> accessed 29 August 2016.

65 Graeme Archer 'You're a geologist, Cait Reilly – which planet are you and your lawyers on?' *The Telegraph* (15 February 2013) available at <www.telegraph.co.uk/finance/jobs/9873470/Youre-a-geologist-Cait-Reilly-which-planet-are-you-and-your-lawyers-on.html> accessed 29 August 2016.

66 Jan Moir 'A human right not to stack shelves? She's off her trolley' *Daily Mail* (13 February 2012) available at <www.dailymail.co.uk/debate/article-2086000/Cait-Reilly-Human-right-stack-shelves-Poundland-Shes-trolley.html> accessed 29 August 2016.

rights protection. The HRA has long been criticised for providing a framework for the inflation of rights into new areas where human rights are inappropriate. Some of this criticism, especially that coming from the political right, has specifically cited the role of discrimination, claiming that the HRA was facilitating a discrimination culture in the UK.[67] Dominic Raab, MP, a leading critic of the HRA framed rights inflation in strident terms describing it as having "undermined this country's liberal tradition of freedom and its approach to human rights, which is founded in [the] Magna Carta . . . towards imposing more and more obligations on government that require it to provide, rather than merely insisting that it refrain from acting in certain arbitrary ways".[68] He criticised the decision in *Reilly* in these terms describing it as "just one illustration of how the HRA has proved rather malleable material for the ingenious twisting of the basic conception of human rights".[69] Commenting on Raab's reaction to the case, Merris Amos noted that "he considers welfare recipients should enjoy a lesser standard of protection, something which prevents them from even bringing an 'inflated' human rights claim before a court".[70] It seemed that the mere ability of benefit claimants to use the HRA was what provoked this criticism. In *Reilly* the claimants won their case in essence on Raab's own conception of what human rights ought to be used for as the judges in the Supreme Court held that basic fairness in the application of state power was not being followed in the administration of the 'back to work' scheme.[71] In other words, the claimant was protesting the arbitrary application of state power, yet Raab still accused her of rights inflation. As Amos noted, in this context claiming that a right was inflated "is simply another way of saying that you don't agree with it".[72]

Conclusion

The chapter examined the persistent attacks against benefit claimants and showed how single mothers, in particular, have been vilified in mass media. Along with disparaging press reporting, reality TV series have emphasised the transformative power of paid work and, in turn, have belittled unpaid domestic and caring labour that women engage in on a daily basis. These representations of unworthy recipients of welfare payments have enabled unprecedented cuts to welfare benefits

67 See Dominic Raab 'Liberty lost democracy denied: The Duel Attack on Britain's tradition of freedom' from Alex Deane (ed.) *Big Brother Watch: The State of Civil Liberties in Britain* (Biteback 2010).

68 HC Deb 9 May 2016 vol. 609 col. 513.

69 Merris Amos 'Do my Human Rights Look big in this? Decoding the Rhetoric of Rights Inflation' *The Human Rights Essay* (27 October 2015) available at <http://humanrightsessay.org.uk/Merris-Amos-rights-inflation.html> accessed 20 November 2016.

70 Ibid.

71 *Reilly* (n.62) [64]-[70].

72 Amos (n.69).

along with wide-ranging austerity measures. Freedom from discrimination is an essential part of the ECHR and a right that is considered to be one of the most important by the British public.[73] In the abstract, the support for freedom from discrimination and even the welfare state seems to be well received. Yet, in practice female benefit claimants such as Reilly and their attempts to enforce rights under the HRA have faced a far more hostile reaction.

The impact of the cuts on those who are dependent on welfare payments has been profound, particularly so for single mothers who find themselves unable to provide adequate care for their children. Since the cuts to welfare benefits were introduced child poverty has risen rapidly, and it is estimated that by 2020 child poverty is set to have risen by 50%.[74] The HRA has provided crucial tools for individuals and pressure groups to challenge not only individual decisions but also the measures more broadly. While the courts have been reluctant to interfere with purely economic policies, claims based on gender and disability discrimination have been allowed. Even if the courts have not declared the measures themselves discriminatory and a violation of the ECHR, the human rights challenges to the bedroom tax and the benefit cap by victims of domestic violence have led to a change in law and policy – demonstrating the importance of subjecting these measures for judicial review using the HRA.

Currently, nearly all challenges to the austerity measures have been brought under the HRA or the Equality Act 2010 and it has proved a particularly important avenue for women who have been disproportionately impacted by the cuts. Lady Hale has repeatedly argued that discrimination is a constitutional issue so challenges to discriminatory austerity measures should be allowed. Yet, as demonstrated by the case law in this area, the courts continue to be reluctant to engage with socio-economic policy so without the HRA most of these judicial review challenges would not have been allowed. This is unlikely to change. Furthermore, the reaction to the Bill of Rights Commission's recommendations on the inclusion of socio-economic rights as part of the human rights framework demonstrate that it would be highly unlikely that such extension would come into existence were a British Bill of Rights be introduced to replace the HRA. This would mean that those most marginalised in society, would have little remedy to challenge the decisions that impact their lives.

73 For polling on this point see Peter Kellner 'Analysis: Which human rights matter most?' *YouGov* (30 March 2016) available at <https://YouGov.co.uk/news/2016/03/30/which-rights-matter-most> accessed 20 November 2016.

74 Institute of Fiscal Studies 'Child and working-age poverty in Northern Ireland over the next decade: An update' (2014) Briefing Note (BN154) available at <www.ifs.org.uk/publications/7448> accessed 28 July 2016.

Part IV

The structural basis of hostility to the Human Rights Act

Chapter 10

Moving away from common sense

The impact of the juridification of human rights

Nicolas Kang-Riou

> If in such cases where human rights and human rights legislation are cited, and the conclusion reached runs counter to common sense, then the conclusion is wrong.
>
> —Lord Falconer[1]

Introduction[2]

There has been a documented series of relentless attacks against the Human Rights Act (HRA) led by right-leaning newspapers in the UK, with headlines such as "How Europe's Human Rights Court Has Made a Mockery of British Justice" (*Daily Mail*, 1 August 2015), "It's Time to Stop Crazy Human Rights Rulings from European Judges" (*The Sun*, 26 July 2014), "Human Rights Madness to End' (*Daily Express*, 3 October 2014) or " 'Rights' that Make a Mockery of Our Courts" (*Daily Telegraph*, 27 April 2013). These newspapers are among the leading opponents of the HRA.[3] Through the qualifiers used (mockery, crazy, mad etc.), they insist that (mostly European) judges have lost 'common sense' when applying the European Convention on Human Rights (ECHR). The usual response from human rights lawyers and others who defend the HRA and ECHR is to challenge the quality of the criticisms made. They highlight the errors, exaggerations and misinformation that many of these articles contain.[4] They tend to

1 Speech at the University of Manchester 2007 cited in Joshua Rozenberg '£25,000 spent on human rights spin' *Daily Telegraph* (London 10 February 2007).

2 This chapter has benefitted from insightful comments from Dr David Rossati and Frederick Cowell, the editor.

3 Liese Gies *Mediating Human Rights* (Taylor and Francis, 2014) 18; Joint Committee on Human Rights *The Human Rights Act: the DCA and Home Office Reviews* (HL 278, HC 1716, 2005–06) 23–24.

4 See David Mead ' "You Couldn't Make It Up": Some Narratives of the Media's Coverage of Human Rights' from Katja Ziegler, Elizabeth Wicks and Loveday Hodson (eds.) *The UK and European Human Rights: A Strained Relationship?* (Hart 2015) 453–472; Adam Wagner 'The monstering of human rights' Talk at the University of Liverpool *Conference*

insist that the attacks are actually a form of "monstering",[5] a demonisation of the HRA and ECHR rather than a proper discussion of controversial issues.

This chapter follows a different approach. It does not challenge the existence of 'monstering' (some of which has been condemned by the courts) but, rather, seeks to complement the analysis of the misrepresentations conveyed by part of the media. This chapter insists on taking the criticism seriously that there has been a loss of 'common sense' in the application of the law because of the HRA. It looks for the reasons behind these claims. Is it a problem with the way the ECHR's rights are phrased or with the judges at the European Court of Human Rights (ECtHR) in Strasbourg interpretation? Or is it a problem with how the British government implements the ECHR, or something else altogether?

Journalists do not always need to express the reasons behind their arguments and may write in a polemic fashion, so it is often difficult to assess what is really meant by the claimed loss of 'common sense'. Fortunately, on occasion they provide a selection of cases; for example, Jack Doyle of the *Daily Mail* chose ten cases illustrating why the judges are "so wrong" when they apply the ECHR.[6] In the descriptions of the cases that are given, the problem appears to be something about the situation of the applicant which makes the outcomes absurd. In a nutshell, this is what the applicants stand for in these ten cases:

1. Hate preacher
2. Sexual abuser
3. Prisoners wanting to use methadone
4. IRA terrorists
5. Spy who was compensated for breach of free expression
6. Murderer and career criminal
7. Murderer
8. Police chief who was doing unethical things who had her phone tapped
9. Criminal not deported because of fear for his physical integrity if expelled
10. Male-to-female transgender person who could not get a pension as a woman

From the cases selected in that article, and in others,[7] three implicit dimensions of the 'loss of common sense' argument appear. The first common element in eight of these cases is that the beneficiary of the human rights law is somebody guilty of having committed serious criminal offenses such as murder, rape, sex

on Human Rights in the UK Media: Representation and Reality (19 September 2014) available at <https://adam1cor.files> accessed 20 December 2016. wordpress.com/2014/09/the-monstering-of-human-rights-adam-wagner-2014.pdf, accessed 25 September 2016.

5 Wagner (n.4).

6 James Slack 'Europe's war on British justice: UK loses three out of four human rights cases, damning report reveals' *Daily Mail* (London 11 January 2012).

7 See also the list provided in 'Case by case: How Europe's human rights court has made a mockery of British justice' *Daily Mail* (London 10 February 2011).

offences, robbery and so on, in other words, a human rights abuser or a 'culprit' claiming to be a victim.[8] The assumption appears to be that human rights should be dependent on past behaviour. According to that view, unlinking rights from duties would be a 'mockery' of justice. The second common element is that each time the Strasbourg court finds a violation of the ECHR in regard to the cases mentioned, critical newspapers and commentators dismiss it as not being serious enough in comparison to what the individual in question has done. Therefore, human rights must deal with serious issues or otherwise fail into 'madness'. The final dimension is that some cases are inspired from liberal values rejected by the press critical of the ECHR.

These dimensions can be explained by the transformation of the common language of human rights into human rights law. The press and the human rights lawyers do not quite speak the same language when they address human rights questions. Both sides purport to discuss human rights issues as being tackled by courts, but one does it from the perspective of the public; the other, from the legal one. This makes a crucial difference, as human rights law is usually not presented as being much different from its media portrayal.[9]

When attacking the ECHR, the media make a series of assumptions, some express, some implied. Of those, many fail to match the premises on which the legal regime created by the HRA and the ECHR actually functions. It can appear that the criticisms made by the press against the court(s) are valid because they relate to a common view of what human rights should be and that human rights law only incidentally follows such a view. In many aspects, these views are actually far apart. Quite often the language used by the ECtHR is substantially different from the 'common view' expressed by the media (hereafter referred to as the 'common human rights language' or the 'common sense' view).[10] As human rights transformed into a legal language, it was taken over by lawyers and legal institutions which altered both its form and substance.[11] The legalisation of human rights produces a modification of the content of the human rights law away from popular intuitions about common sense and justice whilst, at the same

8 Francesca Klug 'A Bill of Rights: do we need one or do we already have one?' (2007) *Public Law* 701.

9 The Equality and Human Rights Commission for instance defines human rights in the following way on its website: "human rights are not just abstract concepts – they are defined and protected by law. In Britain our human rights are protected by the Human Rights Act 1998" available at <www.equalityhumanrights.com/en/human-rights/what-are-human-rights> accessed 26 September 2016.

10 Annabelle Mooney 'Human rights: Law, language and the bare human being' (2012) 32 *Language & Communication* 169.

11 See Saladin Meckled-García and Başak Çal (eds.) *The Legalization of Human Rights: Multidisciplinary Approaches* (Routledge 2006); Nicolas Kang-Riou 'Confronting the legalization of human rights: a counterpoint' from Kang-Riou, Jo Milner and Suryia Nayak (eds.) *Confronting the Human Rights Act: Contemporary Themes and Perspectives* (Routledge 2012) 9.

time, giving expert judges powers which traditionally rested in domestic politics. Human rights law has moved away from a shared will to use human rights as a method to fight potential totalitarian practices such as the atrocities committed during and in the wake of the Second World War[12] towards a more technical and managerial[13] legal language.[14] This is something Frederick Cowell analyses in more depth in the next chapter of this book, but in this chapter I want to examine the technical and managerial-led transformations of human rights law and explain the four key situations where the press may find a particular decision under the HRA nonsensical.

The first point is that the legal human rights language breaks the direct connection between the past behaviour of the applicant and their claim – in contrast to other branches of the law. For many critics of the ECHR, criminals should not be found to be victims of human rights violations as they should primarily be seen as culprits. Unlike the structure and form of criminal law where third parties, like victims, can participate in the procedure, human rights law severs the link between the victim of a human rights abuse and the culprit. It only asks itself whether the government has unduly restricted the rights of the applicant. The second point is that the media often presumes that for a human rights question to be dealt with by the courts it should be sufficiently serious. This is a politically sensible argument which is shared by many member states and the Council of Europe itself. However, the seriousness of the issue is only one factor among others for deciding the admissibility and the substance of the claim under the ECHR. The third point is related to the second. Not only can a court find a violation of human rights even when the restriction of the right can seem to be trivial, but it can also find a violation when a court is unsure if there has been a violation of a human right at all. This may seem highly counter-intuitive to the non-lawyer but, legally speaking, a violation of the ECHR does not mean that an individual's human rights have been breached. Finally, some cases are seen as 'absurd' because of differing political values, which are expressed in defining what human rights are. I conclude by mapping out some possibilities to bridge the gap between the two sets of discourse on human rights.

12 See A.W. Brian Simpson *Human Rights and the End of Empire: Britain and the Genesis of the European Convention* (OUP 2001) ch. 4.

13 This is how Martti Koskenniemi describes this process of expert rule: "The fate of the rule of law as power in international institutions is increasingly wielded by expert regimes and networks looking for 'optimal' outcomes that tend to be situation-specific". Martti Koskenniemi 'Human Rights Mainstreaming as a Strategy for Institutional Power' (2010) 1 (1) *Humanity: An International Journal of Human Rights, Humanitarianism, and Development* 47.

14 Ed Bates *The evolution of the European Convention on Human Rights* (OUP 2010).

(1) Human rights law obfuscates the link between the past behaviour of an individual and his or her right to human rights

The first 'common sense' statement, which has been widely put forward as an argument behind the proposed UK Bill of Rights, is that rights should be connected to the past behaviour of an individual making a rights claim.[15] Rights should not be disjointed from responsibilities, doing anything else would go against common sense. In this area the conflict between human rights law and its opponents seems to be at its clearest. Most of the media pieces attacking the HRA and the ECHR are based on cases where criminals have been able to win for a breach of their human rights. This has been derided as making "a mockery of justice".[16] Cases where convicted criminals are able to escape deportation on the basis that it would breach their right to private and family life are particularly targeted in this context.

At first glance, the difference in perspective seems to be insurmountable. Newspapers opposed to the HRA clearly state that individuals who committed serious crimes should not be able to claim that they have suffered a human rights violation because of what they did to their victims. For Tony Parsons, in a 2014 *Sun on Sunday* column,

> [t]he Human Rights Act is an affront to human decency. It contradicts everything the British believe about fairness and justice. It gives succour, comfort and aid to the perpetrators of evil and insults the good, the innocent and all the victims of crime. Foreigners who come to this country who murder, rob or rape should FORSAKE their right to a 'family life'.[17]

This statement denies that convicts still have human rights, or at least it is an argument that they only have a limited number of rights. At a cursory level, it is contrary to the nature of human rights law which asserts the unqualified and universal nature of human rights: all humans have rights regardless of their qualities.[18] Of course, on closer examination, the operation of qualified rights contained in the ECHR, such as the right to private and family life under Article 8, allows for restrictions. Human rights lawyers know very well that paragraph 2

15 For a recent general discussion of the link between human rights and duties see Stephan Parmentier, Hans Werdmölder and Michael Merrigan (eds.) *Between Rights and Responsibilities: A Fundamental Debate* (Intersentia 2016).

16 Daily Mail Comment 'Great week for the Tories . . . now finish the job' *Daily Mail* (London 3 October 2014).

17 Tony Parsons 'Why the Human Rights Act is just so wrong' *The Sun on Sunday* (London 14 December 2014).

18 Universal Declaration of Human Rights UNGA Res 217A(III) 10 December 1948 Article 1.

of the right to private and family life, right to freedom of religion and the right to freedom of expression as set out in ECHR, allow the government to restrict these rights if there is a legal basis, a legitimate aim and a necessity for such a restriction in a democratic society. Therefore, a government can justify restrictions on the rights of a convicted criminal for public interest reasons, such as guaranteeing public safety. The evidence of the danger to the public is the past criminal behaviour. This is where a link between the rights and the responsibility of an individual appears, even though it is only an indirect and relative one. The British government has won many cases in Strasbourg or in front of British courts on the basis of such a link.[19]

Critics of the media are quick to point out that cases where governments win and courts allow the deportation of criminals, or some other measure, are generally unreported.[20] Thus, the reader of the press hostile to the HRA could be forgiven if they concurred with the statement regarding the operation of Article 8 of the ECHR, that "[i]t doesn't matter if you come to this country and rape, murder and steal".[21] If this were true, it would go against the 'common sense' approach to what immigration should be about. Most people would agree that a serious breach of criminal law is as bad as behaviour can get in a democratic society. In a world with borders, the immigration compact is based on the premise that upon an individual's entry into the territory of another state they are required to respect its laws, especially its criminal legislation. It is therefore reasonable to refuse to let a person stay in a state if he or she committed a breach of the terms on which he or she was allowed to come in in the first instance. This is also what the ECtHR has consistently stated, noting that "the Convention does not guarantee the right of an alien to enter or reside in a particular country and, in pursuance of their task of maintaining public order, Contracting States have the power to expel an alien convicted of criminal offences."[22] In that same case, the Grand Chamber of the ECtHR explicitly refused to assimilate long-term migrants to nationals. Therefore, it could seem that the critics have just failed to do their homework.

The difference of opinion comes from the way the Strasbourg court has interpreted the operation of Article 8 in such circumstances. It balances the rights of the individual with the public interest by taking into account a series of factors, where the severity of the offence committed is only one of them. The other elements are the length of the applicant's stay in the country from which they are to be expelled, the time since the offence was committed and the applicant's conduct during that time, the applicant's family situation and solidity of the applicant's social, cultural and family ties with the host and destination countries.[23] Therefore, the two sides that are being balanced by the court are the crime on

19 For an analysis of the appeal against deportation decisions in the UK and in Strasbourg in 2011 and 2012 see Klug (n.8).

20 Mead (n.4).

21 Ibid.

22 *Uner v Netherlands* ECHR 2006-XII GC [54].

23 Ibid. para. 57 and 58.

one hand and the extent of the applicant's integration on the other. The legal version no longer fits with the simpler test espoused by the media.

In legal terms, what critics of the ECHR are pointing at is a divergent view on how the proportionality test should operate by insisting on the pre-eminence of the past behaviour, as per the criminal law. The ECHR demands that restrictions of rights to be 'necessary in a democratic society'. What that test entails is subject to interpretation. A plausible view could be that some crimes are so severe that in the case of foreign criminals they should always lead to an expulsion. This would be a legitimate restriction in legal terms and one which could not be so easily dismissed by human rights advocates. In fact, such a reading is entirely possible under the Convention,[24] making it arguable that the Strasbourg judges' interpretation of the ECHR lacks common sense as it fails to integrate the operation of the ECHR within its wider societal context.[25] Many believe that some crimes are in and of themselves sufficiently serious to allow for the balance to be tipped in favour of the protection of public order.

The majority of the Strasbourg judges disagree. They have only recognised that crimes like rape or drug trafficking are generally a sufficient justification while at the same time allowing for exceptional individual circumstances to prevail over deportation.[26] The interpretation of the ECHR stems from a liberal perspective of law and justice. In particular, it has rejected retributive justice to encompass a stronger view on restorative justice.[27] When a convict claims a breach of right, the crime committed is assessed under its current impact and not the past impact on the victim. Furthermore, as the case is based on a breach of human rights law, the convict is no longer seen in that perspective and the victim disappears from the procedure. What seems reasonable or 'common sense' thus changes, as the liberal view insists on the importance of the character of the human rights violation rather than on the context in which that violation occurred. Thus, it is structurally difficult to reconcile these two sets of views regarding the impact of the breach of past duties on the enjoyment of human rights.

(2) A breach of human rights law is not necessarily a serious human rights issue

In the 'common sense' discourse, when someone speaks of a human right violation it relates to something important, deeply affecting the individual concerned.

24 In a case where an individual was deported after being convicted for drug trafficking, the court stated that "[i]n view of the devastating effects of drugs on people's lives, the Court understands why the authorities show great firmness with regard to those who actively contribute to the spread of this scourge", *Baghli v France* ECHR 1999-VIII.

25 For an academic view supporting this argument see Marc Bossuyt *International Human Rights Protection: Balanced, Critical, Realistic* (Intersentia 2016).

26 *Beldjoudi v France* [1992] Series A no 234-A.

27 For a study on restorative justice see Holly Ventura Miller (ed.) *Restorative Justice: From Theory to Practice* (Emerald Pub 2008).

This is how charities and non-governmental organisations dedicated to human rights such as Amnesty International or Human Rights Watch report human rights abuses taking place internationally.[28] This is also what human rights institutions focus on when they circulate press releases, the media choosing to report on matters seen as important by the public. Therefore, if a finding of a human rights violation is publicised then it has to be deemed serious.[29] This is one of the major criticisms of the HRA which can be seen in the cases cited as lacking 'common sense' and is summarised by Dominic Raab, a Conservative MP, as follows:

> The British tradition of liberty has been conflated as swathes of other comparatively minor grievances, claims and interests have been shoe-horned into the ever-elastic language of inalienable, unimpeachable and judicially enforceable rights. In place of our most basic – fundamental – freedoms, steadily eroded and undermined since 1997, we have witnessed the expansion of a range of novel, often trivial, rights.[30]

The finding of a breach of the ECHR does not mean that it necessarily constitutes an important case in relation to the applicant. The ECtHR has always considered the severity of the breach for the applicant as only one element to be taken into account in order to decide the admissibility of an application. Prior to Protocol 14,[31] the only test in that respect was that an application should not be 'manifestly ill founded'.[32] This covers many components, including the importance of the right restriction complained of.[33] This has not prevented the ECtHR from finding violations of the ECHR where at first sight the behaviour of the state does not seem to have been wrong. Technically it is sufficient for the court to find an illegal restriction of the right. Often the operation of the law fails to distinguish between serious breach of a provision and a minor breach.

A case usually cited by the British press in this context is *McCann v United Kingdom*.[34] The case concerned IRA members in Gibraltar who were killed by

28 On Amnesty International see Stephen Hopgood *Keepers of the Flame: Understanding Amnesty International* (Cornell University Press 2006).

29 Of course different NGOs will see problems differently, see Sarah Stroup *Borders among activists: International NGOs in the United States, Britain, and France* (Cornell University Press 2012) ch. 4.

30 Dominic Raab *The Assault on Liberty: what went wrong with rights* (Fourth Estate 2009) xviii.

31 Protocol no. 14 to the ECHR, CETS no. 194.

32 Leo Zwaak 'The procedure before the European Court of Human Rights' from Peter Van Dijk et al. (eds.) *Theory and Practice of the ECHR* (4th ed. Intersentia 2006) 198–199.

33 Antoine Buyse 'Significantly Insignificant? The Life in the Margins of the Admissibility Criterion in Article 35(3)(b)' in Yves Haeck, Brianne McGonigle Leyh and Clara Burbano Herrera (eds.) *The Realisation of Human Rights: When Theory Meets Practice* (Intersentia 2014) 107.

34 (1995) Series A no 234. This case is listed among the 10 cases cited (n.6).

the Special Air Service who genuinely thought they were in a middle of a car bombing attack, whereas they were only preparing for a future bombing. The court did not refute that the killing was absolutely necessary to prevent a crime and therefore was compatible with Article 2 of the ECHR – the right to life. Still, it found a breach of Article 2 because of the government's behaviour leading to the attempted arrest. In particular, it pointed at the decision to not try to arrest the IRA members when they landed at the airport in Gibraltar, where it would have been less risky. The tabloid press later claimed that the case "outraged the public".[35] The *Daily Mail* was also dismayed[36] by the decision in *Blackstock v the United Kingdom*.[37] The Strasbourg court found a breach of the right to liberty guaranteed by Article 5 of the ECHR because there was no review of an individual's continued detention after the minimum tariff of imprisonment had expired. Failure to conduct such a review, the ECtHR held, constituted a breach of Article 5 even if there was no evidence that an earlier review would have led to an earlier release.

In both cases, the press did not seem to see that the restrictions of these rights warranted the finding of a breach. Interestingly this criticism has borne fruit within the system itself through the introduction of the *de minimis* criterion of admissibility with Protocol 14, which allows the ECtHR to dismiss a case if "the applicant has not suffered a significant disadvantage".[38] Still, even in these circumstances the Strasbourg court is not bound to dismiss a case if it believes that admission is demanded for the 'respect for human rights'.[39] It can thus continue to examine cases that the press would find unreasonable or lacking in common sense. For instance, the ECtHR has agreed to deal with a case even though the original dispute concerned 17 euros, because it was important for the national courts to know the correct interpretation of the ECHR.[40] If this case had concerned the UK, there is no doubt that it would have been rejected by the press as nonsensical.

(3) A breach of human rights law is not necessarily of breach of human rights

The media tend to conflate violations of human rights law with violations of human rights. However, lawyers know that the transformation of anything external to law into law, such as human rights, necessarily result in structural changes regarding the meaning and application of the imported concept.[41] This is also

35 *Daily Mail* (n.7).
36 Slack (n.6).
37 App no 9152/00 (ECtHR, 21 June 2005).
38 Protocol 14 (n.31); Article 35 ECHR, para. 3(b), Buyse (n.33).
39 Article 35(2) ECHR.
40 *Nicoleta Gheorghe v Romania* App no. 23470/05 (ECtHR, 3 April 2012).
41 For a general sociological account see Niklas Luhmann *Law as a Social System* (tr KA Ziegert OUP 2004) especially ch. 2.

true regarding the application of the ECHR. Two cases vilified in the press illustrate this problem well: *Averill* and *Hirst*.[42]

In *Averill v the United Kingdom*[43] the UK was found in breach of the right to a fair trial (Article 6 ECHR) because the applicant did not have access to a lawyer during the first 24 hours of his interrogation, contrary to an (extensive) interpretation of the ECHR affirmed by the Strasbourg court.[44] However, he stayed silent during the whole time. He was then found guilty of murder. It is doubtful that the failure to follow procedural rules had a negative impact on the applicant in that case, even if the trial judge did make an inference from his silence in the first 24 hours.[45] As he stayed silent even after being represented, it is very unlikely that even if he had been assisted earlier by a lawyer that the outcome would have been different. The fact that he was not awarded any pecuniary damages by the ECtHR is significant as this suggests the Strasbourg judges believed that the applicant did not suffer any adverse impact. Of course, what the Strasbourg court is after in such cases is to make sure that the procedural guarantees are in place regardless of the circumstances so they can benefit society at large. This is an example of a case being used as a tool to ensure general compliance from the defending state rather than to provide an individual reparations for breaches of his or her human rights. From a 'common sense' view it can seem wrong to find a breach of human rights in Mr Averill's case; from the perspective of the ECtHR it was necessary for the rule of law that the procedural guarantee of a right to a lawyer is in place in all circumstances.[46]

One case which has generated strong opposition, not only from the press[47] but also from both the Conservative and Labour Parties is *Hirst*.[48] The finding of a violation was based on the absolute ban for all prisoners to vote regardless of their personal circumstances. The Strasbourg court recognised that legislation banning certain categories of prisoners was compatible with the ECHR. Mr Hirst had been convicted to a life sentence for murder and therefore would have clearly fallen within these categories. Removing his individual right to vote would have been completely acceptable under the ECHR, as confirmed later by the Strasbourg court in another case.[49] Therefore, Mr Hirst had not been subject to a violation of his human right to vote in the substantive sense. In that case, the ECtHR targeted a general issue in the UK, both the lack of specific parliamentary

42 Both cases are listed in the 10 cases mentioned above (n.5).

43 ECHR 2000-II 212.

44 *Murray (John) v the United Kingdom* ECHR 1996-I.

45 *Averill v the United Kingdom* [2000] ECHR 212 [48].

46 Explanation provided about the rule in *Salduz v Turkey* App no. 36391/02 (ECtHR, 20 November 2008) para. 55

47 Tim Shipman '6,000 Perverts and Thugs to Get the Vote: Tory Rebels' Fury at Plans to Let Inmates Cast a Ballot' *Daily Mail* (6 January 2011).

48 *Hirst v the United Kingdom* ECHR 2005-IX, GC.

49 *Scoppola (No. 3) v Italy* App no. 126/05, GC (ECtHR, 22 May 2012).

discussion of the prohibition to vote for all detainees and its absolute character regardless of the individual circumstances. Again, from a 'common sense' perspective, it could seem absurd to find a breach of Mr Hirst's right to vote, as even if legislation had been passed to allow for some prisoners to vote, it would never have included individuals sentenced to long prison sentences.[50]

There are many caveats to be added to the statement that a violation of a human rights treaty was found by an international human rights court. It may sound substantively similar to stating it was found that there was a breach of universally accepted human rights, but it is rather different. Some of the reasons for this difference are quite simple and linked to the development of a highly specialised and technical language. The ECtHR is tasked with the interpretation of the ECHR and not the interpretation of human rights in a more general or wider sense. The Strasbourg court is bound by the vocabulary used in the text of the ECHR, and more important, it tends to follow its own case-law.[51] Regarding the former, the ECtHR has been quite happy to effectively ignore or rewrite some of parts of the ECHR using interpretative tools.[52] So the latter is more decisive. As a consequence, a finding of a violation by the Strasbourg court is relative and specific to the ECHR itself – it is not necessarily a statement that a universally accepted human rights norm has been breached.

This was the case with the breach of Article 3, Protocol 1[53] in *Hirst* which can only be understood in the context of the development of the case law regarding that provision but also, more generally, in the development of the ECHR. For instance, the ECtHR has developed the procedural dimension of Convention rights by insisting that the restrictions placed on rights are discussed and justified by parliaments or domestic judges.[54] Furthermore, the ECtHR has several objectives when making an interpretation of the ECHR. They are broadly defined within the preamble of the ECHR: the rule of law, democracy and human rights. The protection of human rights is only one of the elements to be taken into account by the ECtHR. It believes that human rights are truly protected only in a society which respects the rule of law and democracy.[55] The aim of the ECHR as interpreted by the Strasbourg court is not only about protecting the

50 The bill made in order to comply with *Hirst* at best offered the vote for prisoners with a sentence of less than four years' imprisonment. See Draft Voting Eligibility (Prisoners) Bill 2012 Cm 8499.

51 See Alistair Mowbray 'An Examination of the European Court of Human Rights' Approach to Overruling its Previous Case Law' (2009) 9 *Human Rights Law Review* 179.

52 George Letsas *A Theory of Interpretation of the European Convention on Human Rights* (OUP 2007); Alistair Mowbray 'The Creativity of the European Court of Human Rights' (2005) 5 *Human Rights Law Review*, 5.

53 Protocol No. 11 to the ECHR, CETS no. 9.

54 Eva Brems 'Procedural protection: an examination of procedural safeguards read into substantive Convention rights' from E Brems and G Janneke (eds.) *Shaping Rights in the ECHR* (Cambridge University Press 2014) 156.

55 See for instance *Malone v the United Kingdom* [1984] Series A no 82, para. 79.

individual rights of the applicant but, more generally, to ensure the protection of human rights within the state party to the Convention. In *Hirst*, the ECtHR asserted that a fundamental aspect of democracy had not been respected as the link between the loss of the right and the individual had not been explained by the UK Parliament. Regarding the rule of law, one key dimension of the ECHR is the development of procedural obligations. There, the Strasbourg court is targeting the operation of the state as a whole, rather than looking at any individual situation. Any refusal of the application of the law, even if benign in a particular case, is wrong when the wider situation is taken into account. The state should always abide by accepted rules, including the ones stemming from an evolutionary interpretation of the ECHR, which was the issue in *Averill*.

The development of the interpretation of the ECHR in both its rule of law dimension and its procedural components ineluctably leads towards a wider disconnect with the 'common-sense' understanding of what human right violations are. In these two examples, the extent of the infringement of the rights is not the basis of the breach of the Convention. In *Averill* and *Hirst*, the breach comes first from a deviation from the constructed obligations of the state towards all, regardless of their individual situation. This is contrary to the perspective on the cases taken by the media and politicians who discuss the limitation of the rights in relation to the behaviour of the state complained of. In that respect, the ECtHR's decisions, even though fully aligned with the objectives the court has set itself, can seem to lack common sense as the decisions appear to be going beyond the individual situations. Through its case law the Strasbourg court has thoroughly extended the range of rights protected, far beyond the 'bare' human rights of the individual whereas part of the media has stayed with this original vision.[56]

(4) Finding a breach of human rights law can be politically influenced

Several cases have been selected by the *Daily Mail*[57] as examples of bad decisions by the ECtHR because the judgments reflected a (liberal) view of society seemingly at odds with the (conservative) values of the newspaper. Two cases illustrate this: *Tyrer*, a case about corporal punishment, and *B and L*, a case relating to the right to marriage.

In *Tyrer v the United Kingdom*,[58] the UK was found in breach of Article 3 of the ECHR as corporal punishment was inflicted on a child in a school on the Isle of Man. This judgment was criticised for undermining the concept of "reasonable chastisement" in national law which allowed parents to "smack" their children,

56 Mooney (n.10).
57 *Daily Mail* (n.6).
58 (1982) 4 EHRR 232.

and also led to changes in law limiting parents' corporal punishment.[59] Even though international legislative trends points towards a limitation of physical punishment[60] this is still resisted by part of the population and by some Conservative and Labour politicians.[61] Critics of the judgment warned that a 'nanny state' was being developed from Strasbourg.[62] This generated a divide between what seemed to be reasonable in the UK and reasonable among Strasbourg judges.

In *B and L v the United Kingdom*[63] the ECtHR court found a breach of Article 12, the right to marriage, because of the prohibition of marriage in UK law between a father-in-law and daughter-in-law. The *Daily Mail* argued against this claiming that "[c]enturies-old rules banning marriage between children and their parents-in-law were swept aside . . . [T]he ban had been cemented in law for more than 400 years in the Book of Common Prayer".[64] This was presented as a case of traditional values being challenged by the Strasbourg court, even though the Labour government at the time had been looking at changing the law. In both cases, the disagreement as to what counts as 'common sense' is imbued with values. Liberals approve whilst conservatives oppose, both sides believing they represent what common sense should be. This division is traditionally at the centre of the political divide between left and right across Europe. What this highlights is not so much an issue of common sense but of politics and relates to what many lawyers have noted concerns the political dimension of decisions taken by the ECtHR.[65]

Even within the discourse of human rights law, there are various politics at play in terms of how rights should be interpreted and how they should be applied. In many situations there is no accepted single view within the human rights law community of what the correct interpretation of human rights law should be. One needs to look no further than at the dissenting opinions of Strasbourg judges to see that even they can be divided.[66] There are also oppositions to the

59 Ibid.

60 See P.R. Ghandhi and J.A. James 'Parental rights to reasonable chastisement and the European court of human rights' (1999) 3 *The International Journal of Human Rights* 97.

61 Ibid. 98.

62 Christina Lyon 'Spare the Rod – care for the child: A consideration of proposed changes to the Law on reasonable chastisement of children in the different jurisdictions of the UK' (2001) 7 *Child Care in Practice* 193.

63 [2006] 42 EHRR 195.

64 *Daily Mail* (n.6).

65 Gunnar Beck 'Human rights adjudication under the ECHR between value pluralism and essential contestability' (2008) *European Human Rights Law Review* 214; Nicolas Valticos 'Interprétation juridique et idéologies in Protection des droits de l'homme: la perspective européenne' from Paul Mahoney et al. (eds.) *Mélanges à la mémoire de Rolv Ryssdal* (Carl Heymanns Verlag 2000) 1471.

66 Robin White and Iris Boussiakou 'Separate opinions in the European court of human rights' (2009) *Human Rights Law Review* 37–60.

European view of human rights stemming from the national legal profession.[67] The discourse of human rights law tends to present itself as technical, as a matter of correct application of the rules for the situation in question. This is only partly true. Judgments are also the result of the application of political preferences by judges. What is meant by political is that when a proportionality test is conducted the courts' decisions are made through a mechanism very similar to the one used by politicians. The outcome of such a test depends on personal views as to what the good life is, of how society should function.[68] This process is bound to lead to differences as to what is the 'common-sense' answer to a particular question. Generally speaking, in a democracy it is elected representatives who are tasked with resolving diverging views on how to achieve a good society. According to the media hostile to the ECHR, the ones to make this kind of judgments should be British.[69] This disagreement is then more about who decides what 'common sense' is than how it is decided.[70]

Conclusion: Limiting the rule of experts

This chapter has looked at some of the structural reasons why the legal discourse of the ECtHR often moves away from a common sense understanding as to what human rights violations are. Media outlets hostile to the ECHR are quick to point out apparently absurd decisions which insufficiently take into account the overall context of the case or fail to provide convincing reasons as to why there was a breach of human rights. The language of human rights law has transformed finding of a violation of the ECHR into an exercise which is quite different from the one the tabloids' conduct, which tends to be based on a minimalist version of human rights. Of course, there are many biases within the media as well. They are, for instance, much more prompt to recognise human rights violations abroad than those in the UK[71] or need to feel a sufficient emotional proximity to the victim to side with them. But that does not explain away the gap in perception between the two. The differences between the premises behind the operation of the human rights law according to 'common sense' or according to lawyers are so important that it is unavoidable that the role of Strasbourg-led interpretation of the ECHR in the UK constitution continues to be challenged.

Nevertheless, there are ways to close the gap between the two perspectives without needing to leave the ECHR. This can be done by both member states and the ECtHR. On the states' side, they need to claim their full role in the

67 See for instance Anne Lise Kjær, Lene Palsbro 'National identity and law in the context of European integration: the case of Denmark' (2008) 19 *Discourse and Society* 599–627.

68 Duncan Kennedy *A Critique of Adjudication (Fin de Siècle)* (Harvard University Press 1997) 58.

69 Of course some of the decisions that have been attacked were made by British judges without following direct guidelines from Strasbourg, but the argument still stands.

70 Koskenniemi (n.13).

71 Gies (n. 3).

operation of the ECHR by developing their domestic interpretations of rights within the language of the ECHR. As was discussed in the first part of this chapter, decisions dealing with the potential breach of Article 8 protecting the right to private and family life are mainly about setting the boundary for the application of a proportionality test. With the Immigration Act 2014,[72] the UK government has understood that well, providing domestic judges with clear guidance as to how the test should operate. This is one avenue for states to fully use the margin of appreciation granted by the ECtHR to balance the interests of different parties.[73] This could limit judge-made policy in domestically sensitive areas.[74]

Another way to bridge the gap is for the Strasbourg court to be more careful when selecting the cases they use to evolve case law. It would have been easy for the ECtHR to dismiss the application made by Mr Hirst as manifestly ill founded, leaving only applicants who have been detained for short periods of time as the battleground for discussing prisoner's voting rights. The Strasbourg court should be more politically savvy; it should know that the implementation and respect of its decisions is not something that can be taken for granted. It should be better at taking a pragmatic view of how legitimacy impacts its efficacy, in particular in a time where many states have continuously failed to implement decisions.[75] Finally, the court also needs to define the limits of its judicial creativity if it wants to continue to keep its role as the provider of a concrete level of human rights protection in Europe, and continue to expand it without endangering the system itself.[76] The debate which arose between Sir Gerald Fitzmaurice and the other judges of the ECtHR in the 1970s about the interpretative role of the court has not been definitively settled.[77] What was acceptable in the 1980s or 1990s, an era of further European integration and of the intellectual supremacy of the liberal model (at least in the West), seems to have changed in the new millennium. The June 2016 UK vote to leave the European Union is a clear example of a growing popular rejection of the liberal discourse of European integration through legal institutions. Because of the issues highlighted here, and the more general

72 Immigration Act 2014, s 19.

73 Dean Spielman 'Allowing the Right Margin. The European Court of Human Rights and the National Margin of Appreciation Doctrine: Waiver or Subsidiarity of European Review?' (2012) *Cambridge Yearbook of European Legal Studies* 381.

74 This idea of a wider margin has been actively pursued by the British government at the time of the presidency of the Council of Europe in 2012. See 'High Level Conference on the Future of the European Court of Human Rights' *Brighton Declaration* (20 April 2012) available at <www.echr.coe.int/Documents/2012_Brighton_FinalDeclaration_ENG.pdf> accessed 26 September 2016.

75 Parliamentary Assembly of the Council of Europe, Committee on Legal Affairs and Human Rights *Implementation of judgments of the European Court of Human Rights* (9 September 2015) Report Doc. 13864

76 For an example of scholarship geared towards setting boundaries, even if they are vague see Brenda Hale 'Common law and Convention law: the limits to interpretation' (2011) *European Human Rights Law Review* 234

77 See Bates (n.14) 319.

problems with the human rights discourse,[78] the debate about what human rights are is much wider than the legal realm; it must go beyond lawyers. At the same time one must deal with the tension between limiting the potential excesses of expert rule whilst continuing to allow for an external control on national governments' behaviours that restrict human rights.

78 Martti Koskenniemi 'The Effect of Rights on Political Culture' from P Alston (ed.) *The European Union and Human Rights* (Oxford University Press 1999) 99.

Chapter 11

'Why should criminals have human rights?'

The underserving rights holder and the case against the Human Rights Act

Frederick Cowell

Introduction

Since the abolition of the death penalty in England and Wales the sentence for murder has been a mandatory life tariff. The precise length of imprisonment prior to parole on this tariff is determined by the trial judge in a murder case, and in very rare cases (there are about 31 at the time of writing) they may issue a 'whole life order', meaning that the convicted individual dies in prison. The judgment of the European Court of Human Rights in Strasbourg (ECtHR) in *Vinter and Others v the United Kingdom* held that life imprisonment without the possibility of parole was perfectly legitimate under the European Convention on Human Rights (ECHR), but, in the absence of a review mechanism, it would not be compatible with Article 3 (the prevention of inhuman and degrading treatment).[1] There was a horrified reaction to this ruling from MPs opposed to the Human Rights Act (HRA) and right-wing newspapers where it was denounced for allowing "dozens of killers [to] launch bids for freedom".[2] *The Daily Telegraph* journalist Alison Pearson, commenting on the judgment, posed the rhetorical question "what about the rights of those they murdered" before detailing the story of one of the victims of the applicants in *Vinter* who "unfortunately . . . is unable to appeal to the ECHR because . . . her human rights were extinguished forever".[3] Contrary to what Pearson maintained, at no point in the ECtHR's judgment were the Court 'favouring' the human rights of those who "abuse humanity" nor were they doubting that the applicants would serve very long prison sentences,

1 *Vinter and Others v the United Kingdom* App no. 66069/09 (ECHR 9 July 2013).
2 For a summary see 'MPs blast Strasbourg ruling on whole-life terms' *The Week* (9 July 2013) available at <www.theweek.co.uk/europe/54031/mps-blast-strasbourg-ruling-life-terms> accessed 26 September 2016.
3 Alison Pearson 'Human rights prisoners: what about the rights of those they murdered?' *The Daily Telegraph* (10 July 2013) available at <www.telegraph.co.uk/news/uknews/crime/10171557/Human-rights-prisoners-what-about-the-rights-of-those-they-murdered.html> accessed 26 September 2016.

with most of them dying in prison.[4] What appeared to provoke such hostility was the idea that individuals such as the applicants in *Vinter* could use the HRA. The backlash against *Vinter* was part of a wider trend within criticism of the HRA motivated by the notion that undeserving individuals can utilise the HRA to the detriment of deserving individuals in the rest of society. The Equality and Human Rights Commission's report on the HRA's first ten years noted that surveys on perceptions of the HRA showed there was "mistrust" from the respondents and a widespread view that "the HRA is implemented to benefit what they perceive as undesirable or undeserving groups".[5]

Previous chapters in this book, such as Siobhán Lloyd's exploration of deportation and Laura Lammasniemi's examination of how welfare claimants have used the HRA to protect their rights, have touched on the problem of the undeserving rights holder. 'Undeserving' can mean a variety of different things, but this chapter focuses on the basic conundrum of why those who harm society, by committing a crime or are otherwise deemed to be a risk to society, should have the same rights as the rest of society. As Lord Dyson noted in a 2011 speech concerns about the HRA were "not confined to decisions in relation to crime, terrorism and immigration", there was a wider sense that the Act had led to a litigation culture which was to the "detriment of the interests of the wider community".[6] It is this sense that certain undeserving individuals ought not to use human rights law because it is detrimental to the wider interests of society that this chapter examines. As the first section notes, the undeserving rights holder has its equivalents in other jurisdictions, and whilst often discussed in relation to the media portrayal of the HRA it is not solely caused by media misreporting. Rather an important, and often neglected, element of the concept of undeserving rights holders is how the HRA resolves the question of who ought to possess human rights in the first place. The EHCR, as the second section identifies, never provided a definitive grounding of rights that could implicitly answer the question of why all individuals ought to possess rights. From a strict blackletter law perspective, it is not important that this question is settled, merely that the individuals that possess rights are identified. However, as the third section argues, the HRA creates rights holders effectively by legal fiat. Absent a broader social construction, human rights holders are effectively identified through technical legal arguments, such as resolving jurisdictional questions, which provide an insufficient grounding of rights when there are strong political pressures to remove rights from groups of people deemed undeserving of rights due to their conduct. The final

4 Ibid.

5 Alice Donald, Jenny Watson and Niamh McClean *Human Rights in Britain since the Human Rights Act 1998: A Critical Review* (Equality and Human Rights Commission, Research Report 28 2009) xvii.

6 Lord Dyson 'What is wrong with human rights?' Speech to Hertfordshire University (3 November 2011) available at <www.supremecourt.uk/docs/speech_111103.pdf> accessed 26 September 2016.

section argues that as instruments which create rights holders by fiat become more unpopular it is much harder to justify rights protection for individuals considered undeserving.

(1) Explanations of the undeserving rights holder under the HRA

It is important to note that the issue of the undeserving rights holder is mirrored in other jurisdictions. Trinidad and Tobago withdrew from the jurisdiction of the Inter-American Court of Human Rights in 1998 after the court upheld an earlier decision of the Privy Council that keeping individuals on death row for prolonged periods amounted to inhuman and degrading treatment.[7] In defiance of the court order the government commenced executions and even though there is serious concern about the legitimacy of the practice the death penalty remains law.[8] Support for the death penalty is framed in the media and popular discourse in terms of reducing crime and punishing unidentified rights-less criminals and international human rights courts perceived as interfering with this process.[9] Similar trends can be seen in other countries' domestic law. Judgments by the US Supreme Court which have provided protection for individuals in police custody or protected the rights of those accused of crimes have often been framed as 'giving rights' to criminals at the expense of the wider community. *Miranda v Arizona* clarified the rights of suspects regarding confessions and put an obligation on law enforcement to ensure that confessions were not coerced.[10] The decision was described by Justice O'Connor as "a carefully crafted balance designed to fully protect both the defendant's and society's interests".[11] William Rehnquist, who was later to become chief justice of the Supreme Court, in a memo to John Dean, the deputy attorney general in the Nixon administration, described the decision as having "tilted the scales of justice too far in favour of criminal suspects" and went on to imply that it would impede the conviction

7 For background see Joanna Harrington 'The Challenge to the Mandatory Death Penalty in the Commonwealth Caribbean' (2004) 98 *American Journal of International Law* 126.

8 Roger Hood and Florence Seemungal 'Experiences and Perceptions of The Mandatory Death Sentence For Murder In Trinidad And Tobago: Judges, Prosecutors And Counsel' from Hood et al. (eds.) *A Penalty without Legitimacy: The Mandatory Death Penalty in Trinidad and Tobago Papers Prepared for a Conference held in Port of Spain* (7 March 2009) available at <www.deathpenaltyproject.org/assets/7/original/09.08.10_Trinidad_Publication.pdf?1259080068> accessed 12 October 2016.

9 See Lizzie Seal et al. 'Themes from Trinidad and Tobago' (Caribbean Death Penalty Research 2015) available at <https://caribbeandeathpenaltyresearch.wordpress.com/themes-from-barbados/> accessed 12 October 2016.

10 *Miranda v Arizona* [1966] 384 U.S. 436.

11 *Moran v Burbine* [1986] 475 U.S. 412 [469].

of the "guilty".[12] Although the context is very different in the US, as the role of constitutional jurisprudence and the political role of the judiciary bear little resemblance to the situation in the UK, this is in essence the debate about the deserving and undeserving rights holder. The Rehnquist position does not deny necessity of the right against self-incrimination but articulates the concern that undeserving individuals ("Criminals", "the Guilty") utilise rights in a manner that would be detrimental to the rest of society. This view, Russell Covey argues, has been reinforced by the presence of *Miranda* in popular television shows and action films as an impediment to justice and empowering rights for criminals, which, in turn, has shaped politics and the popular understanding of the law.[13] The general perception that there can be an 'undeserving' rights holder can then be framed as a problem for the lawmakers to fix by presumably removing rights from such a person.

Empirical research on attitudes to the HRA in the UK reveals that the public seem to support the notion that undeserving rights holders exist. In one piece of research where a series of statements about rights and rights holders were put to the public the vast majority of people agreed that the prohibition against torture was important but this number dropped when the question was whether suspected terrorists should be tortured.[14] Research carried out by Amnesty International in 2014 identified that over a quarter of Britons were prepared to countenance torture in some situations, and in a subsequent press conference Amnesty drew an explicit connection between this and a willingness to see the prohibition on torture weakened for terrorist suspects.[15] Outside of the often controversial topic of terrorism, research cited by the Equality and Human Rights Commission showed that a majority of people believed in the existence of undeserving rights holders, with more than half the public saying that the HRA was used by people "when they're trying to get something they're not entitled to".[16]

The role of public perception is important as reporting in the media and popular culture shapes the notion of the undeserving rights holder. The Equality and Human Rights Commission's report notes that there is a culture of reporting

12 Opp Cite Yale Kamisar 'On the Fortieth Anniversary of the Miranda Case: Why We Needed It, How We Got It-And What Happened to It' (2007) 2 *Ohio State Journal of Criminal Law* 163, 197.

13 Russell Covey 'Miranda and the Media: Tracing the Cultural Evolution of a Constitutional Revolution' (2007) 10 *Chapman Law Review* 761.

14 William Jordan 'Scepticism about human rights as well as the ECHR' *YouGov* (20 July 2014) available at <https://yougov.co.uk/news/2014/07/20/scepticism-about-human-rights-well-echr/> accessed 12 October 2016.

15 Amnesty International 'Stop Global Torture Survey: Attitudes to Torture' *Amnesty International* (2014) available at <www.law.ox.ac.uk/sites/files/oxlaw/oscola_4th_edn_hart_2012quickreferenceguide.pdf> accessed 12 October 2016. For details of media coverage see BBC UK 'Amnesty poll finds 29% say torture can be justified' *BBC News* (13 May 2014) available at <www.bbc.co.uk/news/uk-27387040> accessed 12 October 2016.

16 Donald (n.5) 174.

around the HRA which has contributed to "popular mistrust and misperceptions about human rights".[17] Adam Wagner, in a trenchant critique of the coverage of human rights in the media, argued that whilst "misreporting is not entirely responsible for public antipathy towards human rights" it has potentially "caused irreparable damage to human rights protections in the UK".[18] The link between the Act's supposed failure and undeserving rights claimants is sometimes explicitly drawn; in 2012 the *Daily Mail* warned that because "criminals and parasites" were using it 75% of the public had lost trust in the HRA.[19] Later in 2012 the Commission on a Bill of Rights produced a wide range of evidence indicating a more mixed picture of support and hostility towards the Act across the UK that varied considerably according to regions.[20] Media misreporting is not just limited to the HRA; the debate about 'compensation culture' in the UK has often focused on dubious press reports about frivolous lawsuits and statistics about the amount of compensation awarded in personal injury claims, which have given a distorted picture of the law of negligence.[21] The level of misinformation about the HRA has encouraged the growth of projects, such as Rights Info (which was founded by Wagner) to try to provide accurate information about the HRA.[22] Yet, as useful as these measures are in terms of improving public understanding of the law, focusing on this as principally a knowledge deficit ignores the wider issue, discussed in the third section of this chapter of why, beyond statements of legislative fiat, there are few justifications presented in human rights law about why individuals perceived as undeserving ought to possess human rights.

The perception, as Steve Foster puts it, that the HRA has "become a 'rogues' charter' – being employed by the 'undeserving' who should only enjoy their rights subject to them exercising their responsibilities, towards society and others" has also received some tacit level of official endorsement.[23] The 2009 white paper *Rights and Responsibilities* did not call for the repeal of the HRA but proposed the creation of a complementary 'Bill of Rights and Responsibilities' which could

17 Ibid. xviii.

18 Adam Wagner 'The Monstering of the Human Rights Act' *Keynote Address Human Rights in the UK Media: Representation and Reality* University of Liverpool 18–19 September 2014 available at <https://ukhumanrightsblog.com/2014/09/22/the-monstering-of-human-rights> accessed 12 October 2016.

19 Jack Doyle 'Human rights laws are a charter for criminals, say 75% of Britons' *Daily Mail* (London 16 April 2012).

20 Commission on a Bill of Rights *A UK Bill of Rights? The Choice Before Us* vol. 1 (December 2012) available at <http://webarchive.nationalarchives.gov.uk/20130128112038/http:/www.justice.gov.uk/downloads/about/cbr/uk-bill-rights-vol-1.pdf> accessed 12 October 2016.

21 Annette Morris 'Spiralling or Stabilising? The Compensation Culture and Our Propensity to Claim Damages for Personal Injury' (2007) 70 *Modern Law Review* 349.

22 See *Rights Info* <http://rightsinfo.org/> accessed 12 October 2016.

23 Steve Foster 'Repealing the Human Rights Act – no not delay, just don't do it' (2015) 20 *Coventry Law Journal* 9, 10.

"highlight the importance of factors such as the applicant's own behaviour and the importance of public safety and security" in the protection of human rights.[24] Whilst the white paper was careful not to call for legally enforceable duties that would limit rights for individuals perceived to be undeserving, it nonetheless attempted to highlight the concept of reciprocity and responsibility as something that was lacking from the HRA. When the Conservative Party published its proposals for repealing the HRA and replacing it with a British Bill of Rights in 2014 it contained two indirect references to the undeserving rights holder. First, the new bill of rights would "reflect a proper balance between rights and responsibilities", noting that this was intended to protect the "mainstream understanding" of human rights, the implication being that non-mainstream understandings of rights would include extending rights protections to undeserving individuals.[25] Second, and perhaps more directly, the proposals referred to limiting "the use of human rights laws to the most serious cases".[26] As Mark Elliot noted in response to the publication of the proposals references "to what criteria seriousness and its observe, triviality" were lacking.[27] As Lord Stewart Wood argued more directly, the implication of this proposed provision was clearly "that the state [should] distinguish between deserving and undeserving bearers of human rights".[28]

Many of the arguments about the existence of undeserving rights holders often identify the category of undeserving individual – convicted criminals, welfare claimants and asylum seekers being common targets for the underserving tag – and assume from that it follows that certain individuals ought not to use the HRA.[29] This is, however, part of a wider lacunae in debates about the HRA; there is little consideration of who *ought* to have rights and why individuals can be considered rights holders. Instead, arguments on these questions are conducted by proxy in technical legal debates about the operation of the HRA. Some critics have highlighted the use of the HRA in cases against the UK military in relation

24 Ministry of Justice 'Rights and Responsibilities: developing our constitutional framework' Cm 7577 (March 2009) para. 2.25.

25 Conservative Party 'Protecting Human Rights in the UK: The Conservatives Proposals for Changing Britain's Human Rights Laws' (2014) available at <file:///C:/Users/ubf-cow01/Downloads/HUMAN_RIGHTS%20(3).pdf> accessed 12 October 2016, p. 5.

26 Ibid. 6.

27 Mark Elliot 'My analysis of the Conservative Party's proposals for a British Bill of Rights' *Public Law for Everyone* (3 October 2014), available at <https://publiclawforeveryone.com/2014/10/03/my-analysis-of-the-conservative-partys-proposals-for-a-british-bill-of-rights/> accessed 12 October 2016.

28 Stewart Wood 'Conservatives attacking the Human Rights Act have forgotten their party's tradition of defending liberty' *The Telegraph* (30 May 2015) available at <www.telegraph.co.uk/news/worldnews/europe/11639548/Conservatives-attacking-the-Human-Rights-Act-have-forgotten-their-partys-tradition-of-defending-liberty.html> accessed 12 October 2016.

29 This is discussed in earlier chapters of this book see Gearty (ch. 7); Lloyd (ch. 8) and Lammasniemi (ch. 9).

to operations in Iraq and Afghanistan as an example of the Act being used for purposes and being applied to people for which it was not intended.[30] A report from the Policy Exchange think tank criticised what they perceived as the "judicialisation of war" and the judiciary for expanding the jurisdictional scope of the ECHR but did not mention the rights of the claimants, focusing instead on the question of jurisdiction and the appropriate legal regime for combat operations.[31] The question of who should have rights was simply not a component of its criticism of the HRA because the jurisdictional issue was the only relevant matter to resolve in deciding whether the HRA could protect an individual's rights. The failure to establish a coherent answer to the question of who is entitled to rights means that when it is raised the rights holder is established in the negative – by identifying particular categories of individual that ought not to have rights.

(2) Identifying the rights holder under the ECHR

Without the right to have rights, Hannah Arendt famously argued, the "rights of man supposedly inalienable proved to be unenforceable".[32] Arendt's argument was aimed against the transcendental construction of rights that were "supposed to be independent of citizenship and nationality" which Arendt argued, had been shown by the rise of fascism in 1930s Europe to be weak declarations.[33] Recent scholarship on the concept of the right to have rights has focused on considering this in the context of the removal of rights and remedies from individuals.[34] In analysing the way rights holders are identified by a human rights instrument it is important to refer to the distinction that Seyla Benhabib outlines between juridical universalism, the statement that a law should be universally applied, and justificatory universalism, which seeks a conceptual justification for the juridical application of rights as universal.[35] The tendency to seek metaphysical foundations for rights and hence a transcendent justification for the universality of rights under an international human rights instrument are means of creating some form of justificatory universality for such an instrument. States can justify being bound by an international agreement which legally constrains them if it represents a set of commonly agreed-on higher principles about the importance of rights and the individuals who possess them. Unlike the ephemeral nature of the rights of man

30 For examples see *Serdar Mohammed v Ministry of Defence* [2014] EWHC 1369 (QB); *Smith v Ministry of Defence* [2013] UKSC 41.
31 Richard Ekins, Jonathan Morgan and Tom Tugendhat *Clearing the Fog of Law: Saving our Armed Forces from Defeat by Judicial Diktat* (Policy Exchange 2005) 20.
32 Hannah Arendt *The Origins of Totalitarianism* (Harcourt Books 1976) 293.
33 Ibid.
34 See Eva Ersbøll 'The right to a Nationality and the European Convention on Human Rights' from Stéphanie Lagoutte, Hans-Otto Sano and Peter Scharff Smith (eds.) *Human Rights in Turmoil: Facing Threats Consolidating Achievements* (Brill 2007).
35 Seyla Benhabib *Dignity in Adversity Human Rights in Troubled Times* (Polity 2011) 11.

Arendt critiqued, international human rights treaties have legal force. However, the existence of a legal obligation to provide rights does not automatically resolve the question of why people ought to have rights and who has rights, hence the need to ground them in some form justificatory universalism, which implicitly answers these questions.

The HRA does not specify who the holders of human rights are or seek to engineer some form of transcendental foundation to the rights it protects as it is an instrument for incorporating the ECHR into UK law and therefore implicitly relies on the justificatory framework of the ECHR. The ECHR, however, does not really concern itself with a justificatory universalism beyond a reference in the preamble to a "profound belief in those fundamental freedoms which are the foundation of justice and peace in the world".[36] The preamble then infers the existence of rights holders in instrumental terms, stating that values such as "justice" and "peace" are necessary for "democracy" and as a consequence are best protected by a "common understanding and the observance of human rights". This, Marie Dembour argues, allows one to be "nihilist" about human rights which involves seeing them not as representative of any clearly identifiable principle or purpose but, instead, as useful instruments for achieving particular outcomes.[37] The circumstances of the ECHR's drafting do point towards a highly instrumentalised version of human rights and rights holders. Speaking in May 1948 at the Conference of the Movement for European Unity Winston Churchill said that "the idea of a Charter of Human Rights" was at the centre of the movement which drew "its strength from our common spiritual values."[38] The nature and content of these shared "spiritual values" appeared less important than what and who they were projected against – the message to Europeans released at the end of the conference warned of divisions on the continent alluding to communist-controlled Eastern Europe.[39] When the European Movement published a pamphlet on the creation of a Charter of Human Rights in July 1949 it made a number of references to protecting democracy from an outside threat. Later in the summer of 1949 the British delegate to the Consultative Assembly of the Council of Europe, Lord MacNally, warned that any human rights instrument developed by the Council of Europe must be capable of resisting "attempts to undermine our democratic way of life from within or without" and that such an instrument would have to "give Western Europe as a whole greater political stability".[40]

Therefore, 'nihilism' of the sort Dembour describes is an appropriate way to view the ECHR's justificatory universalism as it was designed as an instrument

36 European Convention on Human Rights, 1950 Preamble.

37 Marie-Bénédicte Dembour *Who Believes in Human Rights: Reflections on the European Convention on Human Rights* (CUP 2006) 12.

38 Opp cite. Ed Bates *The Evolution of the European Convention on Human Rights* (OUP 2010) 47.

39 The European Movement and the Council of Europe (Hutchinson & Co. 1949) 37.

40 Collected Edition of the "Travaux Preparatoires of the European Convention on Human Rights" vol. I 'Preparatory commission of the Council of Europe committee of Ministers Consultative Assembly 11 May – 8 September 1949' (The Hague, 1975) 30.

to protect states against a return of fascism or communist takeover rather than grounded in a broader philosophical project. It is possible to trace alternate definitions for ECHR's justificatory universalism in jurisprudence on the question of why certain individuals should be protected by the ECHR. In *Limbuela* Lady Hale described the prohibition on torture and the right to life in the ECHR as being "fundamental values of a decent society, which respects the dignity of each individual human being".[41] This formulation roots the rights contained in the ECHR within an overarching transcendental conception of human dignity, and significantly Lady Hale went onto say that this dignity belonged to individuals "no matter how unpopular or unworthy she may be".[42] Jurisprudence from the ECtHR also shows a similar trend with references to dignity being described as the "very essence" of the ECHR.[43] This, however, is not derived from the text of the ECHR which, as Christopher McCrudden notes, is unusual amongst international human rights instruments in that it contains no references to human dignity.[44] There is in fact some basis for thinking that the concept of dignity is a much later judicial construction that has relatively little to do with the foundation of the ECHR.[45] In the ECHR's Travaux Préparatoires the majority of discussions at the different meetings of the Council of Europe in the summer and autumn of 1949 concerned the protection of European democracy and the importance of democratic values, with scant consideration of the possible philosophical justifications for individuals possessing human rights.

Yet, if the politics of the Convention's founding implicitly answer the question of *why* people should have human rights (albeit in somewhat instrumental terms) there is still the question of *which* people should have their rights protected under the Convention. This is addressed in part by Article 1 of the Convention which requires state parties to secure Convention rights to everyone within their jurisdiction making rights holding contingent on an individual's geographic location at the time of the alleged abuse.[46] In *Banković v Belgium* the Grand Chamber of the ECtHR held that Article 1 protected "all persons in the territories of the signatory States, even those who could not be considered as residing there in

41 *R (Limbuela) v Secretary of State for the Home Department* [2005] UKHL 66 [76].

42 Ibid.

43 For examples see *Christine Godwin v the United Kingdom* Application no. 28957/95 (ECHR 11 July 2002) [90]; *Pretty v United Kingdom* Application no. 2346/02 (ECHR 29 July 2002) [65].

44 Christopher McCrudden 'Human Dignity and Judicial Interpretation of Human Rights' (2008) 19 *European Journal of International Law* 655.

45 See Antoine Buyse 'Dignified Law: The Role of Human Dignity in European Convention Case-Law' Keynote Lecture at Utrecht University (11 October 2016) available at <http://echrblog.blogspot.co.uk/2016/10/the-role-of-human-dignity-in-echr-case.html> accessed 12 October 2016.

46 Lucius Caflisch 'The Iraqi Cases: Further Elements and Thoughts concerning 'Jurisdiction' under Article 1 of the European Convention on Human Rights' from Rüdiger Wolfrum, Maja Seršić and Trpimir Šošić (eds.) *Contemporary Developments in International Law Essays in Honour of Budislav Vukas* (Brill Publishing 2015).

the legal sense of the word".[47] Article 1 is also capable of granting protection to individuals where they were under arrest by agents of a state party to the ECHR in another jurisdiction.[48] In *Al-Skeini v the United Kingdom*, a case arising from the British occupation of Iraq, the ECtHR held that where "the State through its agents exercises control and authority over an individual" they were under an obligation to secure for that individual "the rights and freedoms . . . relevant to their situation".[49] What is significant about *Al-Skeini*, as Pauline Collins notes, is that in the cases where Article 1 comes into effect because state agents are involved rather than the state having "effective control over an area".[50] Yet, in spite of this distinction, it is clear that rights in the case of an individual being under the power of state agents are being granted to them as a necessity due to their connection with public institutions.[51] In other judgments the ECtHR has blurred the distinction between the geographic and the personal in terms of exercise of jurisdiction under Article 1.[52]

This means that the justificatory universality of rights holders is tied up within the exercise of administrative power by state parties. Little is said about the importance of human rights for the subject, instead the claimants in both *Jaloud* and *Al-Skeini*, became rights holders because of what was being done to them and who was doing it, not because of who they were or some other philosophical justification. This can be contrasted with the reasoning involving the interpretation of Article 3 in deportation cases which take a more teleological approach to the justificatory universality of rights holders. Since *Soering v the United Kingdom* the ECtHR has held that Article 3 obligations prohibited individuals being extradited to face the death penalty because it constituted a form of inhuman and degrading treatment, although this did not apply to cases where an individual might die from other causes were they to be deported.[53] The reasoning for this was that even though the UK authorities did not have any "power over the practices and arrangements" of another country the extradition would result "by reason of its foreseeable consequences" in a violation of an individual's Article 3 rights.[54] In *Othman* this was extended beyond the practice of torture to prevent the deportation of an individual to a country where they would be subject to a trial which would use evidence gained from torturing a third party.[55] The judgment held that

47 *Banković and others v Belgium and Others* No. 52207/99, GC, decision 2001, paras. 19 and 20.
48 *Öcalan v. Turkey* no. 46221/99, Grand Chamber ECHR 2005-IV.
49 *Al-Skeini v the United Kingdom* [2011] 53 EHRR 18 [137].
50 Pauline Collins 'Case Commentary: Al-Skeini v the United Kingdom' (2012) 16 *Australian International Law* 267, 275.
51 See Lea Rabile 'The extraterritoriality of the ECHR: Why Jaloud and Pisari should be read as game changers' (2016) 2 *European Human Rights Law Review* 161, 167.
52 See *Jaloud v Netherlands* (47708/08) [2015] 60 EHRR 29.
53 *Soering v the United Kingdom* no. 14038/88 (ECHR 1989).
54 Ibid. [90].
55 *Othman (Abu Qatada) v. the United Kingdom* Application no. 8139/09 (ECHR 2012).

"no legal system based upon the rule of law can countenance the admission of evidence" gained from torture and referred to other international instruments, and the status of the prohibition of torture as a peremptory norm of international law, concluding that there was a duty on states to "eradicate torture and remove all incentive for its practice".[56] These cases justified the creation of rights holders on broadly teleological grounds, couching them in terms of the universal eradication of undesirable practices or in terms of the maintenance of a broader notion of the international rule of law.

In summary, the ECHR and subsequent ECtHR caselaw do not contain much by way of a justificatory foundation explaining who should be a rights holder or why they should have rights. The origins of the ECHR in the late 1940s as an anti-totalitarian instrument essentially fused the questions of who *should* and who *does* have rights, by implying that human rights were enjoyed by citizens living in non-totalitarian Western European states.[57] Britain, however, was a largely stable constitutional democracy that had not experienced fascist or communist rule, and therefore, the tendency was for the British government to see the ECHR as a foreign policy tool and relatively scant attention was paid to how the ECHR could be used domestically. As Dominic Grieve notes, at the time of the accepting the jurisdiction of the Strasbourg court in the 1960s the official advice from the UK Foreign Office was to caution against accepting its jurisdiction out of fear that "communists, crooks and cranks of every type [would] bring actions" against the British government.[58] The idea of the undeserving rights holder was therefore present from a very early stage in discussions about the ECHR's role in the UK, and there is little evidence that at the time of the HRA's drafting there was a meaningful attempt to provide any additional grounding to the existence of rights holders beyond that found in the ECHR.

(3) The construction of a rights holder by legislative fiat under the HRA

To understand why the omission of justificatory basis for rights holders in the ECHR becomes a problem for the HRA it is important to examine its construction through the lens of social construction theories of human rights. This contextualises the rather contingent nature of the anti-totalitarian argument outlined in the preceding section and helps explain how the HRA became reliant on a very legalistic notion of rights holders. Benjamin Gregg argues that human rights cannot be understood as a theological or metaphysical construction because there exists no definitive "universal embrace of human rights" across cultures

56 Ibid/ [266] and [264].

57 Bates (n.38) 46–49.

58 Dominic Grieve QC 'Can a Bill of Rights do better than the Human Rights Act?' (2016) *Public Law* 223, 224.

and there are grounds for believing that "social constructionism" better allows for the moral agency of individual rights bearers".[59] To understand the basis of this argument it is important to distinguish between cross-cultural universality and a cross-cultural consensus on rights protection. As An-Na'im notes it is possible to observe a cross-cultural recognition of different forms of human dignity; for example, the belief that inhuman and degrading treatment and torture are morally wrong is present across many different communities.[60] An-Na'im concludes that this can indicate the existence of a cross-cultural consensus on the prohibition of torture. This does not, however, mean that there is a universal cross-cultural acceptance of what human rights are or who should hold human rights. Instead, it indicates that in the specific case of the prohibition of torture there can be near-universal agreement that the practice is wrong but gives little ground to believe that beyond that there is a universal consensus about rights holders. The other problem with seeking a metaphysical or theological basis for the question of who should be a rights holder is that this is invariably premised on the question of agency. Theological and metaphysical conceptions of rights, Gregg argues, struggle to protect minorities "from [human rights] violations in communities that have not accepted them" because it is possible under both a theological and a metaphysical foundational argument to hold that individuals ought to be rights-less because of their agential status.[61] James Griffin makes a similar point noting it is possible that "a person can be denied religious freedom, even be cruelly persecuted, without ceasing to be an agent".[62]

Therefore, Gregg argues it is necessary to construct a non-agential conception of human rights. This can be done in three ways: First, it can be done by fiat which is to simply state that everyone has rights, in a manner not entirely dissimilar to the text of the ECHR. Second, rights can be used as a moral language to articulate and define social goods. Third, rights can be used to create the conditions for allowing communities, and, in particular, the marginalised in communities, to shape their society following what Gregg describes as the social constructivist approach where people "have human rights, if as a group or community, they collectively choose to embrace them".[63] Gregg sees the latter two non-agential constructions as interrelated although there may be grounds for seeing them as distinct. Taking Dembour's typology outlined in her article "*What Are Human Rights?*" discourse scholars, who believe that human rights exist "only because people talk about them", would be inclined to believe that the second part of

59 Benjamin Gregg *Human Rights as Social Construction* (CUP 2012) 17.

60 Abdullahi An-Na'im 'Towards a Cross Cultural Approach to Defining International Standards of Human Rights: The Meaning of Cruel Inhuman or Degrading Treatment or Punishment' from An-Na'im (ed.) *Human Rights in Cross Cultural Perspectives: A Quest for Consensus* (University of Pennsylvania Press 1992).

61 Gregg (n.59) 30.

62 James Griffin *On Human Rights* (OUP 2008) 46.

63 Gregg (n.59) 33.

Gregg's argument is distinct from the third.[64] Whereas deliberative scholars who, Dembour argues, believe that "human rights come into existence through societal agreement", would be inclined to stress the importance of the third part of Gregg's argument.[65] This would require some form of common political project which society as a whole can agree with or buy into as the basis for constructing rights, such as an appeal to universal human dignity or teleological appeals of the sort outlined above in section two of this chapter. Whilst this does not completely eliminate concepts of deserving and undeserving from the political sphere it provides a sufficient ground on which to contest the removal of rights from particular individuals. The first component of Gregg's argument – the idea that human rights can be founded by judicial fiat – should be treated with some scepticism as a grounding for human rights. As Conor Gearty argues, whilst declarations of universality contained in human rights law may look "solid" the foundations of these instruments are built on "flimsy foundations".[66] Gearty's argument is that the claim instruments like the ECHR make about the universal application of rights is important in the context of human rights acting as a form of ethical "commitment gadget" designed to offer some type of normative guidance in the modern world.[67]

The HRA, Klug argues, whilst having its origins in a much broader project defining a set of constitutional rights for the UK, was presented as a "tidying up exercise" to determine the UK's relationship with the ECHR.[68] Klug noted that discussions about the nature of the HRA were subject to a process of "triangulation" by the government, with it being presented as a radical or a technocratic reform depending on the audience. As Benedict Douglas notes this was in part because the HRA did not emerge "in the aftermath of a widespread state disregard for rights . . . no statement of a deeper, more fundamental basis for rights was perceived to be necessary".[69] The overwhelming impression created was that of a largely technocratic instrument for facilitating rights, rather than a bill of constitutional rights creating fundamental freedoms. However, the operation of sections 2 and 3 of the Act changed the way that courts interpreted the relationship between the individual and the state in a manner which resembled a

64 Dembour 'What are Human Rights? Four Schools of Thought' (2010) 32 *Human Rights Quarterly* 1, 3.

65 Ibid. 4.

66 Conor Gearty 'Human rights the necessary quest for foundation' from Costas Douzinas and Gearty (eds.) *The Meaning of Rights: The Philosophy and Social theory of Human rights* (CUP 2014) 25.

67 Ibid. 26.

68 Francesca Klug 'The Human Rights Act: Origins and Intentions' from Nicolas Kang-Riou, Jo Milner and Suryai Nayak (eds.) *Confronting the Human Rights Act: Contemporary Themes and Perspectives* (Routledge 2012) 35.

69 Benedict Douglas 'Why Human Rights Have Not Been Accepted in the UK' *U.K. Constitutional Law Blog* (4 May 2015) available at <http://ukconstitutionallaw.org> accessed 12 October 2016.

constitutional bill of rights because it created what Keith Ewing termed a "new hierarchy of rights".[70] As Martin Loughlin argues the tensions inherent between rights and democracy can be resolved by maintaining that legislatures respect rights "because this is what citizens demand", making the protections that rights offer a representation of political consensus.[71] There was, as the second section of this chapter outlines, a consensus (albeit a thin one) against totalitarianism in the formation of the ECHR's justificatory universality. The HRA, as Loughlin notes, attempted to create what he terms a "pre-commitment strategy" which would limit the scope of decision-making by parliament and the power of the executive in order to protect rights.[72] But there was little sense at the time of the HRA's passage as to why that commitment was necessary or what kind of political consensus it represented. There was also little consideration given to what might happen if the consensus behind a pre-commitment strategy were to change or were to be reoriented around the exclusion of certain individuals from being rights holders. The question of who is protected is thus inexorably related to the issue of who rights holders are, as a pre-commitment strategy of the sort that the HRA attempts depends on the identification and preservation of a series of shared assumptions and values about the importance of rights.

(4) The politics of the 'undeserving': The limits of legislative fiat

The creation of rights holders by legislative fiat in the HRA was intended to create what Kate Nash described as a form of "cosmopolitan citizenship" where all individuals would be recognised as having a form of universal humanity, defined by the rights that they held.[73] In actual fact, Nash argued the way that the HRA was applied created categories of "quasi-citizens" (long-term residents who the state attempts to remove) and "sub-citizens" (asylum seekers) whose rights the HRA had defined or protected, often in opposition to existing policies removing or limiting rights for individuals in these categories.[74] This problem is discussed in a different direction by Etienne Balibar who noted that there was a significant shift from citizenship as being the subjects of a nation, to political citizens of a state, to a 'social citizenship' in the twentieth century.[75] At each stage of the evolution of the concept of citizenship, the individual was gaining more complex rights, culminating in social and economic rights in contemporary iterations of

70 Keith Ewing 'The Unbalanced Constitution' from Tom Campbell, KD Ewing and Adam Tompkins (eds.) *Sceptical Essays on Human Rights* (OUP 2001) 107.
71 Martin Laughlin 'Rights, Democracy and Law' from Campbell et al.
72 Ibid. 46.
73 Kate Nash 'Between Citizenship and Human Rights' (2009) *Sociology* 43 1067.
74 Ibid. 1076–778.
75 Etienne Balibar *Citizenship* (Thomas Scott-Railton Tr. Polity Press 2015).

citizenship, yet at each stage there was still the concept of the excluded or non-citizen. Some, such as Walter Mingnolo, argued that this is true of cosmopolitan forms of citizenship in the Kantian sense, which were predicated on identifying and classifying non-citizens in the processes of colonial imperialism, and then using this as the basis for constructing a form of universalism which could then serve as a basis for identifying rights-holders.[76] Whilst this was true historically the foundations of modern human rights law aim for a much more inclusive conception of rights holder. Yet, as Balibar argues, the extension of the rights of man to every individual does not eliminate the notion of exclusion, but rather, the "line drawn by exclusion" becomes focused on defining the existence of the "abnormal" among citizens using "psychiatric [and] criminological" terminology to essentially generate a closed category of rights holder.[77] What the HRA did was to try to protect individuals from the effect of this political line drawing – but in practice this meant using the HRA to claim that legislation enacted by the government of the day excluded individuals and their entitlement to rights. This leads to the dilemma Douglas outlines; when "unpopular minorities have their rights vindicated the question is asked, "[W]hy are we giving rights to them?"[78] There is no effective answer to this question because, as Douglas concludes, there has been no real attempt to ground the "recognition of the universal and inalienable possession of rights" in the HRA.[79] This echoes the problem originally identified by Arendt, detailed at the start of the second section of this chapter, of how to protect the right to have rights.

The language describing undeserving rights holders explicitly uses the reference frames Balibar describes earlier – contrasting the closed deserving rights holder of the citizen with the undeserving rights holder who uses the HRA to gain entitlements. This was starkly illustrated by the front cover of *The Sun* newspaper on the 27 May 2015 whose headline claimed "European Court Puts Terrorists and Murderers First" and juxtaposed pictures of convicted criminals who had successfully used the HRA with labels such as "Peado Rapist" with pictures of the victims of crime.[80] The individuals pictured who had been convicted of crimes had not become in any legal sense rights-less, but there was nevertheless a sense that they ought not to be able to use the HRA because of their undeserving status. Anti-HRA MPs have continually raised the figure of undeserving rights holder – commenting on the deportation of criminals who were foreign nationals Peter Bone, MP, said that it was "wrong they can claim their human rights were affected when they didn't care about the human rights of the people

76 Walter Mignolo 'Citizenship Knowledge and the Limits of Humanity' (2006) 18 *American Literary History* 312.
77 Balibar (n.75) 80.
78 Douglas (n.69).
79 Ibid.
80 'The Sun Says' *The Sun* (Print Edition) 27 May 2015.

they committed [their] crime against".[81] When proponents of the HRA have attempted to use the foundational argument for rights holders, described earlier by referring to the ECHR's genesis after World War II as a bulwark against totalitarianism, opponents of the HRA have undermined the pre-commitment strategy using the rhetoric of British exceptionalism (described by Colin Murray in Chapter 2 of this book). Chris Grayling, MP, the former justice secretary who had introduced the Conservative's bill of rights proposals, has said that there is no prospect of Britain turning into a "totalitarian nation" as a result of HRA repeal.[82] One anti-HRA journalist argued that British traditions of civil liberties made the HRA redundant and that European states needed the ECHR as it gave "continental Europeans liberties that many of them had never enjoyed".[83]

The lack of a justificatory foundation beyond legislative fiat poses problems when human rights as a concept are increasingly questioned. According to research carried out in 2014 around 58% of people living in the UK thought that people deserved human rights "simply by virtue of their humanity", but this number declined sharply amongst Conservative Party voters and UK Independence Party voters.[84] Cosmopolitan notions of citizenship, upon which notions of universal human rights often depend, have been coming under increasing pressure as governments have become more sceptical of the legal regimes underpinning them. The hostile politics around the UK's referendum to leave the European Union in June 2016 were driven in part by a rejection of the construction of a European citizenship by instruments such as the 2004 EU Citizenship Directive, and a counter-assertion of an exclusive national identity premised in part on the exclusion of others.[85] Further empirical research conducted in 2016 identified a sharp decline in the trust in human rights generally and a rise in what can be described as authoritarian populism in many parts of Europe, a component of

81 Ian Dury 'More than 1,300 foreign criminals, including killers, rapists and paedophiles have used human rights laws to stay in the UK' *Daily Mail* (15 November 2016) available at <www.dailymail.co.uk/news/article-3939970/More-1-300-foreign-criminals-including-killers-rapists-paedophiles-used-human-rights-laws-stay-UK.html> accessed 12 October 2016.

82 Hardeep Matharu "UK will not turn into a totalitarian nation as result of human rights reforms', insists Chris Grayling' *Epsom Guardian* (6 October 2014) available at <www.epsomguardian.co.uk/news/11516919._UK_will_not_turn_into_a_totalitarian_nation_as_result_of_human_rights_reforms___insists_Chris_Grayling> accessed 12 October 2016.

83 Phillip Johnston 'In the land of Magna Carta, individual liberties already exist – Human Rights Act or no' *The Telegraph* (2 June 2015) available at <www.telegraph.co.uk/news/uknews/law-and-order/11644576/In-the-land-of-Magna-Carta-individual-liberties-already-exist-Human-Rights-Act-or-no.html> accessed 12 October 2016.

84 See *YouGov* (n.14).

85 See Eddie Bruce-Jones 'Citizens of Nowhere? Fear, Race, Migration and the Dangers of Formalism' *JuWiss Blog* (16 November 2016) available at <www.juwiss.de/84-2016/> accessed 12 October 2016.

which is a strong distrust of human rights as a concept.[86] Cumulatively this makes appeals to universality as represented by the ECHR, particularly difficult as both supranational legal structures containing rights protections and philosophical ideas of universality are increasingly coming under strain. This leads to the kind of exclusionary identification of rights holders described by Balibar and Arendt which in many ways is the antithesis to the universality generated by international instruments.

Conclusion

The problem of a lack of philosophical grounding for the rights holder and its subsequent compensation by creating rights holders though legal fiat, is a general problem of international human rights law. The ECHR arguably suffers this problem more acutely than other instruments because it fails to appeal to concepts such as dignity, which offer some form of basis for justificatory universality situated in human intuitions. Instead, it utilises a justificatory universalism built on anti-totalitarianism. This is at best historically contingent and in the context of the UK open to other forms of refutation. When justificatory universality is constructed by way of legislative fiat without any necessary underlying social construction of rights it cannot Act as a counterweight to the political dynamics described in the final section of this chapter.

The problem of the undeserving rights holder is in many ways a structural feature of the very notion of rights protection; it is always going to be difficult to justify an individual widely perceived as being harmful to society having access to rights and entitlements from that society. Yet, at the time of the HRA's creation in the late 1990s there was a failure to develop any kind of foundation for rights or develop any kind of rights culture (something discussed in the next chapter of this book), and the presentation of the Act as a technical instrument became a missed opportunity to potentially lay the foundation for the social construction of rights. Given the context described earlier it is unlikely that a British Bill of Rights offers much of a solution. In fact, as noted in the first section of this chapter, a central claim of the Conservative's proposal for a bill of rights is the removal of rights from undeserving rights holders. If anything, arguments about those who do not deserve rights are likely to escalate the more that rights holding is linked to citizenship.

86 Joe Twyman 'Trump, Brexit, Front National, AfD: Branches of the Same Tree' *YouGov* (16 November 2016 available at <https://yougov.co.uk/news/2016/11/16/trump-brexit-front-national-afd-branches-same-tree> accessed 12 October 2016.

Chapter 12

The Human Rights Act and the failure to construct a 'rights culture' in the UK

Trudy Morgan

When the Human Rights Act (HRA) was introduced, its political architects claimed it would in time create "a culture of human rights" in the UK.[1] The Act would introduce fundamental changes in the relations between individuals and public authorities, and it was expected that the relationships between these actors would be construed through the framework of an institutional and ethical meaning of human rights associated with the HRA.[2] Yet the cultural politics of human rights in the UK are today dominated by deep divisions amongst institutional actors, civil society, the public and media over the extent to which human rights values (if any) should shape their interrelationships. The proposal to repeal the HRA, emblematic of a broader 'backlash' against human rights, has its roots in these conflicts.[3] Charles Moore, the former editor of the *Daily Telegraph*, described human rights culture under the HRA as "beginning to look like tyranny".[4] It was not just individual judgments he was critical of but the way those judgments were being used to change the practices of schools and charitable organisations. In numerous pieces of empirical research on the HRA (some of which are discussed in the following) the Act is perceived either in narrow legal terms or as an instrument that empowers underserving rights holders. As discussed by Frederick Cowell and Nicolas Kang-Riou in the previous chapters in this book, the

1 Home Secretary Jack Straw 'Human Rights Bill 3rd Reading' from Cooper and Marshall-Williams (eds.) *Legislating for Human Rights: The Parliamentary Debates on the Human Rights Bill* (OUP, 2000).

2 Francesca Klug *Values for a Godless Age: The Story of the United Kingdom's New Bill of Rights,* (Penguin, 2000).

3 Susan Marks 'Backlash: the undeclared war against human rights' (2014) 4 *European Human Rights Law Review* 319.

4 Charles Moore 'Our human rights culture has now become a tyranny' *The Telegraph* (18 December 2009) available at <www.telegraph.co.uk/comment/columnists/charlesmoore/6840557/Our-human-rights-culture-has-now-become-a-tyranny.html> accessed 4 September 2016.

structure of legal arguments and indeed the structure of the law itself has contributed to the perception that the HRA exists for undeserving claimants and lacks 'common sense'.

Yet the existence of a backlash also suggests that the HRA's aim of bringing about "a culture in which there is a widely shared sense of entitlement to human rights, of personal responsibility and of respect for the rights of others" has not been achieved.[5] The parliamentary Joint Committee on Human Rights noted that growth of a culture of rights protection had been important for the development of legislation on race and sex discrimination introduced in the UK during the 1970s. Whilst legislation was an important spur for change the committee noted that "shifts in public perception about the acceptability of sex and race discrimination have been at least as important in bringing about social and cultural change as the law itself", leading it to conclude that a "culture of human rights" needed to be built on the legal framework of the HRA "to take concepts of human rights beyond the legal sphere and into the currency of everyday life."[6] A culture of rights describes how the law entrenches itself within society, moving rights beyond their narrow legal iteration and into social interactions and entrenching this was a key aim of the HRA. This chapter assesses this cultural aim of the HRA through an analysis of the cultural politics of human rights, focusing on the sectors of public life intended to be transformed by the Act.

The first section of this chapter will set out an approach to understanding and assessing a 'human rights culture', drawing on the work of Pierre Bourdieu and Kate Nash to describe how the concept of the human rights field can be used to analyse the cultural politics of human rights. After discussing the 'institutional' and 'ethical' meanings of human rights the HRA was intended to promote, this section discusses how the success of that aim can be assessed using the concept of the human rights field. The chapter considers research into public perceptions of the HRA and assesses what this tells us about key values in the human rights field and how these both reflect and diverge from the institutional and ethical meaning of human rights associated with the HRA. It then looks at two areas the HRA intended to transform – legal culture and public service delivery – to examine how contests within the human rights field have limited the ability of the institutional meaning of human rights to gain legitimacy, whilst the ethical meaning of human rights has been subsumed into greater contests over who is permitted to have rights.

5 Joint Committee on Human Rights *Thirty Second Report* (2005–6, 140) available at <www.publications.parliament.uk/pa/jt200506/jtselect/jtrights/278/27810.htm> accessed 4 September 2016.

6 Ibid. para. 142.

(1) Building a human rights culture: What did the HRA intend to create, and how can we analyse it?

Nash notes that the concept of a 'human rights culture' articulates the importance of intersubjective understandings of rights to their realisation: to establish human rights they need to be "one of the forms through which people live their lives".[7] In order to analyse whether the HRA realised its cultural aims, we need to assess how the meaning of human rights the HRA intended to create is reflected in cultural politics.[8] Understanding culture as a process where meanings are constantly reworked "places emphasis on language and power, showing how the terms of the discourses are constructed and contested".[9] Thus, the problem to be explained is how certain meanings of rights become authoritative in specific historical circumstances.[10] Pierre Bourdieu's theory of social fields provides a conceptual space for mapping who has the power to construct and contest discourses and the locations in which these contests take place. For Bourdieu "a field is a relatively autonomous domain of activity that responds to rules of functioning and institutions that are specific to it and which define relations among agents".[11] Within this "set of regularised social interactions . . . the *value* of what is at stake is shared".[12] The agents within the field have, to a greater or lesser extent, capital of 'recognition' of their status and power within that field. Changes to the rules which define legitimate activity within the field result in shifts in that capital. Consequently 'struggle' in a field is a process of imposing a definition of legitimate recognition and victory in this process leads to a more or less monopolistic control of the definition of the forms of legitimacy prevailing in the field'.[13] Applying the concept of the field to human rights, Nash identifies four subfields within which different principal actors compete for status: governmental (government, parliament, public authorities), juridical (judiciary), activist (civil society groups) and the mediated public.[14] The courts and the media are

7 Mertus, quoted in Kate Nash *The Cultural Politics of Human Rights: Comparing the US and UK* (CUP 2009).

8 Nash uses the term *cultural politics* to reflect the impact that culture has on human rights but also to distinguish from the bounded concept of culture implied in the term *human rights culture* and to reflect that practices of communicating meaning through symbolisation are inherently political (Ibid. Nash). In this chapter I use the term *human rights culture* to refer to the specific aim of promoting a particular meaning of human rights associated with the HRA.

9 Susan Wright 'Culture in Anthropology and Organisational Studies' from Wright (ed.) *Anthropology of Organisations* (Routledge 1994) 26.

10 Ibid. 21–2.

11 Mathiu Hilgers and Eric Mangez *Bourdieu's Theory of Social Fields: Concepts and Applications* (Routledge 2015).

12 Nash (n.7) 30.

13 Hilgers and Mangez (n.11) 6.

14 Nash (n.7) 40–58.

the prominent sites of contests of meanings between these different actors, but each is active across the subfields.[15] The shared value in the human rights field is not human rights but the authority to decide what they mean. Competing in the human rights field allows the participants to construct authority, understood as "the ability to speak effectively, to define human rights in a way that impact on state formation".[16]

The HRA changed the rules of functioning within the human rights field by changing the balance of power between certain institutional agents (governmental actors and judiciary) and imposing new obligations on governmental actors (public authorities) towards individuals (the public). The 'culture-building' aim of the HRA intended that the prevalent form of legitimacy in the human rights field would reflect a particular meaning of human rights. The change in rules within the field that the Act introduced would be one mechanism by which this particular meaning of human rights could gain legitimacy. The Parliamentary Joint Committee on Human Rights (JCHR) set out the key features of this particular meaning in its sixth report of the 2002–3 session.[17] The JCHR identified two limbs: an 'institutional' meaning, that human rights should shape the goals, structures and practices of public bodies and an 'ethical' meaning, comprising a sense of entitlement to rights accompanied by personal responsibility and social obligation.

The 'institutional' limb closely relates to the concept of positive obligations, which requires states to have reasonable systems in place to prevent breaches of fundamental rights, envisaging proactive rights protection.[18] Realising positive rights (and contingent state obligations) was a key aim of the HRA. McCrudden highlights the revolution in understanding this required: "human rights are primarily about . . . freedom from arbitrary or unjustified *state* action . . . a positive rights interpretation confuses this by smuggling in an approach that relies on the state to *intervene* more".[19] The intended driver of this change was section 6 of the HRA, which imposed a duty on public authorities to Act in accordance with the European Convention on Human Rights. As Klug noted, there was expected to be a culture shift towards a greater understanding of, and respect for, the

15 For example, whilst the judiciary give authoritative meanings in the juridical subfield, governmental actors and civil society actors actively contest meanings (seeking to influence judicial pronouncements) through involvement in human rights cases.

16 Nash (n.7) 30–1.

17 Joint Committee on Human Rights *The Case for a Human Rights Commission (sixth report)* HL 67-I (2002–3) 3–8 available at <www.publications.parliament.uk/pa/jt200203/jtselect/jtrights/67/67.pdf> accessed 4 September 2016.

18 Francesca Klug anticipated that public officials, rather than just being prohibited from breaching rights, would be expected to respect them in their everyday decision-making. Klug *Values for a Godless Age* (n.2) 48.

19 Christopher McCrudden 'Mainstreaming Human Rights' from Colin Harvey (ed.) *Human Rights in the Community: Rights as Agents for Change* (Hart 2005) 15. Emphasis in the original.

principle of universal human rights in the public sector which would in turn promote a rights culture within society.[20] It was hoped this would lead to changes in legal culture, where pre-HRA the common law placed little restraint on executive power, reflecting the tradition of 'negative liberty'.[21]

The 'ethical' limb envisaged a high public awareness of rights and an association of rights with responsibilities. The effect of this 'ethical' meaning is to foreground the relationship between rights holders, switching the focus away from the role of rights in structuring the exercise of state power towards individuals. The coterminous emphasis on responsibilities was a calculated choice by the Labour government when introducing the HRA, anticipating that the 'individualism' of rights would be criticised. Discussing the motivations behind the 'cultural' aspects of the HRA, Croft noted that the government intended to link rights with responsibilities to discourage potential litigants.[22] This thinking was influenced by Amitai Etzioni's communitarian ideas, which maintained individuals should feel moral responsibilities towards their communities and that rights flow from these duties. Consequently, an individual should feel dissuaded from asserting their rights as against the rights of others in the community.[23] However, this communitarian approach narrowly construes individual's actions to enforce rights as self-interested, ignoring the potential for rights litigation to benefit the entire community by facilitating changes to law, policy and the delivery of services.[24]

As culture is a continuous process of contesting and reworking meanings, analysing the extent to which the HRA succeeded in its culture-building aims cannot be answered simply by the existence of dissent. Competition for authority within the human rights field does not end contests over meanings. Rather, the issue is the extent to which the particular meaning of the human rights culture aimed for by the HRA has become authoritative within that field.[25] As actors in the field compete for status and power, an appeal to that particular meaning of human rights indicates the latter is a form of legitimacy within the field. At the same time, one particular meaning of human rights may gain greater legitimacy if promoted by actors in the field with the highest status and power. To understand

20 Klug *A Magna Carta for All Humanity: Homing in on Human Rights* (Routledge 2015) 249.

21 Defined by Lord Donaldson in the *Spycatcher* case: 'Every citizen has the right to do what he likes, unless restrained by the common law or statute', quoted in Klug *Values for a Godless Age* (n.2) 35.

22 Jeremy Croft 'Whitehall and the Human Rights Act 1998' (UCL Constitution Unit Research Paper 2000) 15–6.

23 Amitai Etzioni *The Spirit of Community: Rights, Responsibilities and the Communitarian Agenda* (Crown 1993). Klug discusses the influence of Etzioni in *Values for a Godless Age* (n.2) 57–61.

24 For detail on this argument see Tom Campbell 'Human Rights: a culture of controversy' (1999) 26 *Journal of Law and Society*, 11.

25 Nash (n.7) 31.

how this occurs, Nash uses Luc Boltanski and Laurent Thevenot's idea of 'justification' which argues that as actors compete for status they reference particular values in order to confer legitimacy on the actions they have taken.[26] In other words, actors justify their behaviour by expressly linking it with certain shared values which they believe will confer legitimacy by association. Consequently, the principles the actors appeal to reveal the ideas they believe have value and will command respect within their field of activity. These justifications necessarily appeal to existing mutual understandings and as such also involve "the contention of fundamental values and interests".[27]

The success of the project of promoting these particular 'institutional' and 'ethical' meanings of human rights may be assessed by analysing the extent to which actors in the human rights field articulated or used justifications that appealed to these particular meanings of rights. To reflect the 'institutional' meaning we might expect public authorities to have framed their public service obligations with reference to human rights and the HRA and for the public to have used the same framings to critique or demand changes in those services. The 'ethical' meaning may be reflected in justifications which appeal to an understanding of rights being linked to responsibilities.

(2) Public perceptions of the HRA

Reviewing public attitudes to human rights in 2005, Frances Butler noted that "within wider civil society" the purpose and value of "human rights are contested rather than assumed".[28] Since the enactment of the HRA, various studies have been carried out into public perceptions of rights.[29] The research revealed common themes. Human rights were associated with abuses in countries overseas, particularly countries which are not democracies. There was general recognition of the importance or relevance of human rights but at the same time a majority of respondents felt that too many people took advantage of the HRA.[30] In general, empirical research on perceptions of the HRA showed that awareness of

26 Luc Boltanski and Laurent Thévenot *On Justification: Economies of Worth* (Princeton University Press 2006).

27 Nash (n.7) 59.

28 Frances Butler 'Improving public services: using a human rights approach' (Institute for Public Policy Research 2005) 11.

29 Ipsos MORI Social Research Institute 'Public perceptions of human rights' (EHRC, 2009); Constitution and Strategy Directorate 'Human Rights Insight Project' (Ministry of Justice Research Series 1/08, 2008); Alice Donald, Jenny Watson, Niamh McClean, Philip Leach and Jörn Eschment 'Human rights in Britain since the Human Rights Act 1998: a critical review' (EHRC Research Report 28 2008).

30 According to an Ipsos MORI survey quoted in the Ministry of Justice 'Insight Project' research paper, those who are most felt to take advantage are asylum seekers/refugees (46%), foreigners (not specified) (21%), people seeking financial reward (14%), lawyers (11%) and criminals (10%).

human rights and the HRA was generally low. In these surveys, the statements put to respondents framed the parameters of the discussion. The choice of framing, in the selection of specific issues to explore in the research, and the greater or lesser extent to which these issues had resonance, are all broadly indicative of the human rights issues which have prominence in what Nash terms the mediated public subfield. This term reflects the role the media plays in structuring and framing the public debate as the media is both the source of information and an actor (through media practitioners) involved in the struggle over the authority to define human rights.[31] Lieve Gies, work on the portrayal of human rights in the media identified how the media often creates the reference frames through which subsequent debates about human rights are constructed.[32] For example, on the role of human rights in relation to the criminal justice system, the framing of the stories – which is defined by Gies as a "process of storytelling . . . promoting a particular viewpoint" – was often highly negative, regardless of the facts of individual cases involving the HRA.[33] Therefore, public perceptions of human rights are not solely determined by media presentations, but the media is a key symbolic space where contests over the meanings of rights take place.

The Equality and Human Rights Commission's (EHRC) 2009 research into perceptions also included deliberative research which aimed to gather participants' own language and conceptions about human rights.[34] When asked to consider the values and principles important in society, none of the participants explicitly used the terminology of human rights law, although the principles and values they picked out (mutual respect among all people, family/community, fairness and natural justice) were closely related to human rights.[35] The deliberative research also reflected the view that people can use human rights to take advantage of society and that human rights issues were more relevant overseas than in the UK.[36] The deliberative research sessions also highlighted the contestability of rights. Whilst participants often expressed support for universalist understandings of rights, the concept of 'fairness' was closely linked to the perception of people taking advantage of human rights. In this sense, the participants perceived 'fairness' requiring factors such as a person's previous conduct to be taken into account when deciding the extent to which they exercised their rights.[37] The views revealed in the research have parallels with the 'communitarian' idea underpinning the intended 'ethical' meaning of human rights. This link between rights and responsibilities shifts the focus of the debate away from the duties of the state to realise rights

31 Nash (n.7) 50–2.
32 Lieve Gies *Mediating Human Rights: Media, Culture and the Human Rights Act* (Routledge 2014).
33 Ibid. 19–20.
34 Ipsos MORI Social Research Institute 'Public perceptions of human rights' (EHRC 2009) 3–4.
35 Ibid. 24–5.
36 Ibid. 43–50.
37 Ibid. 36, 43.

towards rights holders and whether, or to what extent, they may be permitted to exercise their rights. The groups specifically identified in the Ministry of Justice's Insight Project research are predominantly non-citizens, followed by unpopular minorities.[38] This reflects Nash's observation that "the idea that citizens and non-citizens should have equal rights appears to be difficult to countenance".[39]

Public perceptions on human rights were also prominent themes in media representations of human rights. A study of positive and negative human rights messages in the UK in 2013 found that around 70% of stories had a negative message.[40] This research analysed the human rights messages appearing in tabloid and national newspapers, political blogs and parliamentary speeches and classified the messages into key 'frames' which were concepts that had emotions and values attached to it. Frames are used consciously or unconsciously to provoke a particular kind of reaction to that concept and echo the 'values' appealed to in Boltanski and Thevenot's justifications discussed earlier. The frames identified in this research as positive messages of human rights were 'protect basic rights', 'promote tradition and patriotism', 'defend British democracy', 'everyone has human rights', 'prevent discrimination' and 'balance competing interests'. The frames identified as containing negative messages about human rights were 'decrease security', 'reduce our sovereignty', 'increase unfairness', 'increase cost', 'damage British tradition' and 'harm religion'. Consequently, appeals to tradition and Britishness were often invoked to legitimise or delegitimise human rights. A positive presentation of human rights would try to associate it within British tradition, whereas a negative portrayal would argue it harmed that tradition. This highlights the way that 'Britishness' and tradition were considered to be shared values that confer status and legitimacy in the human rights field. These appeals to familiarity and consistency occur in the context of changes in the balance of power between institutions in the human rights field introduced by the HRA. This chapter now considers two areas the HRA intended to transform, legal culture and public services delivery to consider how those changes had an impact on the cultural politics of human rights.

(3) Legal culture

The participative human rights culture envisaged in the 'institutional' meaning of human rights was intended to expand the law's reach beyond the familiar limits

38 See n.29.

39 Nash (n.7) 185.

40 The 70% was for the UK overall. Broken down into the devolved regions, the picture varied substantially, from 37% negative message stories in Wales, rising to 82% in England. The research was carried out by Counterpoint, Public Interest Research Center and Equally Ours. Rachel Krys 'Research-based messaging changes public support for human rights' *Open Democracy Net* (3 July 2015) available at <www.opendemocracy.net/openglobalrights/rachel-krys/researchbased-messaging-changes-public-support-for-human-rights> accessed 1 September 2016.

of state interference to contest the extent of the state's positive obligations. As a significant departure from the UK common law tradition of 'negative' liberty, the new obligations introduced by the HRA made the judicial subfield a location of contest over meanings of rights. The concept of positive obligations had to compete in the judicial subfield with other values drawn from the common-law tradition. In 1999, Murray Hunt anticipated that two features of UK legal culture, loyalty to parliamentary sovereignty and the belief in the private, rather than the public, as the proper sphere of judicial activity, could constrain the realisation of a culture of rights based on positive obligations.[41] Since the introduction of the HRA the courts have become a location of high-profile contests between the government and the judiciary, two actors with high status in the human rights field. As each actor sought to legitimise its position with in the field, the justifications used for their respective position tended to appeal to values of liberty and sovereignty. For the judiciary, which had the task of asserting human rights against the government, the effect of their justifications was to frame human rights within a 'British' tradition of liberty, a value that it believed would command respect in the human rights field.

Lord Hoffman's dissenting judgment in *A and Others* framed the issues in the case with reference to British "traditions of liberties" in direct contrast to doctrines "of European law", arguing that the Convention merely entrenches the same liberties British subjects already enjoyed at common law.[42] David Dyzenhaus criticised Hoffman's misleading equation of the common law with the Convention as "an unfortunate outburst of Anglo-Saxon parochialism".[43] In recent judicial discourse the common law has been promoted as the primary source of rights.[44] Judicial commentators frequently foreground the 'British' influence in the ECHR, placing it in a linear progression of rights from the Magna Carta onwards.[45] This articulates a different meaning of 'bringing rights home', presenting Britain as the birthplace of human rights. The framing of human rights in terms of their complementarity to British traditions translates them from the international sphere into terms which have familiarity in the domestic, making

41 Murray Hunt 'The Human Rights Act and Legal Culture: the judiciary and the legal profession' (1999) 26 *Journal of Law and Society* 89.

42 *A and Others v Secretary of State for the Home Department* [2004] UKHL 56, [2005] 2 AC 68 [88].

43 David Dyzenhaus 'An unfortunate outburst of Anglo-Saxon parochialism', (2005) 68 *The Modern Law Review*, 673.

44 *Osborn v The Parole Board* [2013] UKSC 61 [54]; *Kennedy v The Charity Commission* [2014] UKSC 20 [46] [133].

45 See for example, Lord Neuberger *The Role of Judges in Human Rights Jurisprudence: A Comparison of the Australian and UK experience* (Supreme Court of Victoria Conference, Victoria August 2014); Laws LJ *Lecture III: The Common Law and Europe* (The Hamlyn Lectures, London, November 2013); Joint Committee on Human Rights *Human Rights Judgments* (2011, HC 873 -ii) 6 (evidence of Lord Judge).

human rights 'vernacular'.[46] This increases the power of justifications for judicial acts by appealing to, and reasserting, concepts which already have value and can command respect. These justifications also serve to delegitimise those who criticise the HRA and human rights as 'European' or 'foreign' impositions, antithetical to British values and traditions, such as those discussed in the first chapter of this book. However, this framing by foregrounding liberties, nevertheless reinforces the idea that rights are 'other', outside of this tradition, and obscures the limitations of the common law to secure the same level of rights protection.[47] Instead, common law rights protection is often defined by a preoccupation with property and contractual rights and a relatively weak framework of rights litigation, the expectation being that institutions such as parliament will take civil liberties into account when legislating. The narrative of the civil libertarian tradition of common law serves to reposition the judiciary as the historical developers and guardians of rights, thus gaining status within the human rights field.

Masterman and Wheatle considered that the "judicial reiteration of the value of the common law to the protection of human rights places emphasis on the 'national' in the face of the 'non-national' qualities of the Convention rights".[48] Whilst rights which have a "homologue" in common law can easily be articulated within this national framing, Convention rights and doctrines, such as positive obligations which have no ready counterpart, struggle within a national framing of rights.[49] This framing then serves to emphasise a difference between liberties and rights. The recognition of positive duties is one of the main cultural shifts considered necessary to bring about the 'institutional' meaning of human rights envisaged by the HRA. By framing rights within the concept of 'British liberties', the judiciary (an actor with status in the human rights field) undermines the ability of the 'institutional' meaning to become authoritative. The almost exclusive linking of the positive values of 'Britishness' and 'tradition' to the value of 'liberties' means that there is no express link to a broader meaning of rights which could encompass positive obligations upon the state, decreasing the status of positive obligations within the field. Moreover, the framing of rights solely within the 'British liberties' tradition lends itself to co-option both in broader contests over the relationship between the domestic and the international (e.g. anti-European, anti-immigration) and in the specific campaigns to repeal the HRA. The promotion of the idea that the ECHR simply reflects common law liberties supports the

46 Sally Engle Merry, quoted in Nash (n.7) 98.

47 See Conor Gearty 'On fantasy island; British politics, English judges and the European Convention on Human Rights' (2015) 1 *European Human Rights Law Review*, 2.

48 Roger Masterman and Se-shauna Wheatle 'A common law resurgence in rights protection?' (2015) 1 *European Human Rights Law Review*, 57.

49 The term 'homologue' was used by Lord Mance in *Kennedy v The Charity Commission* [2014] UKSC 20 [46].

contention that the HRA can be repealed without any significant impact.[50] This, in turn, reflects what Gearty terms the "fantasy of English exceptionalism": that the domestic traditions are unique and incompatible with European imports.[51]

The justifications used in the judicial subfield appealed to a continuity of values in legal culture. This is perhaps not a surprising consequence of the struggle for legitimacy by both government and judiciary in the wake of the new balance of power created by the HRA. However, the emphasis on liberties served to place positive obligations outside the domestic vernacular of rights. Therefore, the values appealed to by the judiciary and government did not expressly associate British tradition with the concept of positive obligations, creating a disconnect between this key feature of the institutional meaning of human rights and the values promoted in the human rights field.

(4) Public service delivery and the HRA

A key intention of the HRA was for human rights to inform the delivery of public services beyond simple legal compliance. Government and public authorities (and private entities delivering public functions) would fulfil their positive obligations through respecting human rights in everyday decision-making. Section 6 of the Act placed a legal obligation on public authorities to comply with Convention rights. This required public authorities to "avoid [legal] challenges through auditing and correcting procedures and practices where breaches of the Convention might occur" but did not place any wider obligations on public bodies to promote or create a particular cultural understanding of rights.[52] Over time, it was expected that pressure for change in services would come not only from court judgments but also from service users and community groups able to use human rights to frame their demands.[53] Rather than using litigation to secure the rights of individuals living in care homes, social housing or using the National Health Service, rights would become part of the process of administering those services. Public officials would take into account the impact on rights holders when making decisions and providing services, and people using those services would be aware of their entitlements to rights and rely on these when asking health, social care and other public services to accommodate their needs. The key actors in the human rights field are therefore public authorities (in the governmental subfield) but also the public using those services and civil society organisations which assist

50 The concept of continuity in rights protection was asserted by Michael Gove in evidence to the Justice Committee: when asked about the proposed plans he stated that there were 'human rights before the Human Rights Act' Oral evidence session (15 July 2015) available at <www.parliamentlive.tv/Event/Index/01128a23-eb50-4c34-a4a4-f482abf4ea84> accessed 4 September 2016.

51 Gearty (n.47) 8.

52 Croft (n.22) 15.

53 Klug (n.2) 48.

or promote access to services (mediated public subfield, activist subfield). After the HRA came into force, various governmental and non-governmental bodies commissioned research into its impact on public service delivery: the Audit Commission (2003),[54] the Institute of Public Policy Research (IPPR; 2005),[55] the Ministry of Justice[56] and the Equality and Human Rights Commission (2008,[57] 2009).[58] The primary aims of this research were to identify the extent to which human rights focused service delivery had been established and if there were any obstacles to implementation. The Audit Commission attributed the struggle of public authorities to connect human rights with service improvement in part to the HRA's introduction "without any structured guidance and without a statutory duty to positively promote a human rights culture".[59]

The mainstreaming of rights in the public sector would require significant reorganisation, improvement, development and evaluation of policy processes.[60] However, the Audit Commission found that despite the initial high profile of the HRA before it came into force, by 2003 58% of public bodies surveyed had still not adopted a strategy for human rights. In many local authorities the Act was described as not having "left the desks of the lawyers".[61] Assessing the response of local authorities to the HRA, Clements and Morris identified three approaches: first, to do little or nothing; second, to undertake a protectionist 'Strasbourg-proofing' approach; or, third, to aim to incorporate the legislation into the organisation's functions.[62] Central government failed to take a leading role and centrally developed policy did not reflect or clearly articulate a human rights framework that the wider public sector was expected to follow. Butler notes this failed to comply with the 'culture of human rights' expected from everyone else.[63] EHRC research in 2008 and 2009 found that leadership was important in creating a rights culture within organisations.[64] By failing to provide that leadership by example and promotion, central government, a key actor in the human rights

54 Audit Commission 'Human rights: improving public service delivery' (Audit Commission 2003)
55 Butler (n.28).
56 Constitution and Strategy Directorate 'Human Rights Insight Project' (Ministry of Justice Research Series 1/08, 2008)
57 Donald et al. (n.29).
58 Equality and Human Rights Commission 'The impact of a human rights culture on public sector organisations: lessons from practice' (EHRC Research Report Series 2009).
59 Audit Commission (n.54) 7.
60 McCrudden (n.19) 9.
61 Audit Commission (n.54) 7.
62 Luke Clements and Rachel Morris 'The Millennium Blip: The Human Rights Act 1998 and local government' from Simon Halliday and Patrick Schmidt (eds.) *Human Rights brought Home: Socio-legal Studies of Human Rights in the National Context* (Hart 2004)
63 Frances Butler 'Building a Human Rights Culture' from Colin Harvey (ed.) *Human Rights in the Community: Rights as Agents for Change* (Hart 2005).
64 Donald et al. (n.29) 50–1.

field, missed an opportunity to give status and legitimacy to the institutional meaning of human rights.

In 2005 the IPPR concluded that whilst many public authorities were aware of the need to comply with the Act (and so primarily understood the HRA to signify legal obligations), they lacked "sufficient understanding of the nature and extent of their human rights responsibilities".[65] These were not understood as positive obligations. Murray Hunt considered this to be at the 'root of the problem' of embedding a human rights approach: the question, "[W]hat *should* we be doing?" . . . is a massively important missing dimension in the thinking and the training".[66] The Ministry of Justice's Insight Project of 2008 intended to assess the experiences of service users of public authorities that had implemented human rights mainstreaming, but there were insufficient numbers of public authorities that met this criteria to allow a comparison.[67] The EHRC's Human Rights Review of 2012 identified a lack of understanding of human rights obligations by health and social care providers as an area requiring improvement in domestic rights protection.[68] Instead, negative views of human rights became dominant; as the Critical Review noted, "there is a discrepancy between largely positive staff perceptions of the term 'human rights' and the values of dignity, respect and fairness, and largely negative perceptions of the HRA as a charter for miscreants or as something that's remote, intimidatory, and happens in a court of law".[69]

The preceding research builds a picture of missed opportunities to clearly articulate the institutional meaning of human rights by actors in the governmental subfield. The links between human rights and public service delivery were not communicated clearly or consistently. The research also revealed a language disconnect between the language of human rights and the language of best practice service delivery. Both the IPPR and the EHRC's 2008 reports noted that concepts of fairness, respect, quality and dignity were generally recognised to form the ethos of public services but were not expressly identified as human rights concepts and even less likely to be associated with the HRA.[70] The Insight research also supported these findings noting that service users (32% unprompted rising to 78% when prompted) placed 'being treated with dignity

65 Butler 'Improving Public Services' (n.28) 52.

66 Hunt (in his capacity as legal adviser to the JCHR), quoted in Donald et al. (n.29) 38.

67 Constitution and Strategy Directorate 'Human Rights Insight Project' (Ministry of Justice Research Series 1/08, 2008)

68 EHRC 'Human rights review 2012: how fair is Britain? An assessment of how well public authorities protect human rights' (EHRC 2012).

69 Paul Coen, former chief executive of the Local Government Association, quoted in Constitution and Strategy Directorate (n.67) 82.

70 Butler (n.28) 12; Donald et al. (n.57) 65–8; Constitution and Strategy Directorate (n.67) 64. Dignity and respect are reflected in the ECHR in Articles 3 (prohibition on inhumane and degrading treatment); Article 8 (respect for family and private life); equality and fairness in Article 1 (obligation on contracting states to secure the Convention rights to everyone in their jurisdiction) and Article 14 (non-discrimination).

and respect' amongst the essential factors for satisfactory public services. However, respondents generally did not recognise the links between these principles and human rights.[71] Human rights were more clearly associated with liberty and freedom of speech (reflective of the 'British liberties' framing of rights) and their relevance to provision of adult social care, care for the elderly and other services was therefore less apparent. The research suggests that, against the idea of liberties, the 'institutional' meaning of human rights shaping the practices of public authorities was less authoritative. Had public service values been expressly articulated as human rights values, and had actors in this field used justifications that referenced these values as human rights, the authority of the 'institutional' meaning would have been increased. In turn, this could have given greater legitimacy to the HRA and countered some of its negative associations, by expressly linking the HRA and its introduction of positive obligations to valued institutions such as the National Health Service. Comparative research undertaken in 2016 on the different rights that people living across eight countries valued showed that the top five rights that British people valued the most were the right to vote, the right to a fair trial, the right to free health care, the right to physical safety and the right to education.[72] This suggests that there is a basis within existing public opinion for the HRA to be linked to service delivery. As Alice Donald notes, the obligation on public authorities to Act compatibly with Convention rights is the most important way in which the HRA affects everyday life, and research supports the assumption that attitudes to human rights become more positive when people feel rights are relevant to them personally.[73]

Likewise, negative perceptions of the HRA have discouraged some civil society actors in the 'activist' subfield from openly promoting human rights. A 2010 pilot research project conducted for the EHRC found that voluntary organisations were put off using human rights by the "often heated tone of domestic political and media debate".[74] However, there is evidence of new activity by civil society organisations to promote positive perceptions of the HRA in direct response to its proposed repeal. In these campaigns activists seek to persuade other actors in the human-rights subfield by lobbying (governmental), bringing or intervening in key human rights cases (juridical) and campaigns, publicity and events (mediated

71 Constitution and Strategy Directorate (n.67) 29–30.

72 Peter Kellner 'Analysis: which human rights matter most?' *YouGov* (30 March 2016) available at <https://yougov.co.uk/news/2016/03/30/which-rights-matter-most/> accessed 11 November 2016.

73 Alice Donald and Elizabeth Mottershaw 'Identifying Human Rights Stories: a scoping study' (Middlesex University Research Project 2014) <www.mdx.ac.uk/__data/assets/pdf_file/0021/135318/Identifying-human-rights-stories-July-2014.pdf > last accessed 4 September 2016.

74 British Institute of Human Rights and Equality Diversity Forum 'Human rights and equality in the voluntary sector' (EHRC 2010).

public).[75] In their campaigns supporting the HRA, both Liberty and Amnesty International foreground case studies which expand beyond the frequent media framing of 'non-citizens' (e.g. immigrants, foreign criminals) or 'non-deserving' (e.g. prisoners) and outside the usual setting of the associated human rights issues (national security/immigration/prison). Amnesty International's campaign on the HRA uses case studies, such as an elderly couple and care home, housing for a victim of domestic violence, gay rights and the retention of innocent people's DNA.[76] Amnesty also appealed to 'national pride' when it campaigned on the negative impact that repealing the HRA would have on the UK's standing to raise concerns about other country's human rights records.[77] These justifications place emphasis on the everyday situations where human rights can be relevant, and on the types of people who can benefit from the HRA. In research conducted by the 'Equally Ours' campaign this was found to be the most effective way of encouraging support for human rights.[78] Equally Ours was a campaign set up by eight charities to "talk about the importance of human rights and how they benefit us all in everyday life".[79] These actors are now more prominently framing human rights to make explicit the connections with issues that people value and frequently encounter, which prominently includes public services. To that extent, civil society actors are now articulating a meaning of human rights that parallels the 'institutional' meaning originally intended to be promoted by the HRA.

Conclusion

The justifications used by different actors in the human rights field reveal a positive association with values such as 'tradition' and 'Britishness'. Human rights messages gain legitimacy through association with these values. The 'institutional' meaning of human rights could have gained greater authority if it had successfully linked these shared values to the positive role of human rights in public service delivery. However, by not expressly promoting or articulating such a link, actors in the governmental subfield missed the opportunity to promote a meaning of rights which associated the HRA with best practice public service delivery. The weak association between rights and public service delivery is reflected in the

75 See for example, Richard Maiman '"We've had to raise our game": Liberty's litigation strategy under the Human Rights Act 1998' from Halliday and Schmidt (eds.) (n.62).

76 Amnesty International 'Eight reasons why the Human Rights Act makes the UK a better place' *Amnesty International* (3 October 2014) available at <www.amnesty.org.uk/eight-reasons-why-human-rights-act-has-made-uk-better-place-british-bill-of-rights#.VeDNO_lViko> accessed 28 August 2015.

77 Nash (n.7) 103–4.

78 Bec Sanderson 'Building Bridges: how (not) to talk about human rights' *Common Cause* (January 2015) <http://valuesandframes.org/how-not-to-talk-about-human-rights/> accessed 28 August 2015.

79 Equally Ours 'Everyone's Rights, Every Day' available at <www.equally-ours.org.uk/about-us/> accessed 28 August 2015.

language disconnect in which values and principles important to services such as dignity, respect, fairness and equality are not recognised as being derived from human rights.[80] Civil society actors are now trying to promote this connection, but the failure to strongly articulate it by other actors in the human rights field has led to this meaning of human rights having limited authority. As the 'institutional' meaning has more direct relevance to many people's everyday experience, it had the potential to counter the perception that the rights protected by the HRA are only realised in remote processes such as litigation. The 'institutional' meaning has also struggled to gain authority because of the appeal to the value of 'liberties' as a distinct feature of British tradition in justifications by prominent actors in the human rights field, including the judiciary. This had the effect of presenting the positive obligations crucial to the 'institutional' meaning of rights as something outside of other more traditional values.

Research into public perceptions of human rights and media messaging suggests that the 'ethical' meaning of rights intended by the political architects of the HRA has gained some authority, to the extent that rights are associated with responsibilities. Yet this has contributed the current position where the cultural politics of rights in the UK remains dominated by fundamental contests over who gets to have rights. The failure to establish the rights culture the HRA was intended to introduce is primarily the failure of government actors and not a fault of the legislation itself. The research reviewed in this chapter reveals the limitations of culture building through legislation without institutional support and promotion. This limited its capacity to embed a broader conception of rights, one which articulated their relevance to shared values. Had this aim succeeded it may have prevented or countered the association of the HRA with undeserving rights holders, which has created the conditions where repeal of the act has been seriously considered. It also suggests that replacement with a British Bill of Rights is similarly unlikely to resolve the structural problems affecting the creation of a rights culture detailed in this chapter.

80 Donald et al (n.29) 179.

Index

www.ingramcontent.com/pod-product-compliance
Ingram Content Group UK Ltd.
Pitfield, Milton Keynes, MK11 3LW, UK
UKHW021302190926
475701UK00009B/578
9780367232177